Custody Chaos, Personal Peace

"A gold mine of useful information for one of modern families' greatest challenges."

> —Michael P. Nichols, Ph.D.,
> author of *The Lost Art of Listening*

"A wonderful blend of wisdom, encouragement, and skill-specific advice. Confronts the really intractable problems that are so disheartening in post-divorce relations. I am recommending this book to my clients."

> —Carl D. Schneider, Ph.D.,
> director, Mediation Matters,
> author of *Shame, Exposure, and Privacy*

Custody Chaos, Personal Peace:

Sharing Custody with an Ex Who Drives You Crazy

Jeffrey P. Wittmann, Ph.D.

A Perigee Book

A Perigee Book
Published by The Berkley Publishing Group
A division of Penguin Putnam Inc.
375 Hudson Street
New York, New York 10014

Copyright © 2001 by Jeffrey P. Wittmann, Ph.D.
Book design by Tiffany Kukec
Cover design by Dorothy Wachtenheim
Cover art by Ruth Sofair Kelter

First edition: October 2001

Published simultaneously in Canada.

Visit our website at
www.penguinputnam.com

Library of Congress Cataloging-in-Publication Data

Wittmann, Jeffrey P.
    Custody chaos, personal peace : sharing custody with an ex who drives you
crazy / by Jeffrey P. Wittmann.
       p.   cm.
    Includes bibliographical references and index.
    ISBN 0-399-52710-9
    1. Children of divorced parents.   2. Joint custody of children.   3. Divorced
parents—Psychology.   4. Parenting, Part-time.   I. Title.

HQ777.5 .W58   2001
306.89—dc21
                                                                    00-068475

Printed in the United States of America

10   9   8   7   6   5   4   3   2   1

To my wife, Frances,
who has always been my partner in the pursuit of dreams

Contents

Acknowledgments

Whenever I sit down to write, I am aware that I am not alone. I bring to the task a personal history rich in lessons taught by good teachers and carved into my soul by my own life's meandering through joy and pain. I am grateful to all those who have inspired and guided me.

My wife, Frances, to whom this book is dedicated, not only tolerated the hundreds of hours that I spent secluded in my office but also consistently believed in this project and in all it represented for me. In a sense, she is my co-author; quite simply, this book would not have happened without her encouragement.

The team most central to this book's final gestation and birth was invaluable: My agent, Sara Jane Freymann, offered me deep enthusiasm for this work, crystalline guidance, and a kind of spiritual companionship that kept me focused. Susanna Margolis, my private editor, took a somewhat rough stone and helped me turn it into the gem I was striving for. Her influence is woven throughout this book, and I am very grateful for her extraordinary literary talent, her critical insight, and for many moments of laughter between us. Sheila Curry Oakes, my editor at Penguin Putnam, said "yes" to my proposal for this book, a moment I will not soon forget, and then was the skillful and supportive shepherd of this manuscript through its release.

My colleague and close friend Dr. Randy Cale has served as a sounding board and loving critic, always challenging me to take my thought to a higher level in a way that stretched me. Our partnership, focused on work with divorcing adults and children, has been enormously important to me. Jeffrey Cohen, Esq., has been an enthusiastic supporter of this project and has been a model for me of enlightened and sensitive legal representation for parents and children as they experience divorce. Christine Benton provided early editorial assistance along with very welcome encouragement. Dr. Michael Nichols offered invaluable advice on the process of bringing this work to print, for which I am deeply grateful.

Most important, I am grateful to the several thousand divorced parents who have come to my office as they struggled with navigating their relationships from separate homes. Their creative and thoughtful insights, borne of life in the trenches of divorce, form the foundation of this book and are woven into its very fabric.

Finally, some gratitude for a life experience: After my own dad died, my mother remarried, and my beautiful sister was born of that second relationship. As a twelve-year-old, I saw my little sister, a toddler at the time, trying to cope with the reality that her mother and father had decided to divorce; I was the big brother who watched as she tried to make sense of the complexities and emotional challenges of a divided family. Consequently, some of the thoughts I will share with you in the upcoming chapters flow from my own experience as a teenager observing two loving parents working hard to part, with dignity, while a special little girl stood between them.

PART ONE

Working on Yourself

CHAPTER ONE

How You Got Here

"I felt like I had no life of my own when we were together . . . like I was drowning. I finally couldn't take it anymore and told him I wanted out—but now that I'm out he still finds ways to drive me nuts, especially when we have to talk about the kids . . ."

"It took me twelve years to figure out that I could never do anything right in her eyes, and I just couldn't face that for the rest of my life. I remember the night that we told the kids. . . . I felt like I was dying inside, but at the same time I thought I was finally finding freedom from her endless nagging. Now, after two years apart, I'm amazed at how she continues to make me feel like a worthless father from ten miles away. In many ways, things didn't get easier . . ."

"He pulls up to my house with the kids sitting in his truck, and they never have their seat belts on. Whenever they leave for their dad's home I have a lump in my throat, because he has no brains when it comes to keeping our kids safe . . ."

* * *

"Whenever Jason comes to my house for our weekend together it feels like it takes five hours for him to settle in and warm up to me. No wonder—I know that my ex speaks about me like I'm a vampire, and Jason hears it all . . ."

"My ex is like a screaming maniac whenever I bring up the fact that I need more money for the kids. He acts like he thinks I'll blow his money on partying rather than taking care of Suzy and Jake. When he starts to yell I can see our kids cringe and hide, but there is no stopping him . . ."

"No matter how many times I tell my ex that I need her to be on time and to stick with the schedule for her visits, she keeps pushing the limits, showing up a half hour late, or canceling at the last minute, only to leave me with two disappointed kids."

Sound familiar? The fact that you're reading this book means that you recognize the anxiety, anger, frustration, even desperation that come through loud and clear in these quotes from divorced and separated parents. Your story is no doubt different in the details. What's the same is the extent to which your life is still shadowed by someone you no longer live with, the extent to which you're still driven crazy by an ex-spouse with whom you will be sharing custody for years to come.

I am a psychologist who specializes in the problems affecting separated families, of whom I've counseled or evaluated more than 2,000 to date. As you can imagine, I've heard infinite variations on the theme of sharing custody with an ex who's driving you crazy, but the theme itself is always the same. It prompts feelings of hopelessness and sadness, anxiety and anger, feelings that seem to be always present just under the surface. Even the brief periods of relative calm these separated parents enjoy are darkened by the knowledge that another storm with their ex lies just over the horizon. Too much of their life feels out of their control. For such parents—perhaps for you—where there is custody chaos, there is virtually no personal peace.

This book aims to help you end the chaos and find the peace. It will help you put a stop to the roller coaster of conflict that constantly and consistently interrupts your life. When children are involved, divorce doesn't erase conflicts between ex-partners. Your kids will bind you together for decades after separation; your lives will intersect time and again as you try to rear them from your separate homes through schooling, sports, graduations, weddings, and beyond. Your problems won't disappear, and neither will your ex. Raising children from two separate households provides many opportunities for further conflict and disagreement.

This book will offer a path for reclaiming your life when relations with your ex threaten to make your life miserable, or to drag you down, or to keep you from knowing peace and contentment. It will empower you to fulfill your responsibilities with more confidence—your responsibilities to your children, of course, but your responsibilities to yourself as well. It will give you the wherewithal to believe that you *can* find that peace and contentment, *can* lift yourself up over your despair, *can* work your way out of this misery with your ex.

As such, while this is a book for divorced parents, it is also a book about living. While it teaches you how to try to influence a former spouse to change, it also teaches you how to achieve peace when your former spouse refuses to change.

Reaching that peace within yourself is particularly important—profoundly important—because of your children. Fragile at any time, kids are especially so when their lives are buckled by divorce. The more centered your life, the more centered your child's life will be and the more power you have to deal effectively not only with your ex but also with all the other players: family members on both "sides," a new spouse or partner, or prospective partner.

In the end, you will be doing the greatest amount of work on yourself—on the way *you* think about your ex and about your problems with him or her, on the way *you* respond when your children come home and complain about something that your ex has done, and on how *you* focus your energies and attention in life. When your ex refuses to budge, you probably feel as if you're trying to push against a brick wall. This book gives you ways to walk around the wall.

Throughout the book we will work together toward a number of goals. Achieve them, and you'll almost surely find the peace you seek. Here's what I hope you'll eventually be capable of:

- Influencing your ex, in skillful and compassionate ways, to behave more reasonably.

- Shifting your attention and energy away from problems with your ex that you will probably never control toward those parts of your life that you *can* control.

- Accepting that you create your own happiness and frustrations in life by the way you think about your problems.

- Determining clearly whether a particular problem with your ex belongs on your shoulders or someone else's.

- Empowering others when you decide that a particular problem does not belong on your shoulders.

- Giving to your ex what you yourself want to receive.

- Making your child's needs your primary focus as you try to work out relationship difficulties with your ex.

- Remembering that every decision that you make about your relationship with your child's other parent teaches your child a life lesson.

These goals seem difficult to accept, much less realize. But I'm confident they will make increasing sense to you as you read. That's why I urge you to go through the book in order. Parts I and II are sections that will provide the foundation that is critical to implementing the suggestions offered in Parts III and IV; without a foundation, the lessons taught in Parts III and IV could well collapse.

We'll start by working to define clearly the problem between you and your ex-spouse; after all, it helps to have a clear idea of where you want to go before you can try to get there. Next you'll learn to cultivate ways of thinking about your ex that will reduce your distress level. As with most painful situations, peace begins between our own two ears and is seldom achieved by insisting that the world around us change.

Then we'll look at concrete ways to cultivate cooperation with your ex, to communicate with your ex about "hot" or difficult issues, and to make an effective difference when all attempts at civil communication have failed. How should you respond when you and your ex disagree on raising the children you are both committed to protect and nurture? What should you do when your children's complaints about your ex call forth your impulse to do battle for them?

Your own parents—not to mention your new partner—also have feelings about your children's other parent, and your ex will have feelings about them. At times you may feel stuck in the middle of warring tribes, and so this book will suggest ways to avoid becoming a casualty.

Each chapter of the book ends with key tips to keep in mind as you try to deal with your ex. Also at the end of each chapter are brief scenarios of real dilemmas that parents struggle with. My answers to these dilemmas represent what you would hear from me if we had the opportunity to sit together in my office.

A word about language: Words like "visitation" and "custody" can be damaging and disrespectful to families if misused. "Visiting" parents wipe little noses, make meals, and tell teenagers to be in on time. They parent. They don't visit. And "custody" suggests a winner and a loser. The phrases I prefer are "parenting time" for visitation, and "time-sharing schedule" for custody, but I reluctantly decided to stay with the language that most readers are likely to be familiar with; it seems less cumbersome.

Some of the ideas you will encounter in the chapters ahead may make you uncomfortable. Some may challenge long-held views of your own family dilemma. But as has been confirmed time and again in my practice, in working toward a less conflicted relationship with your ex-partner, feelings of challenge and discomfort may be important signals that you are on the right track.

In any event, be gentle with yourself. You deserve it.

One final, essential note: If your ex has shown violence or abusive behavior toward you or your children, I urge you to explore this book and its suggestions with the assistance of a trained therapist. Many of the tools and techniques offered here are inappropriate for families in which there has been violence or the threat of violence. A trained therapist can help you pick and choose carefully.

CHAPTER TWO

What Drives You Crazy about Your Ex-Partner?

Just as you can't heal a sickness that hasn't been diagnosed, you can't solve a problem that hasn't been defined. Of course, you're quite sure you know what the problem is: your ex. It's he or she who is making you furious or frustrated, hurt or frightened, or maybe just confused. That's crystal clear to you. What more do you need to know?

Actually, you don't need to know more. Rather, you need to be more precise—and more explicit—about *what* you know.

If you take your car to the garage and tell the mechanic that "it just doesn't run right," you haven't given him much help in fixing whatever's wrong. You haven't given yourself much help, either: you'll be without a car for some time while it sits idly in the shop and the mechanic goes through a lengthy checklist of diagnostic tests—a costly process in any number of ways.

But tell the mechanic that, "the wheel shimmies when I go over fifty miles per hour," or the, "clutch seems to stick going from second to third," or, "there's a high-pitched noise when the car takes a sharp right curve but not on a left curve," and both the mechanic and you are far better off. The mechanic knows where to begin the diagnosis and repair; you know what to check for to see if the problem has been fixed.

It's simple: defining the problem empowers you, and the more precisely you define it, the more empowered you will be. Clarity of definition is therefore your all-important first step toward breaking free of custody chaos and finding your personal peace.

Statements like, "He just frustrates the hell out of me" or "She's just impossible to deal with" are far too general. They express annoyance, but they don't tell you anything that might lead to a sensible solution. You end up still beating your head against that brick wall.

Before you can begin to solve the problem of your ex, you must define the problem, analyze it, and dimension it (put it into context).

> *Not to know yet to think that one knows will lead to difficulty.*
>
> —Lao Tzu, founder of Chinese Taoism

Through Pain to Power

Defining the problem is often easier said than done. Separated parents often feel overwhelmed by a confusing mix of emotions. The confusion understandably interferes with their ability to focus clearly, and the lack of clear focus in turn interferes with their ability to act constructively.

Nor is the process of defining the problem free from pain. It requires you to dig deeply into your own feelings. It demands that you look clinically and objectively at situations that have angered you, frightened you, or broken your heart. It means reexamining a history you would probably just as soon forget. But all of this is necessary to understand exactly what bugs you about your ex-partner and how the behavior has impacted your life.

The exercises that follow ask you to define exactly what you find distressing about your ex. If there are several things you find distressing, you will have to go through the exercises several times, but the complete list of defined issues you end up with will prove invaluable to putting you on the path to empowerment and action.

FIRST, DEFINITION: SEEK CLARITY

Clarity of definition—being precise about *exactly* what's bugging you about your ex—is absolutely essential. Without clarity, there is no direction, and the search for relief becomes an aimless thrashing about when what is needed is a purposeful progression along a carefully marked trail.

The object of this first exercise, therefore, is to craft a clear, one-sentence description of the problem by answering the following questions:

- What specific behavior on your ex's part do you find distressing?

- What specific effects does this behavior have on you, your children, or others that you care for?

- What feelings do you or others have when the problem occurs?

What you're doing here is breaking the problem with your ex into three components: your ex's distressing behavior; how it affects you; and how you end up feeling as a result. As with any problem, by breaking it into its parts you can more clearly see how to deal with it.

First, write out a sentence with blanks in it, like this:

When my ex _____,
                    [behavior]

it causes _____,
             [effects]

and I (or my kids, or my partner, etc.) feel _____.
                                                  [feelings]

Let's look at some examples:

"When my ex is late returning the kids, I end up late for work, and I feel furious."

"When my ex doesn't send Jacob's soccer shoes back with him, Jake has to stay on the sidelines, and I feel sad for him and angry at my ex. Jake ends up sad and ticked off too."

"When she's two weeks late sending her support check, I can't afford groceries, and I feel frightened and mad."

Here's one that highlights the fact that the frustrating dilemmas that we have with our ex-partners don't always affect just ourselves and the kids.

"When he yells at my mother when dropping the kids off at her home, the kids hear it and end up sad. My mother becomes afraid of caring for the kids again, and I feel pissed off about what he's doing."

SECOND, ANALYSIS: GO DEEPER

If you're going to achieve personal peace in place of the current custody chaos, things will have to change, and you can change only those things you control—that is, your own feelings. So this is the moment to understand precisely what those feelings are, and that means probing beneath the surface annoyance, anger, and frustration to the deeper, more tender emotions inside you. You may be surprised to find that underneath your anger are old feelings about your ex that you have tried hard to escape. Maybe his tardiness conjures up old feelings of hurt that your feelings didn't matter enough to him. Maybe her criticisms of your parenting as she arrives with the children rekindle old feelings of hopelessness about ever being good enough for her. Or perhaps his forgetting to use seat belts with the kids summons a familiar terror that a terrible accident will occur while they are with him. Behind your fury or indignation with your ex may even lie fragile feelings of embarrassment, humiliation, or sadness.

In analyzing your feelings, it's essential to take the perspective illustrated in the examples cited above under "Definition." Did you notice that the speakers in the examples do not say that their ex *makes them feel* something? It's "I feel furious" or "I get furious" instead of "He makes me furious." This apparently trivial distinction points to an essential idea we'll be discussing at greater length later in this book: in a sense, no one can make us feel anything. We may become furious, frightened, or sad after our ex does something despicable, but that emotion comes primarily from the way we interpret the situation—from what happens between our ears—not from the situation itself.

Although this is an empowering point of view—our ability to consciously change our emotional state by altering our perspective on a dilemma is, after all, one thing that places us a notch above apes on the evolutionary ladder—most people I've counseled resist the idea. They think it means they're letting their ex off the hook in some way. It somehow feels better to blame their ex for what they are feeling. In fact, one mother told me the idea so distressed her that she avoided therapy for two months. Eventually, she saw—as you'll see in later chapters—that nothing could be further from the truth. In fact, when the mother who fled therapy finally returned, she reported that the change in perspective—"I feel," not "He makes me feel"—was a life-changing concept for her.

So be sure your analysis of what drives you crazy about your ex-partner is from the perspective of the feelings you feel—the feelings you own—not just your ex's distasteful behavior.

THIRD, DIMENSION: PUT THE ISSUE IN CONTEXT

Once you have defined your problem with your ex, you'll need to put it in context—that is, dimension the issue, measuring it so that you better understand its size and its limits. To do that, reflect carefully on the following two questions:

- In what situations and under what circumstances does this troublesome problem tend to happen?

- In what situations and under what circumstances does this troublesome problem tend *not* to occur?

In answering the first question, you'll not only gain a better sense of what may lead to the upsetting behavior, you also may discover possible "triggers" for the behavior. For example, you might find that just before your ex blows up at you in front of the kids, you have usually mentioned something about money problems. Or, you might discover that your ex is only late picking up the kids on the weekends when he is angry at you. Whatever the pattern, what is important here is seeing that the troublesome behavior is in some way predictable: certain things tend to happen before it; certain circumstances make it more likely to happen.

The second question, about exceptions to the rule, can actually be as revealing as the rule itself. You might discover that your ex is more faithful about support payments during the busy part of her business year and that she becomes less responsible during the months when business is down. Or, perhaps you'll learn that your usually uncommunicative ex faithfully calls the children during weekends when your new partner isn't around. Search for the situations in which your ex's behavior is reasonable and conciliatory—or at least more tolerable. What brings those situations about? Discovering triggers of good behavior are as important as triggers of problem behavior to understanding precisely what drives you crazy about your ex.

After you have become clear about the problem with your ex, have brought clarity to the feelings that you have about it, and have searched for triggers and exceptions, you will be ready to create peace for yourself.

Remember:
    ✓ Becoming clear about the specific behavior that bugs you and about its effects is an essential first step toward dealing with the problem.

✓ Identifying triggers of your ex's problem behavior can offer important clues for possible solutions.

✓ Looking closely at the times the troublesome behavior does *not* occur can also offer important hints about the nature of your problem with your ex.

Real Life

My ex is just an irresponsible blob. He's late every week when it's his time to pick up the kids, feeds them junk over the weekend, and lets them do anything they want at his house. This stuff just makes me and the children feel rotten. How do I put that into words?

This litany of the many ways your ex is messing up your life tells me that you feel overwhelmed by a confusing mix of emotions, which isn't surprising given the frustrating things you've mentioned. There is a simple way to begin to deal with it. Start by breaking your feelings down into separate specific problems and the emotional effects of each—the behavior-effects-feelings formula discussed in this chapter. Your list might end up looking something like this:

Problem #1: When my ex is late picking up the kids, I am prevented from beginning my afternoon plans. I feel angry, and they feel hurt.

Problem #2: When my ex feeds the children Twinkies for breakfast, they expect the same at my house, and I feel furious.

Problem #3: When my ex lets the children jump on his furniture and run around the house, they often end up with bruises. Since they tend to do the same things at my home, I end up frustrated.

CHAPTER THREE

Walking Around Brick Walls: Empowering Yourself

Since we cannot change reality, let us change the eyes which see reality.

—NIKOS KAZANTZAKIS,
author of *Zorba the Greek*

Does dealing with your ex feel like pounding your head against a brick wall? No matter how hard you pound, the wall doesn't budge; in fact, the only result is a bruised and bloodied forehead: yours.

Similarly, no matter how hard you try to get your ex to make changes, nothing works. You can't get him or her to listen to reason. The brick wall simply deflects your arguments, your concerns, your anger and your frustration. It doesn't yield. And it doesn't move.

Kate loved fruits and vegetables and believed her children should learn to love them too. She made fruits and vegetables part of every meal she served her kids, assuming—correctly—that this would accustom the kids to their taste. And in fact, her children were glowingly healthy.

The brick wall in the equation was Tom, Kate's obese ex-husband, a junk food junkie who was deaf to her pleas, demands, and urgings that he feed the children healthfully on those alternate weekends they were in his custody. At times, Tom actually seemed to listen to Kate. Other times, he argued back. And sometimes he simply pooh-poohed what he called her "nuts and berries non-sense." But his behavior was consistent: he religiously treated the kids to breakfast at Burger King, sausage pizza for lunch, and multiple Happy Meal dinners. Kate pictured her children munching on hamburgers and fries at their father's house, as she replayed in her mind all the bad health effects of high-fat foods. She compiled facts and figures on eating and health, which she set down in long letters to Tom, explained the harm he was doing in their regular phone calls, even mentioned her complaint to a judge when she was before the court on a visitation matter. But the Happy Meals kept on coming. And Kate's frustration kept on growing.

By the time she came to me for counseling, Kate was at her wit's end, certain that her husband's behavior was detrimental to their children, and unable to make the slightest difference in that behavior.

I put the following challenge to Kate:

"Your ex's behavior seems to be telling you that he's not going to change. Imagine the impact on your children if you gathered up all the psychological energy you have put into trying to change this aspect of your ex-husband and invested it instead in the quality of your own parenting. What do you think their life would be like?"

Kate said nothing, but she agreed to take up the challenge, to put her rich imagination to work on my scenario, rather than on her nail-biting visions of grease-soaked French fries, sugar-filled sodas, and rich desserts ruining her children's teeth, bones, and future. She mulled the notion over for several weeks, during which time I began to notice a gradual change in her. She seemed at once more energized and also more at peace with her life. Simply put, Kate had come to a point of acceptance.

First, she accepted that her ex-husband was a man who loved junk food and would probably never be convinced to un-love it. Chances are, he would continue to eat at fast-food restaurants, cook with grease, and shower sweets on the kids. Accepting that reality went a long way toward bringing Kate some peace.

But perhaps even more significantly, Kate also accepted—in her words, "wrapped her arms around"—the reality that can be the most difficult truth for any divorced parent to accept: that her children were walking a separate path with their father, and that this path was through territory over which she ultimately had little control.

This dual acceptance did not mean that Kate did not still wish Tom acted differently with the children. She did; she still wished his eating behavior was more like hers, and in fact, she still occasionally tried to convince him to change. But acceptance did mean that Kate shifted her attention from something over which she had little control—i.e., how her ex decided to parent when *he* had the children—to something over which she did have control: how *she* cared for the children when they were with her.

Finally, acceptance meant recognizing that it was *she* who had the problem with Tom, not her children. After all, like most kids, they were perfectly content eating fast food when they were with their father. For Kate, however, accepting who her ex was and how he behaved, as a man and as a parent, ultimately meant that *she* was more content.

She had stopped beating her head against that unmoving, unyielding brick wall. Instead, she had given herself the resources to simply walk around it.

The "Ex Eclipse"

The first step in learning how to walk around the brick wall is a kind of astronomy lesson. That is, you need to locate two separate universes: the world you can control, and the world you can't.

My colleague, psychologist Dr. Randy Cale, and I are the co-authors of a psycho-educational program for divorcing parents entitled "Kids First after Divorce." Shortly after we had begun teaching the program we began to notice a special kind of distress suffered by separated parents. The distress flowed from the two parents increasingly focusing on parts of their lives they couldn't control. The more divorcing parents we reached with "Kids First," the more evident this phenomenon became. We even gave it a name: The ex eclipse.[1] Here's how it works:

Look at Diagram A and think back to the time you and your spouse were still under the same roof. Back then, there were things that went on in your life together that you could control, and there were things you could not control. Maybe it was up to you to decide whether to give the kids cereal or eggs for breakfast. Or perhaps you took charge of getting the kids dressed for school and deciding what they would wear. You certainly had control over whether you drove the speed limit on the way to day care or took a risk with the gas pedal because you knew you were going to be late for work. While you were together, despite the fact that you certainly had some frustrations with your partner, most of your mental energy was focused on the parts of your life over which you had control.

As to the frustrations with your partner, they were annoying— even maddening. Perhaps years of experience had taught you that no matter how many times you reminded your partner to give the children vitamins in the morning, he would almost always forget. Perhaps it was the way she let the kids "get away with murder" that bothered you, or the way he took out his work frustrations on the children.

Chances are that every now and then when you and your ex were living together, you may have taken a shot at convincing him or her that something should change. In fact, every once in a while, he or she may even have listened to what you said, maybe even shown a willingness to change. But for the most part, you accepted the fact that that there were certain aspects of your partner's behavior that you didn't like but were simply stuck with. That was the marriage; that was "the deal."

Everything changed when you and your ex parted. New frustrations crept into your life. Unexpected worries surprised you. As your children left to be with their other parent, you found that you were suddenly preoccupied with fresh fears and anxieties about their well-being. Would the weekend be filled with junk food?

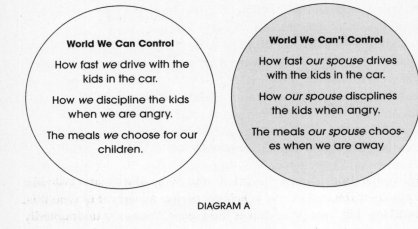

World We Can Control

How fast *we* drive with the kids in the car.

How *we* discipline the kids when we are angry.

The meals *we* choose for our children.

World We Can't Control

How fast *our spouse* drives with the kids in the car.

How *our spouse* disciplines the kids when angry.

The meals *our spouse* chooses when we are away

DIAGRAM A

Would your ex remember to use seat belts? Would your teenager be allowed to stay out until ridiculous hours?

What happened? The separation from your ex seemed to spur you to focus heavily on the world of things you could not control, and that world seemed to be growing larger and larger, the list of things that you couldn't control becoming longer each time your children walked out the door. The very act of separation seemed to give birth to these frustrating new realities—things beyond your reach—and the place where you had your personal power, the aspects of your life that you *could* control, became eclipsed by the world you couldn't control. You had become a victim of the "ex eclipse," illustrated in Diagram B. You were mentally "losing" a most valuable part of your life: the part where you can make a difference. It was sliding into shadow; you could feel the light in your life being eclipsed, the same way the moon can block the light of the sun during an eclipse.

Apple Pie and Emotional Peril

Insisting that your ex should change in some way—and being met repeatedly by your ex's resoundingly defiant unchanged behavior—

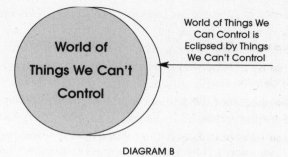

World of Things We
Can Control is
Eclipsed by Things
We Can't Control

DIAGRAM B

is like standing before a custard pie and demanding that it taste like apple pie. The custard pie is being a perfect statement of who it is; ordering it to "be apple" makes little sense. Your ex is undoubtedly a perfect statement of who he is, however unreasonable who he is may seem to you, and he may have neither the desire nor the ability to become the apple pie you want him to be.

Where does this leave you? As you feel your world of control slipping further and further into the shadow created by what you *cannot* control, you're in peril of being blacked out in a kind of emotional darkness created by the ex eclipse.

Of course, your concerns are real. Your worries are understandable. Up to a point. Certainly, these worries and concerns spring from the best of intentions: these are your children, after all; their safety and well-being are the most important thing in the world to you. But does worrying have an impact on the quality of your children's lives? Does your preoccupation with things you can't control make them safer? Not really. Will you still be preoccupied with these frustrations a year from now? Five years from now, will you still be doing nervous laps up and down the living room floor on a Sunday night, waiting for the kids to get back from their time with your ex-spouse, still stewing over the fact that, as always, as has been the case for the last five years, he or she is bringing them back late?

When you're in the ex eclipse, it's all too easy to blame your ex for your own unhappiness. How many times have you thought to yourself: "He knows it makes me angry, but he does it anyway." Or:

"She's a genius at pushing my buttons, and she enjoys doing it." Or: "He just does it to get to me."

Listen to those words. They say clearly that the speaker is a puppet on a string, emotionally yanked to and fro at someone else's whim. Are you so emotionally dependent on your ex? Is your happiness in the hands of the person you used to be married to? If so, it's time to realize you've allowed that to happen. It's time to realize you have choices about how you will respond to your ex-partner's behavior. If you don't, then you are doomed to remain in emotional darkness until your ex decides to change his or her behavior. That doesn't leave you much of a life.

The ex eclipse, in short, is not neglecting what you can control in favor of a preoccupation with what you can't control. It allows your emotional well-being to be determined by the behavior of others; it's the result of surrendering your internal emotional life to others. Ultimately, you do have the power to choose how to feel and act. In the ex eclipse, you've given up that power. What's more, you've given it up to someone you've chosen to stop sharing your life with.

Try:

✓ Noticing any small or large ways in which you have lost parts of your life to preoccupations about your ex's antics. How many moments lost to worrying? How many stomachaches about what she might be doing wrong? How many precious moments with your children swallowed up by anger?

Out of the Shadow: Focus on What You Can Control

Take a good look at Diagram B again. Imagine stretching your arm into the picture and taking hold of the circle that holds all the things in life that you can't control. Picture it as one of those hollow rubber balls kids are forever tossing against walls and steps. Grip

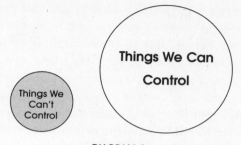

DIAGRAM C
Empowerment: Strategy for Resourceful Living

the ball. Reach it back overhead. Now hurl it to the lower left corner of the page. Throw it so hard and so far that it becomes very tiny.

What you are left with is Diagram C. Have a good look at it. Try to feel what it can do for your life. Here, large and prominent in your mind, are all the things you can control. Over there, down in the left-hand corner where they loom comparatively small in your vision and your thinking, are the things you can't control.

When you do what the diagram suggests—relegating what you can't control to a minor role in your life—life itself becomes quite different. Making the conscious decision to refocus your emotional and mental energies on the things that you can control and away from the things you cannot unties your emotional life from your ex-partner's. You're free.

The Empowerment Shift

The empowerment shift is achieved by *the conscious decision to refocus your emotional and mental energies on the things that you can control and away from the things you cannot.* I call it the empowerment shift. It takes place in your mind. It requires not only that you mentally shrink the frustrating realities of how your ex parents your children, but also that you vigilantly search for all the small and large ways that *you* have a positive impact on your children. It's step two toward learning how to walk around the brick wall.

It would be painful to watch a recently disabled person try, over and over, to walk in the same way he used to, insisting that his life doesn't have to change, only to see him fall again and again. At some point, you would want to say: "My friend, it may be time to accept that you can't walk as you used to . . . to accept that you have a disability, to get a cane, use the power of your good leg, focus on all of the things that you *can* do, and get on with your life." You would want your friend to make the empowerment shift.

Kate made the empowerment shift by focusing not on her ex's eating habits but on the wonderful gifts *she* gave to her children— how *she* fed them, how *she* watched over their health, how *she* searched out the freshest vegetables, fruits in season, the best ingredients to keep them safe and strong. You can make the same mental shift.

Start by accepting your ex for who he or she is. Acceptance does not mean resignation. It means recognition of the fact that each of you has chosen to behave in a certain way as parents, and neither of you is likely to dramatically change how you approach life with the kids. You know that you've exhausted your creative possibilities for influencing your ex, and instead, you're deciding to reinvest your energies in things you do have control over. This means that you will not sacrifice another moment of your precious life with your children to preoccupations with things about your ex that you cannot control. Is it possible for you to believe that, for every maddening thing that your ex does with your children, there are two, five, or hundreds of gifts that *you* offer the kids, and that it is in these gifts that you have your real power as a parent? One father I worked with put it this way: "I finally realized that I had to take my mind off her and get a life."

The empowerment shift means replacing thoughts like, "I can't believe she lets them be so wild," with thoughts like, "I am making sure my kids behave well and don't get out of control." Like Kate, remind yourself of your own parenting—how *you* keep them safe in the car, how *you* make sure that they are in at a decent hour, how *you* behave with them when you are angry. When you make the empowerment shift, you mentally and emotionally reclaim the part of your life you lost when you became preoccupied with your ex-partner's behavior. You notice that it's possible to walk around that brick wall—and take back your life.

Your real power lies in how *you* choose to raise your children, not in trying to change your ex as a parent. Acceptance does not mean resignation.

MAKING THE EMPOWERMENT SHIFT: A LIFE DISCIPLINE

The conscious decision that the empowerment shift entails is a critical turning point for many parents, and it is the change that most promotes personal freedom and family healing. But making the empowerment shift is not easy, nor is it something that will be accomplished overnight.

In fact, you don't really "accomplish" the empowerment shift at all. Rather, it is one of those life-changing mental disciplines you will come back to again and again—not just when looking for personal peace out of the chaos of your custody situation with your ex, but in many other spheres of your life as well.

It's important that you view the empowerment shift as such—as a life discipline that will require practice and focus, and that will persist as part of your life. The exercise you're about to undertake is the first step on a path of living you will come back to again and again. In a very real sense, the empowerment shift involves recognizing that you'll need this discipline a thousand times over the course of your life with your children.

As you embark on this path of living, be aware that staying on the path requires three steps: recognition that you're straying; acknowledgment without punishment; and return. If you have ever engaged in meditation, you'll recognize this sequence; it's like coming back to the breath each time you wander off it. The analogy to making the empowerment shift is this: your mind will wander off from time to time—away from the things you can control to the things you can't. When this happens, acknowledge the wandering, accept it, even celebrate your acknowledgment and acceptance. Then gently bring your mind back to a concrete focus on what you can control.

It's a quiet command, a soft-spoken reminder: "I've let my mind focus on my ex's irresponsibility, or bad temper, or poor judgment. I'm now going to return to *my* source of power, which is the way *I* parent—*my* behavior, not my ex-partner's."

Over time, with practice, the discipline grows easier. This time, you must force your mind to return to your own empowerment. Next time, you don't have to force it quite so hard; it returns more smoothly and easily. Eventually, the shift will become almost automatic. As we'll discuss in greater detail in the next chapter, lasting peace and freedom almost always come from changing the world within us, not the world around us. Making the empowerment shift can be a giant step around the brick wall of frustration with your ex. Imagine the life your children would have if they experienced your parenting infused with the energy you unleashed when you directed your attention away from things about your ex that are beyond your control!

MAKING THE EMPOWERMENT SHIFT: THE PAPER CHASE

Here is an exercise that can kick-start your empowerment shift. Doing some parts of the exercise may make you feel foolish, but consider this: Nothing is more foolish than being a puppet on a string that is controlled by your ex-partner's behavior.

Gather three sheets of paper, one 6 inches by 6 inches, another 8½ inches by 11, and another as large as you can find—but no smaller than 1½ feet by 2 feet. The dimensions of these sheets are important, so be sure to gather the right materials. In addition, get a notebook or composition pad you feel comfortable with. You'll want to use it as a journal.

On the smallest sheet of paper, write down all the things you can think of that you wish you could change about your ex, but that you know in all honesty will probably never change. This is your brick wall. Fill the sheet up if you can, and write small enough that you can avoid using a second sheet (unless absolutely necessary).

On the medium-sized sheet, list all the things that you would like to change about your ex that you think you have a chance at influencing—the bothersome things that your ex might actually someday be willing to consider changing.

Finally, on the largest sheet of paper, make a list of all of the things that you clearly control in your life. As you work on this, remember two things:

First, control is in the eyes of the beholder. You have control over many things; you just have to choose to see them.

Second, don't just look for large issues—like the kind of person you think you can become. Think small. It might help to think in three categories, one at a time:

- things in your own life you have control over—how fast you drive, or which side of the bed you will get out of in the morning.

- things in your children's lives you have control over—the cereal you buy for them, the school they attend.

- things in your relationship with your ex that you have control over—the words and tone of voice *you* will use when you complain about the sugary cereal she buys the kids.

The smaller you think, the more items you will have.

Here's a sample of one parent's sheets:

Sample Empowerment Sheet

Brick Wall Items:
Jack lets the kids run wild and won't listen to me about it. They act out when they return to my house, and I end up feeling overwhelmed and depressed.

He insists that 10:00 PM is an okay time for bed on a school night, and never listens to me about it. They end up tired, and I end up furious.

Things I Might Have a Shot at Getting Jack to Change:
Getting the support checks here on time.
Remembering to give Katie her asthma medication.

Things I Have Real Control Over:
The clothes I choose to wear in the morning.
What cereal I'll have.
Who I'll smile at today.
Whether or not I'll do housework.
How I'll tell the boss the bad news about the quarterly project.
The rules I have around the house for the kids.
The bedtime I set for them.
Being faithful myself with the medication for Katie.
The good foods I choose to prepare.
The vitamins I buy to keep them healthy.
The attention I give to Jimmie's difficulties with math homework.
The table manners I teach them.
The soothing songs I sing to Katie during bath time.
The way I always try to mention several things that my children did
    that I appreciated right before they go to bed.
How I choose to handle spirituality in the family by being at church
    with the kids every Sunday morning.
Making sure Jimmie knows how much I love his smile despite his
    braces.

Talking nicely to the kids about their dad despite what a jerk he is.
Following through on my responsibility to give Jack insurance
    cards for Katie and Jimmie.
The way I always bite my lip and stay calm when Jack says
    something infuriating to me and the kids are nearby . . . I want
    them to learn how to be civil with people that bug them.
What I choose to say when Jack insults my mother.

Once all three sheets have been carefully filled out, do the following:

Set the medium-sized sheet aside in a safe place where your children can't find it but where you can easily refer to it later. You'll want it when you begin to practice some of the lessons of later chapters on ways to creatively influence your ex.

Place the smallest sheet of paper—the brick wall—in the middle of the floor. Fold it. Now fold it again. Fold it repeatedly, until you have reduced it to a tiny speck of paper. Step on it—yes, I mean that literally—to make it even more compact. Take this speck of paper to a safe outdoor setting. Place it on the ground and light it with a match. Burn it. As you watch the smoke rise, make a gesture up to the sky, as if you are commending these problems to the heavens. Now walk away.

Take the largest sheet of paper and do something memorable with it. Hang it on your private mirror, so you have to look at it over and over. If you're feeling spirited you might tape it to your forehead and dance about the room or wear it on your back for an afternoon. Most important, whatever you do, end by hanging this sheet of paper in a prominent place where you can look at it easily. (A good place is the inside of a closet door, so the kids won't read along.) In a very real sense, this sheet of paper expresses your power. Honor it. Celebrate it. And, as much as you can, keep coming back to the points that are written on it.

Take it one week at a time at first. As you go through your week, you will find yourself occasionally becoming lost again in thoughts about things you cannot control, things like: "I know she doesn't have their seat belts on, and I'm scared as hell," or "How long is he going to continue to be late coming to pick up the children and making me late for work?"

Here's where the notebook comes in. Keep a journal of these thoughts and the feelings they produce, simply jotting them down whenever they occur. After you have been keeping the journal for a few weeks, take the next step: Whenever one of these disempowering thoughts enters your mind, simply notice the thought. Don't judge yourself. Then, quickly immerse yourself in an activity that speaks of the power you *do* have in the lives of your children. This can be a very small and simple activity—check your list inside the closet for hints—anything from perhaps spending a few minutes planning your vacation with the children to looking up a new recipe to surprise them with when they return home from school.

Maybe you'll have the disempowering thought in the middle of a heated discussion with your ex in which she is, as usual, attacking you verbally even though the kids are in the next room. Of course, you're furious—which means you're concentrating on *her* behavior. Center yourself by immediately shifting your attention to your breathing. Are you breathing fast? Probably. Calm down. Then focus on how *you* want to behave in front of your children. It's not your ex's behavior that's at issue; after all, you know by now that there's little you can do about it. What will your response be during the verbal barrage and when she stops screaming at you? *That's* the issue; that's the behavior you can control.

If you can make that mental empowerment shift in mid-argument, you'll continue to make a difference in the lives of your children despite the behavior that your ex is choosing.

Try:

✓ Finding ways to "get a life" again. Time with friends. Small kindnesses for yourself. A class you've always wanted to take. Bubble baths. A health club. Counseling. Bottom line: Your children will be emotionally okay to the extent that you are emotionally okay. Take care of yourself and you take care of them.

Remember:

✓ Accepting that there are aspects of your ex that are beyond your control is a critical first step toward achieving peace.

✓ One of the greatest powers of the human mind is the capacity to choose where to place one's attention.

✓ Making the empowerment shift means diverting your attention away from frustrating realities about your ex that are unlikely to change and toward parts of your life where you can make a difference.

✓ Making the empowerment shift does not mean giving up: you can still wish things were different with your ex and try to create change in the relationship.

✓ Lasting peace always comes from changing the world within us, not the world around us.

Real Life

What about situations where what your ex is doing with the kids is downright wrong? She screams at our eight-year-old over minor issues and seems to enjoy bad-mouthing my girlfriend to her. How do you surrender about stuff like that?

Your question goes to the heart of a difficult dilemma for separated parents: How do you let go of or accept frustrating and sometimes harsh realities about your ex and your children? First, remember that you can still try to make a difference with your ex, and the upcoming chapters will give you many tools for doing so. Second, remind yourself that you can still deeply wish these realities would change; in fact, if you want to, you can even hang on to your anger about them. Finally, you may have to gently embrace the truth that your ex's screaming and bad-mouthing, while undesirable and certainly insensitive to your children, may also be something you simply are not able to protect them from. It may just be a part of the path they have to walk with their mother. Life sometimes simply isn't fair, and for your children, a mother who is insensitive at times may just be the way it's going to be. Of course, if what your ex is doing with your children is abusive, you should immediately contact child protective officials or a mental health professional who can help you sort through the risks to your kids.

Whenever I try to shift my attention away from the stuff about my ex that sends me up a wall, I find my mind returning over and over again to the thoughts about him that make me furious. What can I do?

Here is an opportunity to use a shift in behavior to help you make a mental and emotional shift. Find small or not-so-small things you can immediately begin to do that will make you feel that you are making a difference in your life or in the lives of the children. You might plan a trip to the museum, or bake cookies that will please and surprise them. Any fast and doable action like this will remind you of the possibilities that are open to you despite preoccupations with your ex. Remember also that focusing on what you can control is a discipline that takes practice. Be patient with yourself.

CHAPTER FOUR

Going Headfirst:
Making Your Own Peace

Man is made by his beliefs. As he believes, so he is.
—BHAGAVAD-GITA,
Hindu Sanskrit poem

The path to peace with your ex starts and ends between your own two ears. The first steps on the journey take you to an understanding of your own mind-set, to an acceptance of what you can and cannot change, to an acknowledgment of the uncomfortable feelings that have overpowered you. That's why these first steps are among the toughest you'll ever take—and the most important. They'll get you ready to take back control of your inner life; instead of being bounced around like a marionette by your ex-partner's antics, *you* will determine how you feel inside.

Did you ever rappel down a mountainside? Even with someone securing you at the other end of the rope, even though you know you've checked and rechecked your equipment, that moment when you first step backward off the edge of a cliff into nothingness is difficult, to say the least. Your leg seems paralyzed. An oppressive physical resistance locks you to the spot. You're aware that all you have to do is move one leg back a few inches—simplest thing in the world—and you'll be on your way, bouncing down the mountain, moving swiftly to where you want to go. Just a few inches. And still your leg won't move.

Mountain climbers call that first backward shift the "commitment step." And the commitment, as any climber will tell you, occurs not in the quadriceps or hip joint or foot muscles but in your brain. It's a change in *perception*. A change from: "I'm about to go over the side of a cliff backward" to "I'm setting out to where I want to go." Not "I'm going to step into thin air and descend eighty feet," but "I'm going to walk down a mountainside, well-trained and well-equipped, and I cannot fall because this rope will catch me."

Free your thinking, and you unlock your leg. Change your perception, and you can take the first step toward where you want to go. It's the same approach to finding peace with your ex.

Indeed, sharing custody with a former spouse who drives you crazy may sometimes *seem* like going backward over a cliff. But it's only by taking charge of your own mind-set that you can transcend this painful situation. It's only through self-mastery that you can conquer the stress and anxiety of this ongoing relationship. It's the ultimate paradox. Your relationship with your ex, which threatens daily to drag you down, may actually be an opportunity for growth and a vehicle for your personal evolution.

The chances are good that your current perspective is actually amplifying your distress, that your mind-set is adding pain to a situation—dealing with your exasperating ex-spouse—that is already painful enough. Psychologists call that a cognitive distortion; it means you are clinging to a set of assumptions about how the world *should* work, and since the world invariably does not work that way, the clinging sets you up for regular disappointment and constant frustration. Of course, it would be nice if your ex acted reasonably. Of course, your life would feel better if he controlled his temper. But he seldom has, and he is unlikely to change overnight. Until you accept the reality of who he is, you remain in a paralyzing cage forged by your own rigid perspective.

So here are tools to help you shift your perspective in a way that frees you to find contentment whatever the situation and however static it remains. Here are critical, irreplaceable skills—Life 101 stuff—that you can carry with you whenever you take up arms against your personal sea of troubles. Here are mechanisms that will help you learn to understand what you can control—and then control it . . . that will teach you what you can change—and help you change it . . . that will show you how to examine your own feelings, relieve and reclaim your emotional life for yourself—so you begin to find peace. Best of all, this can happen without a single change on the part of your ex!

You have more power to change your own mental perspective than to change your ex.

Be Compassionate With Yourself: Embrace Your Feelings

Here's a rule of thumb so powerful it's virtually a universal principle: deny an uncomfortable thought or feeling, and it controls you; acknowledge it, and you can let it go. The first step in finding the path to peace with your ex is to find peace with yourself. That means giving yourself permission to feel what you're feeling.

Sharon's ex-husband, Jack, seemed to regard their carefully worked-out visitation schedule as his personal space, a room in which he could move around at will. He would phone at the last minute to say that something had come up, or his plans had changed, or he was suddenly exhausted, and he couldn't possibly take the kids that day as planned—how about the next day instead? Or he simply wouldn't show up, leaving Sharon feeling angry and hurt, forcing her to bear the burden of explaining things to the children.

Jack's actions wreaked havoc with Sharon's life. Her boss was becoming impatient with Sharon's own schedule changes and with the amount of time she spent making arrangements and rearrangements. The man with whom Sharon was attempting to start a new life was also not pleased—both because Jack's shifts in schedule interrupted his life with Sharon, and because she expended so much energy and *angst* being upset about the issue. Sharon found it outrageous, that Jack still "played fast and loose" with her life, and she suspected that he did it partly to provoke her. Then she would quickly remind herself that Jack was "the father of my children," and would feel guilty for her suspicions. She would remember that "Jack always acted like an airhead, and it always drove me crazy," and that, therefore, she "shouldn't be feeling this way." "I didn't really mean to say that about him," she would confess remorsefully or "I have no right," to feel injured or distressed by his behavior.

But the fact is: Sharon *does* have a right to her feelings, however ungenerous or dark they may seem.

Like a lot of us, Sharon had grown up believing that it is wrong to feel anger. She had spent a lifetime—and certainly all of her married life—running away from her feelings of injury and hiding her feelings of being hurt. Until she allowed herself to feel those feelings—and it took a long time to get to that point—she remained locked out of her own soul.

Resisting your own feelings is what turns pain into suffering. Suppose you've injured your knee. You know you're injured because you feel pain. Resisting or ignoring the pain, telling yourself it shouldn't be there and tensing your body against it, insisting you can still jog two miles with stiffened muscles can lead to real suffering and even permanent damage.

The same with emotions. We create suffering when we resist emotions and run from their reality, telling ourselves that we shouldn't be feeling a certain way. But in resisting the flow of our internal experience and trying to dismiss or ignore the pain, all we do is disengage from part of ourselves, pushing that part away under the notion—sheer fantasy—that the emotion will leave us. Of course, it doesn't leave us; rather, it comes back with renewed and more powerful force.

The first step toward relief is to admit what we are feeling, to allow the tide of emotion to wash over us and then recede naturally, as tides do. Simply saying aloud to ourselves or to someone else that we feel frightened, hurt or injured, furious or enraged, hopeless or sad is like relaxing into the pain of an injured knee. The pain doesn't go away, but by allowing it to be there, we rob it of some of its power over us.

When Sharon stopped running away from her feelings of injury and hurt each time her ex acted in a distressing way, she said it was as if she had "finally opened the door to my own home and let myself in."

Emotions can be painful. But telling yourself that you shouldn't be feeling them can create unnecessary suffering.

What are your feelings about your ex? They're sometimes subtle, sometimes powerful. Let them enter your consciousness; try to put words to the feelings. But don't be tricked. Explore under the surface. Are you angry at your ex? Look carefully at the events that triggered your anger. Just before the fury set in, did you perhaps feel dismissed, hurt, belittled, even frightened? Did you experience a sense of shame? Had the sense you were being set aside? Felt excluded, or underestimated, or put down? Anger is easy to see, but it is those subtler feelings, often expressed as anger, that are especially important to allow into your consciousness. Embrace them and say their name aloud and they will instantly lose their secret control over you.

Steve felt ready to explode with anger when his ex-spouse, Patty, handed him a list of do's and don'ts every time he picked up his young children. When he looked deeper, however, it became clear that he saw every list as a put-down, a loud statement that he was an incompetent father. It was shame and hurt he was really feeling; after all, he had been the parent who worked outside the home during the marriage and who spent less time with the kids. Maybe it was true after all that, when it came to the kids, Patty knew more than he did. The do's and don'ts lists galled him because the fear that he was an incompetent father was in his head; it was his own fear. The anger the lists spurred was only the surface expression.

Anger often masks subtler feelings of embarrassment, humiliation, or shame.

Once Steve embraced his emotions and recognized the subtle feelings beneath the sensation of rage for what they were—his own sense of inadequacy, his own hurt—he was able to take action that actually influenced his ex. He told her that he wanted to become more confident as a dad, and he asked her not to overdo the lists because while he admitted that he had weak spots as a parent, he also felt competent in many of the areas listed. Having given himself permission to feel what he was feeling, and setting his ego aside for a moment, Steve could at last accept his ex's communications as simple attempts to help ensure a good life for the children.

Of course, some thoughts and feelings are particularly repugnant—even frightening—to contemplate. It's not unusual for separated parents to feel so wronged and frustrated that they fantasize about hurting each other. That's a distressing thought, to be sure; violence is wrong in virtually all circumstances. But there is an essential difference between thought and actions. Thinking or fantasizing about revenge and retribution may simply be your mind's way of coping with a very difficult situation. When such thoughts emerge, first gently acknowledge them and quickly remind yourself that you have an absolute commitment never to act on them. Watch the thoughts pass by and recede like clouds on the horizon; observe them without entering into them. Remind yourself that you can let them go as quickly as they entered your mind. Simply acknowledging your feelings, awful though they may be, without necessarily acting on them, is the first step toward reclaiming your inner life and disentangling from your ex.

NO ONE MAKES US FEEL THE WAY WE DO

"Failing the test made me so depressed."

"My son made me so mad when he threw his potatoes across the table."

We've all made statements like these, because we all tend to see a strict cause-and-effect connection between an event and the feelings with which we respond to the event. But not everyone who failed that particular test is depressed, and not every parent will become furious at a child for throwing mashed potatoes. It is not the events themselves that cause us to feel a certain way; rather, our way of thinking about those events creates the feelings.

That person who failed the test and refused to give in, resolving instead to do better next time: What was she saying to herself that was so different from what was going on in the mind of the person felled by the failure? What was the difference in thought process between the parent who was *not* enraged as the mashed potatoes flew across the room and the parent who was red with anger?

> **"Our greatest freedom is the freedom to choose our attitude."**
> —Viktor E. Frankl, *Man's Search for Meaning*

Nothing is easier when struggling with your ex than to fall into the trap of simply saying "He makes me so mad" or "She makes me feel so hopeless." The reality is that your perception about a situation is what creates your anger or hopelessness.

Two people whose ex-partners are perpetually late to pick up their children—by as much as an hour on occasion—respond with diametrically opposed reactions. One becomes livid at each instance of lateness, while the other treats it with patient resignation *and* with contingency planning. What determines the difference?

The difference is in attitude, in way of thinking, in the orientation of the individual's mental compass. The difference is: Are you a victim, who is defeated by circumstances, events, situations before you begin to fight? Or are you the creator of your own experience, able to take some control over your emotions?

The difference is being willing to accept that you can control whether your emotions are chaotic, disturbing, neutral, or pleasurable. How? By reclaiming your emotional life. When you accept that you create your own experience, rather than feeling victimized by circumstances, you gain freedom over those situations in which your ex appears unlikely to change.

Focus less on how your ex "makes" you feel, and more on how you want to feel.

This doesn't mean you should feel guilty about the distress you may be feeling. You certainly didn't sit back and decide to be a victim. Nobody wakes up and says: "I think I'd like to feel miserable today." Most of this happens unconsciously. But you do have the capacity to learn how to free yourself from the cascade of emotions. You *are* the author of your internal experience.

Trust that there is much greater hope for you to feel some sense of peace in your relationship with your ex if you can take the courageous step of assuming full responsibility for your emotional struggle rather than suspending your life while waiting for your ex to change. The power to find relief and happiness is in your hands.

YOU ARE NOT YOUR THOUGHTS AND MOODS

When feelings are intense, they seem to define us. It's easy to think of yourself as a depressed person when you are depressed or as an angry person when you're burning up with rage. But it isn't true. Though feelings well up from within the deepest part of you, they are not who you are; they are simply what you are experiencing. You are not the depression; you are the person feeling sad. You are not the anger; you are the person having angry feelings. You are the witness, not the feeling. The feelings come and go, like a leaf on a river. Depression passes. Anger fades. They only describe what you're sensing at that moment; they don't tell you who you are.

You are the witness to the feeling, not the feeling itself.

Both of these truths—that feelings do not define you, and that feelings pass—are essential to keep in mind where feelings about your ex are concerned. Those feelings, powerful as they may be, don't have to take up permanent residence in your consciousness; they need not be a constant part of your life. Even when they seem to take over your life, it doesn't last and they eventually recede. For that reason, you can let your emotions wash over you. When your ex does something that distresses you, you can always tell yourself: "This distress is not me. . . . I can watch it; it will pass."

When you begin to feel yourself well up with rage, frustration, or sadness about something your ex is doing, close your eyes and imagine a cloud passing on the horizon. It is there for a brief time, then it floats away. Let your feelings about your ex pass in the same way. After all, they always have and you just didn't notice; one minute you were ticked off at your ex, and the next you were thinking about your daughter's dance recital. Allow yourself to feel the feelings, acknowledge them, then feel them ebb, pass like clouds in the sky, vanish. Now you can get on with your life. The feelings may be at the edge of your consciousness, but you're still able to do the work on your desk, fill the baby bottles, shuttle your kids off to their dance class. You've detached yourself from the feeling. It's not you. You're free.

The Four Feel-Bad Buttons: How to Keep Them from Being Pushed

In reality, other people can't make us feel anything. All they can do is push the buttons that we ourselves have turned on for them.

Other people act, and we choose to think about their actions in a manner that causes our distress. It's *our* irrationality, not theirs. There are four buttons in particular that ex-partners tend to present for their former spouses to push, four surefire irrationalities with which they make themselves feel as bad as possible: catastrophizing, absolutist demands, denial, and nothing-but thinking.

CATASTROPHIZING

Catastrophizing[1] means making something much bigger than it really is. It's a practice we all engage in from time to time, imagining the worst-case scenario and embracing it till we're virtually paralyzed into inaction.

When Joan and her husband Chris separated, Chris took the good family car and left her with the jalopy they had used for quick errands. With the full burden of the family's daily transportation needs now upon her and her job more essential than ever, Joan began to catastrophize: "What if this car doesn't start on a morning I have to be at work? I could get fired." "What if I'm on the highway and I get a flat tire? How will I ever fix it?" "What if the baby is in the car with me and the axle freezes, as it did once before? She could be killed!"

Any reasonable person would feel some degree of frustration—even anxiety—over being stuck with an old and decrepit car. But Joan's catastrophizing took her feelings to a new level of fear and terror. Such "awfulizing," as Dr. Albert Ellis has described it, set her up as a perfect patsy. So overpowering were her (irrational) emotions that anyone could easily push her buttons. Just ruffling her feathers even slightly would send Joan into a spasm of terror. And just about anything could ruffle her feathers.

Joan and I reviewed how her awfulizing was focusing on future possibilities, and how she was allowing her emotions to be cranked up to unnecessary levels of intensity by things that had not happened yet—and might never happen. In a sense, Joan had ratcheted up normal worry into sheer fantasy. By catastrophizing, she was bringing an imagined, tragic future into the present and making her own life feel rotten.

> *The mind is its own place and can make a heaven of hell and a hell of heaven.*
>
> —John Milton, 17th century poet

The solution was certainly not to go to the opposite extreme of feeling nothing; rather, Joan needed to recognize that her catastrophic thinking had expanded the tragic possibilities beyond reality. We reviewed the realities: To date, no one in the family had lost a job, suffered a flat tire on a highway, or been killed because of the car. We also looked at more reasonable ideas about what would likely happen in the event the car did break down: Yes, someone *could* be injured—even die—but that could happen crossing the street. More likely, she would have some temporary inconvenience, she would go on breathing, and the world would keep spinning. As acceptance of the facts brought some proportion to her fears, Joan also developed a proactive plan for coping: she arranged for back-up rides, took the car in for a good checkup by a trusted mechanic, and invested in a membership in the AAA. In short, by taking control of her feelings about a situation, Joan was able to take action on the situation.

Choose to treat your dilemma with your ex as a problem to be solved rather than as a catastrophe.

ABSOLUTIST DEMANDS

Absolutist demands are the "musts" and "shoulds" of life: We must be thin to be attractive. We should never lose our temper. We must act in a certain way for others to like us. Of course, if we insist on living according to such absolute rules of behavior, even the slightest imperfection equates to failure and plunges us into unhappiness and disappointment.

Ex-partners in particular tend to make absolutist demands of their former spouses. Of course, there is nothing wrong with wanting respect from your ex, wanting your ex to maintain self-control, or wanting him or her to be a certain kind of person—punctual and even-tempered, for example. But while wishes about other people's behavior are fine, turning them into shoulds and musts is irrational and, in the end, dysfunctional; it creates *our* distress and has virtually no impact on the other person.

Spiritual leader and psychologist Ram Dass once created the following metaphor: On a walk in the woods, we come upon a tree. It is gnarled and bent with age, fat and thick at the bottom and thin and spindly on top, and though it wears some vibrantly colorful leaves, others are brown or shriveled. Yet we stand and simply behold the tree. We observe it, maybe touch it. We appreciate its uniqueness, accepting it as a perfect manifestation of what it is. Shriveled leaves, rough bark, knots, and twists—all are part of the package. We let the tree be as and what it is.

As soon as we leave the forest and enter the realm of human relationships, however, we tend to lose our capacity for such nonjudgmental acceptance. Instead, we impose onto others our mental model of how they should or must be in our eyes, and when they violate these mental rules—this long list of shoulds and musts—we become disappointed or furious. *Our* mental model of others, in short, makes *us* unhappy; it doesn't impact the others at all—they are just being a perfect statement of who they are.

So when your ex-partner acts in ways that offend or distress you, check to see if it isn't your mental model that's causing the offense or distress. Are the shoulds and musts you impose on your ex a little extreme, even irrational? Is there a law carved in stone that states that your ex must behave in any particular way for you? If you have carved one, you are bound to feel rotten. It's *you* who have created the feeling, not your ex.

It is our internal demands that others be a certain way for us that produce most of our suffering.

Of course, dropping your mental rules about your ex does not mean you go along with whatever he or she hands you. Instead of demands, establish realistic preferences: Examine your thinking about your ex's upsetting behavior and transform your *requirements* about that behavior into reasonable wants and desires . . . into preferences.[2]

Joan, for example, could transform her irrational beliefs about the junky car Chris left her into a realistic preference. By reminding herself that no law says her ex must or even should be considerate at all times, she did just that. Here's how Joan put it:

> "It bothers me that Chris took that car, because I would prefer him to think about how it will affect me and the kids before he makes such a decision. I wish he would think about what we need more often, but he just doesn't seem to be doing that lately. Now that this unfortunate thing has happened, I'm going to have to figure out how to deal with it constructively. The fact that he took the car from me isn't the end of the world, and I'm most likely not going to die or have a serious illness because of it. I just wish it hadn't happened, and maybe I'll find a way to complain to him about it."

Notice the softer emotional tone of Joan's transformed dialogue with herself. There is a world of a difference between a demand and a preference. A demand says: "You must be a certain kind of person and act a certain way." A demand *implies*: "You are being a bad person, because you're not living up to my expectations . . . you should be more reasonable for me."

By contrast, a healthy preference says: "I prefer that you act a certain way, although there is no way that I can ultimately control that, and I know that my life can still go on and have meaning even if you do not change." That's simply realism, and it is the key to coping with frustrating behavior from an ex-spouse.

Shoulds, musts, and demands directed at your ex-partner will only intensify your suffering. Realistic preferences will soften your distress.

What is particularly pernicious about absolutist demands is that you tend to hang your happiness on them. You link the rules in your head about how your ex must or should behave to your own chance for happiness. "She must do a certain thing or act in a certain way or be a certain kind of person for me to find peace and contentment." When you think like that, you're making a pretty tough bargain for yourself—a bargain in which you play no role whatsoever.

> *Blessed is the man who expects nothing, for he*
> *shall never be disappointed.*
> —Alexander Pope, 18th century poet

When you transform those demands into preferences, you unlink your ex's behavior and character from the train of your own life. Your happiness will no longer depend on what your former spouse does—or at least, on your idea of what your former spouse ought to do. He or she won't have to change in order for you to lead a happy or peaceful life. You prefer that your ex change, of course, but it no longer hangs you up; you can go on living.

To help you turn demands into preferences, do the following exercise daily for several weeks:

Imagine

. . . that you are sitting in a large movie theater, facing a full-size screen, watching a movie of your ex doing one of the things that most upsets you. Now clear the screen till it becomes blank. Start the movie over and watch the same behavior again. This time, however, imagine a gentle voice speaking over the images. It is your voice, and it is saying: "I can wish this behavior would never happen again, I can prefer that it go away, but I know that there is no way that I can control what my ex chooses to do. Even if he or she decides to continue acting this way, my life will still go on. . . . My life will still have meaning. . . . I can choose to have happiness. . . . There is much more to my life and to my child's life than whether or not my ex decides to act reasonably."

DENIAL

When you deny, you underreact. You pretend that a real problem is not really affecting you at all. A woman kept telling herself that she didn't really care that her ex routinely insulted her at the doorstep because she is strong and can take it. A man whose wife recently left him downplayed his personal pain, telling himself: "She just needs time to be by herself. . . . She'll come around."

Such rationalizations leave us particularly vulnerable when the full reality of a situation breaks through to our consciousness. The woman who kept explaining away her ex-husband's verbally abusive behavior suddenly found herself facing it head-on one Sunday afternoon when the children were returned to her; the outburst prompted her to lose control completely and uncharacteristically. The man who insisted that he was not threatened by his wife's departure later found himself curled up in a corner, weeping and immobilized, consumed with sadness and out of control with rage, because he wasn't psychologically prepared to hear that his wife had gone out on a date.

What makes denial a particularly tough problem is that it usually operates outside our awareness. To guard against it, stay as closely attuned as possible to your moment-to-moment feelings. Keep your feelings above the water line despite all temptation to submerge them and avoid the discomfort they bring.

Unfortunately, precisely because denial is about hiding, it can be a very effective defense mechanism. Our minds work hard at protecting us from realities that, unconsciously, we're afraid may overwhelm us. But when self-protection becomes an ongoing avoidance of dealing with your real feelings about life problems, it may help to work with a counselor, someone whose unclouded eye can more clearly see the truth about your relationship with your ex.

NOTHING-BUT THINKING

Tim ended up with a knot in his stomach after discovering that his ex-wife, Susan, had failed to tell him the whole truth about why she was keeping their kids for an extra day. It wasn't that she had car troubles, as she had led him to believe. No, she had taken the kids to her boyfriend's house for the day. In Tim's eyes, this made Susan "a liar—nothing but a liar." He added: "You can't believe a thing that comes out of her mouth. Not a word."

It's a common reaction: look at the specific and see the universal. In Tim's case, he generalized a single incident of Susan's behavior into a total personality characterization. It's like stubbing your toe after a highly successful day at work and proclaiming the whole day worthless as a result.

When Tim and I went to work on the problem, we began by checking to see whether he was justified in his conclusion that his ex-wife was "nothing but a liar." I asked Tim to tell me what Susan had said in the last four or five conversations they had had at the doorstep. Just about everything was benign—"The diapers are in the diaper bag . . . She's out of formula . . . Jonathan's teacher wants a school conference on Wednesday night . . . I'm sorry, but I couldn't bring back the sweatshirt, because it needed to be washed, you'll have it next weekend. . . . Jennifer is really tired right now, I think she needs a nap"—and at least 99 percent of her statements, as it turned out, were true.

I suggested to Tim that he needed to shift out of nothing-but thinking to thinking about his ex as a sum of parts, a collection of components. Then he could begin to admit to himself that "I hate the part of Susan that lies, but I appreciate the other part of her that tells the truth." I suggested to him that, rather than thinking of his ex as "a liar," a broad and malignant label, he could instead think of her as "a person who lies sometimes." Thinking of her that way neither glossed over nor excused the inappropriateness of her behavior, nor did it dismiss Tim's valid complaint, but it did begin to loosen the knot in his stomach. That's because Tim was no longer seeing his ex as a demonic figure who did "nothing but" lie, but rather as a person who did lie on occasion but who was also capable of telling the truth. He still felt upset about the lie, and he still told Susan that it bugged him. But being "bugged" is a long way from having a stomach tied up in knots. Once Tim invalidated his general conclusion—his nothing-but assessment of his ex as a liar—his emotions softened, and his own distress was reduced.

Another common form of nothing-but thinking overgeneralizes from ways in which *we* have been hurt or betrayed by our ex to ways our children might be hurt or betrayed. One mother spoke with me about how fearful she was for her child's welfare when he went away with his dad for two weeks in the summer. As we reviewed the long history of her ex's relationship with their son, I discovered that the boy had always returned from extended vacations safe, intact, and thoroughly happy. From her own history of having been emotionally hurt by her ex, this mother had extrapolated the possibility of her child being emotionally hurt, even though there was nothing to suggest that her ex was capable of such a thing. She had simply overgeneralized his behavior to her into his overall parenting behavior, convincing herself that he was "nothing but" risky and hurtful.

You can fight nothing-but thinking—calling your ex-spouse a "liar," a "louse," "incompetent" or "neglectful"—by looking for exceptions to the characterization you have pronounced. There are occasions when even a lying parent tells the truth. There are times when even a neglectful parent attends to the children. There are always moments when the ex with a short fuse acts calmly. Take control over your distress by looking for examples that contradict your assumptions. Write them down. Make a list—and keep expanding it.

It is easy to forget that your ex is a more complex, whole person than your mental model of him implies.

One good way to start your list is to imagine your ex-partner walking through a typical day. Visualize him or her as a complex, multifaceted human being going about his or her daily routine. In this movie in your mind, observe your ex doing very simple things: pouring cereal in the morning, smiling at a neighbor, doing his or her job, laughing with your children, eating dinner, preparing for bed. Be sure to include images of your ex doing the *opposite* of what bugs you. The goal here is to see your former spouse in a more complete way without doing what our brains tend to do: highlighting the negative and selectively forgetting the positive.

In all these ways, you can reclaim your emotional life. By letting yourself feel your feelings about your ex, you can recognize the feelings for what they are. By taking responsibility for your feelings, and by fighting the irrationalities that tend to haunt the shared custody relationship, you can come to grips with your own perspective. Do all this, and you will have seized the opportunity to create your own emotional experience through conscious choice. Now it's time to start choosing.

Remember:

✓ Peace begins between our ears.

✓ Embracing the full range of feelings you have about your ex is a critical first step toward being free of them.

✓ Your feelings about your ex-partner are not created by your ex-partner's actions, they arise from how you have chosen to interpret and respond to your ex's actions.

✓ Paying attention to your ex as a whole person and noticing how there is more to that person than troublesome behavior helps create balance in your mind.

✓ Remember that you are not your thoughts and moods.

✓ Extreme ways of thinking about your ex (e.g., catastrophizing, absolutist thinking, denial, nothing-but thinking) make your feelings extreme and uncomfortable.

Real Life

It makes sense to clean up my own act if I am making things worse between myself and my ex-wife. Sometimes I do like to stick it to her by reminding her of the rotten things she did to us as a family. She just dumped me and the kids. I can work on that. But once I stop doing my part we still have her part left: She lies to me and the kids over and over about why she canceled visits and I later find out that she's with her new boyfriend. Isn't there still a problem here?

Yes, there may be a lingering problem: your ex may still continue to behave in ridiculous ways even if you are "doing your part" and there are sensible ways that you can try to influence her. However, the first step is to look in the mirror, admit that you probably fan the flames of conflict, and eliminate this behavior. It also sounds like you may have an irrational "should" bouncing around in your head, as if you're saying to yourself: "Now that she's gone, she should still always be completely honest with me and the children about her personal time." Consider converting this to a realistic preference: "I *prefer* her to be honest with me and the kids about why she is canceling, but she doesn't have to always be honest for my life to go on and for my children to enjoy reasonably happy lives." Finally, remember that one good lesson for your children is better than none, so even if your ex continues to model dishonesty, you can choose to stop "sticking it to her" as a way of teaching your kids how to let go of the past.

Let's say I do all this work on my own head and my ex contin-ues to act like a fool and screw my life up on a weekly basis. What good will I have done?

You will have at least eliminated or reduced your own mental contribution to your anguish. A pound of anguish is better than a ton of it.

CHAPTER FIVE

Seven Strategies for Your Head

There's a poster I saw once, never forgot, and haven't seen again that offers a fitting epigraph to this chapter. The poster shows a giant wave rising up where the ocean breaks hard against a reef. Riding the wave is an Indian swami on a surfboard. The swami wears flowing robes. Lotus petals are woven into his long white hair. He is the very picture of an ascetic mystic, but he is hanging ten with the best of the hotdoggers in high breakers. YOU CAN'T CONTROL THE WAVES, the poster proclaims, BUT YOU CAN LEARN HOW TO SURF.

The seven strategies in this chapter teach you how to surf.

There are tools here for helping you become fully aware of yourself as the author of your own experience. There are tools that will help you untether your emotional life from your ex's shenanigans. And there are tools that will help you turn toward a freer future. Keep the tools in your toolbox. Carry them with you. Whenever you're feeling distressed, anxious, or angry because of your ex, you can just reach into the toolbox and grab what you need. Then you can apply it in complete privacy. Without saying a word to your ex-partner or former spouse, you can give yourself emotional freedom from behavior your ex seems unlikely ever to change.

This is tougher than trying to change your ex-spouse—work we'll get to later—but it is also more powerfully transforming. Of course, these seven strategies also tend to be tougher to wrap your mind around, so be prepared to be challenged. In fact, if you feel the discomfort of being emotionally stretched, that's a good sign. It's your mind telling you that you're on the verge of growth. Press on.

Strategy 1: Stay Here and Now

Dennis was a vibrant man engaged in a range of meaningful activities. He had an active career in which he served needy people, was the father of two beautiful children who were doing well in life, had a new partner whom he loved, possessed friends and co-workers who cared for him. He also had an ex-wife who called him at least once a week to insist that she had to change the times she would pick up the children. More than a minor annoyance, this caused Dennis a number of frustrating, pain-in-the-neck problems with day-care providers and with his own schedule. It also left him feeling both angry and hopeless—angry about his ex's behavior and hopeless that she would ever change.

One beautiful autumn day, Dennis and his children went apple-picking out in the countryside. The day was crisp and cool, the leaves on the trees were just turning to flame, the children were enchanted with picking their own basketful of apples. But Dennis couldn't concentrate on any of that; he was consumed by a slow burn of anger and frustration over his ex's infuriating behavior. The latest upsetting "change of plans" simply wouldn't work its way out of his mind. It was as if his ex-wife were with him in the apple orchard. In a sense, she was, for his anger at her had taken control of his day, and his entire life felt heavy and distressed as he pondered the last weekly frustration and thought about the next frustration to come.

It plunged him into gloom. What should have been a sunny, wonderful morning with his children was ruined. Dennis wasn't really there. In telling me about it, he spoke wistfully about the lost moments with his kids that he could never recapture. Dennis regretted the lost time. Above all, as he eloquently put it, he regretted the sense that he was allowing his ex-wife's behavior "to steal the apples" from him.

Does this sound familiar? Have you ever noticed that you are spending a large part of your day focusing on something that happened in the past or worrying about something you are afraid will happen in the future? If so, you're dealing in fantasy.

Think about it. Regrets about the past and worries about the future are abstractions at best, delusions at worst. The past is already done and cannot be changed; no amount of mental retrofitting can alter it or make it go away. The same is true of worry about the future. If you worry about whether your ex will do the same dumb thing this week as she did last week, or whether she'll act in the same upsetting way this Christmas as she did last Christmas, you are focusing on an imagined possibility. There is simply no way of knowing what anyone will do this week or next Christmas, and no amount of imagination or supposition can make your ex-spouse do or not do something in the future. The only certain thing about these fantasies is that they can become a preoccupation that is both dispiriting and disabling.

For every moment you spend thinking about a painful past with your ex or an imagined painful future with your ex, you lose a moment in your present life, which is more real than the upsetting thoughts in your head. In his wonderful book, *Time Shifting*[1], Dr. Stephan Rechtschaffen, a founder of the world-renowned Omega Institute in New York's Hudson River Valley, suggests that, in the present, there is no stress. Stress happens only when we allow our minds to shift into thoughts about the past or into worries about the future. When we are fully focused on the present, there is no distress. The reason is fairly obvious: The mind cannot be in two places at once, cannot focus on two separate times simultaneously.

When we are fully focused on the present moment, there is no stress.

So remind yourself that *each and every moment you spend preoccupied with your ex's behavior is a moment you are losing in your own life and in your life with your children.*

How do you drag your mind back to the present? The most effective way I know of is to try to focus on the riches and beauty you can find near you—the good things available to you here and now. For Dennis, that could have meant focusing on his daughter reaching for an apple in the sunlight. For you right now, it might mean glancing over at some object or heirloom you're particularly fond of. At work or when out with friends, it might mean looking at the face of a co-worker or friend and appreciating what it is about that relationship that means something. The more you do this—the more often, the more intently—the more you'll realize that you don't have to allow any sense of satisfaction in your life to be drained away by your ex's irritating behavior.

The Next Time

. . . you find yourself preoccupied with upsetting thoughts about your ex's irksome behavior, search diligently for beauty or harmony somewhere near you. You're bound to find it. It may involve turning your attention to a nearby bed of flowers, or watching the bees arrive to pollinate the flowers, or letting yourself melt inwardly as you watch your child watching the bees and the flowers. Your mind will no doubt tug you back to thoughts about your ex. Try to notice the tugging; acknowledge it and then gently bring your attention back to the beauty you had found. Imagine a rope tightening as a boat drifts away from its mooring; the tightened rope pulls the boat home again, keeps it close to shore. That's how you want your mind to pull you back to the here and now.

Flowers, bees, your child's sense of wonder may seem trivial in the context of a conflict-ridden relationship, but as you pull your mind back, you remind yourself that they are anything but trivial. In fact, these are the wondrous parts of your existence. In your distress, you've allowed your ex's antics to dominate what really counts. Come back to the here and now; focus on the beauty that already fills your life.

Strategy 2: Count Your Blessings

One of the most damaging consequences of becoming lost in painful or upsetting emotions is how much time it takes and how much energy it consumes. When you're angry, frustrated, or anxious, it's all too easy to lose track of the many other aspects of life, of its rich gifts and moments of quiet contentment. So intense is the anger you feel towards your ex at such a moment, so discouraging is your frustration, that you all too easily forget the rest of your life, letting the problem with a former partner become all of who you are.

It is not all of who you are. It is probably only a very little part of who you are. So a second strategy for your head is to count your blessings.

Dennis pursued this strategy along two parallel tracks; I recommend them both.

First, he literally counted up the time spent on the unhappy exchanges with his ex. Remember, Dennis complained that his ex-wife changed arrangements and thus disrupted his life "at least once a week." He repeated this so often I finally suggested he measure the portion of his week consumed by this frustrating weekly incident. Here's how it computed: Out of the 10,080 minutes in every week, the infuriating and upsetting exchanges between Dennis and his ex lasted anywhere from ten to twenty minutes. That left 10,060 minutes that were *not* infuriating or upsetting, yet for Dennis, the twenty minutes colored virtually the entire 10,080.

Dennis and I then began to look hard at the remaining 10,060 minutes of his week. Some 3,000-plus minutes were taken up by sleeping—Dennis likes a good seven hours a night. That still left about 7,000 minutes. What filled them?

It quickly became obvious that Dennis's life was filled with warm relationships with co-workers and friends, his children and his work. Against these many blessings, Dennis could resoundingly remind himself that his upsetting exchanges with his ex-wife represented only a small part of the reality of his life. Twenty minutes out of 7,000 minutes is not so much time; the twenty need not overwhelm the other 6,080.

As a way to focus on the many blessings that remain with him no matter what happens with his ex, Dennis began to write daily in a "gratitude" journal. He disciplined himself never to go to sleep without first making at least ten entries—either something that had happened that day for which he was grateful, or something about his life in general, or a sudden realization, or a dawning understanding. Dennis developed an ability to remind himself, as he began to feel upset about his ex, that there was more to his life than the frustration of the moment. He was able to remember that his life was gifted and wonderful and full of blessings, and he understood that the blessings far outweighed the brief upsetting exchanges. Over time, as Dennis repeatedly counted his blessings, he began to develop a new view of his life, a view in which the brightest, most dominant parts of his life-picture were those gifted, special parts—children, friends, work—and the tiniest portion began to be those upsetting times with the mother of his children.

Try:
- ✓ Remembering all the small and large blessings that are part of your life, which that your suffering over your ex's behavior has made you forget. Make an inventory—on paper—of what is wonderful about your life. Think small—"it's spring and my garden is gorgeous"—and large—"my child is the most precious gift that I have." Consider doing a daily gratitude journal.

There is always much more to your life than the problem you are having with your ex.

Strategy 3: Take One Problem at a Time

After a number of sessions characterized by anxiety and rage, Deborah suddenly showed up looking notably relieved. She had originally come to me with a long list of her ex's infuriating habits: he would phone her home at 6:30 AM to chat with the children . . . he repeatedly failed to pay for their medical insurance . . . he would insult her mother—the children's grandmother—in their presence at his home . . . he purposely called Deborah at work during hours when he knew it would cause her problems with her boss. Her sudden calm was in marked contrast to her usual frustrated recitation of the latest annoyance, but Deborah had a simple explanation, which she gleefully reported.

As a result of our discussion during the previous session, she had made a simple decision: she would disconnect her phone and answering machine during the early morning hours. As she reported this decision, Deborah made a circular motion with her hand, as if drawing in midair. "I decided to take charge of one small part of my life at a time," she told me. "I'm not going to let myself get wiped out by trying to solve all of these problems at once. Just turning off that machine in the morning made me feel like I still had some control over my life. I'm going to just enjoy this little bit of freedom I've given myself before tackling the other ridiculous things he does."

Has there ever been a time in your life when it seemed that you were being attacked on all sides by life's problems? Have you ever felt as if there were so many things going wrong that you felt frozen stiff, not knowing where to begin trying to make things better? Your relationship with your ex was probably one of the things going wrong—conceivably one of the biggest things, or the thing going wrong in the worst way. In any event, it was easy to see all of your life's problems congealing together around your relationship with your ex.

When life crowds us with problems, we feel overwhelmed by them; feeling overwhelmed, we can easily despair; despairing, we can become paralyzed and unable to deal with our problems at all. Instead, we may decide to curl up in a corner and do nothing. Or, we might lash out at all the problems indiscriminately, like a frightened cat surrounded by angry dogs.

Deborah's response, however, embodied one of the most basic strategies for your own head. It's this: Focus on one slice of the problem pie at a time. Break the overwhelming barrage of things-going-wrong into small pieces, then deal with just one very small, very manageable piece, one solvable issue at a time.

In dealing with a troubled relationship with an ex-partner, this doesn't mean that the rest of the trouble will automatically be solved as well. Nor does it mean the rest of it will go away. But it does mean that you will feel less overwhelmed and more effective. It means you can at least find relief from the troubling aspects of the relationship—and you might just find peace for yourself. And while you solve the one small, manageable thing, the rest of your troubles can just "be there" for a while until you're ready to deal with them one at a time as well.

There are three simple reasons why this strategy makes sense and why it provides great relief:

First, doing something—even a tiny something—distracts your attention from the long laundry list of problems and thus reduces the seeming enormity of your difficulties with your ex partner. A problem that is less at the forefront of your mind seems less of a problem.

Second, there is tremendous personal power to be found in focusing all your energies on a single problem rather than two or three—or ten—because all of your personal resources are then being invested in the difficulty you have *chosen* to work on. Your choice, your energy: You're in charge.

Third, if you begin by working on smaller, less challenging problems with your ex, any success that you do achieve energizes you with a sense of your own competence. You're then that much stronger for the next problem you tackle.

Here's a good way to approach this strategy:

Make a list of the various difficulties you are having in your relationship with your ex. You might use the list you developed in Chapter 2. Then rank the problems in order from least solvable to most solvable. You're guessing here, but these are educated guesses. Look closely at the most solvable difficulties. Find one item—one slice of the problem pie—and decide to invest your energy there and to ignore the other slices until you have achieved some resolution of your chosen slice.

Remember that the best place to begin, almost always, is with yourself. The problem you'll have the best chance of resolving is one that requires you to work on your own beliefs and attitudes rather than on your ex's behavior. The reason is simple: You have power over your own beliefs and attitudes, and you have no real power over your ex's behavior. In addition, a problem that requires you to work on your own beliefs and attitudes is muted or even solved once you've found a new way to think about it.

Strategy 4: Glance in the Mirror: Do You Contribute to the Problems?

It's a human trait to want to feel good about yourself. When things are going wrong, it's all too human to decide that the problem resides outside ourselves rather than to admit that we might have had a hand in creating it. It is far easier and more pleasant to believe that "circumstances," not our own actions, have created our failures or disappointments.

Unfortunately, in problem relationships with ex-spouses, it is typically both sides that contribute to the discord and distress, with each side unaware of their own contribution and more than ready to say it is all the other person's fault.

Michael insisted that he was completely puzzled by his ex's

propensity for finding something to argue about every time he picked up their daughter. But as he told me about these occasions, I began to notice how often he referred to the antics of his stepson—"the little creep," as he invariably called him—as being responsible for the death of the marriage. I suggested that he might be peppering his conversation with his ex-wife with similarly offensive references and asked him to promise to not even mention the boy to his ex for the next month. Sure enough, the arguments dwindled; Michael agreed that he had been guilty of lighting his ex's fuse by getting in a dig about her son. While his ex was still responsible for her extreme or irrational responses, he now realized that he had contributed to the mess between them.

It takes more courage to look in the mirror than it does to point a finger.

Glancing in a mirror may not sound like much of a strategy for your head, but in fact it is basic to all human relationships. Every relationship is a two-way street. Every conversation is a two-way street. Every conflict is a two-way street. As you glance in the mirror, have an honest and open conversation with yourself about ways in which you may subtly—or not so subtly—contribute to some of your ex's upsetting behavior.

Sometimes, the contribution takes the form of actively pushing an individual's buttons so that he or she ends up doing things you can then complain about or find distressing. Or, your contribution may simply be to become so upset at your ex's troublesome behavior that your reaction acts as a reward for your ex; it's unfortunately true that human beings sometimes find it pleasurable, in an unhealthy way, to get a rise out of others. Doing things that upset you can be your ex's conscious or unconscious way of expressing old resentments, and your extreme reactions can actually reward such behavior.

Think Back

... to your last three upsetting exchanges with your ex. Try to list everything both of you said. Pay particular attention to all that you said and did: your words, your facial expressions, your tone of voice. Review any contributions you may have made to poisoning the conversation or pushing your ex's buttons. Embrace these discoveries, not as reasons to criticize yourself, but rather as aspects of yourself that you now can improve in order to facilitate peace. If you find it hard to do this exercise, you may want to ask a close friend—someone who knew you and your ex as a couple—to tell you about any ways in which they perhaps saw you making things worse with your ex. If you're feeling really courageous and open to some personal growth, you might even ask your ex for some feedback.

Have the courage to look in the mirror at your contribution to this relationship with your children's other parent. Then think what it would mean to be the first to take care of your part of the painful dance the two of you are doing together. Remember, this is the one thing that you have control over.

Strategy 5: Trade Eyeballs with Your Ex

Lois Gold, author of a well-known book on divorce, tells a moving story about what happened as her own divorce was coming to completion.

"I flew with my husband to Seattle to obtain a Jewish divorce, called a 'get.' It was strange traveling together, sitting side by side at a proximity that was both familiar and alien. We were on our way to end our marriage. What do you say? There were no distractions and nothing to argue about. All dressed up together and going nowhere, for the last time.

"We arrived at the synagogue and were ushered into a small library, where several holy men were sitting around a large oak table. Ivan and I were seated next to each other. No one spoke. The men barely looked up from their prayer books. The solemnity of the occasion hung from everything in the room, from the dark mahogany paneling to the deliberateness of the rabbi's every movement. There was no escaping. The final reality of ending our life together stood starkly before us. As the elders began to chant the prayers, Hebrew words that I didn't understand, tears began to fall. Not the familiar tears of rage, frustration, or hurt, but of a profound sorrow I had not known before. I looked over at Ivan. He was crying also—Ivan crying! I had never seen him like this. For the first time, I felt his pain and saw him in his humanity, vulnerable, imperfect, and struggling. His tears touched me deeply, evaporating my shield of anger. At that point, I could hate him no more for doing what he had to do. I was filled with sorrow, but it was a sorrow that contained no blame; it was deep and pure and cleansing.

"The rabbi asked if we wanted to continue. Unable to speak, we both nodded yes. The long silence that followed was broken only by muffled sobs and Ivan's words, then mine: 'I'm sorry, I'm so sorry.' The words reverberated, as if for the first time they were genuinely true."[2]

Remember the person you married? It isn't easy now that you've separated, now that your relationship is characterized by conflict, anger, and resentment. That's why one of the hardest things to do—and one of the most powerful paths to peace when you're in conflict with an ex-partner—is to step into the other person's experience and see the situation through his eyes.

I call it "trading eyeballs" with your ex—really seeing the world as your ex sees it, really understanding how he perceives the problem and what he is truly looking for. The goal is not to adopt your ex's point of view; it is to reach an *understanding* of that point of view—especially because you know that your ex thinks he's right!

How does the dispute look to your ex? What are his interests in this matter? If you can at least understand his perspective, you don't have to resist it quite so hard, and maybe both of you can then craft fair and effective solutions.

As a strategy, trading eyeballs is one of the most effective ways there is for achieving the outcome you want in your relationship with your ex. As we'll discuss in greater detail in Part III, any strategic negotiation must start with an understanding of what the other person is looking for in the dispute. But to be able to answer the question "What is she really after?" you need to start by trying to understand her needs, her desires, the way she looks at the dispute.

It's tough under any circumstances to step into someone else's shoes and see with their eyes. But it's particularly tough after separating from someone you once cared for or loved, someone with whom you share a complicated history. All the injuries that the divorce process creates can cause people to demonize their ex-partners, to deny their humanity and vulnerability, to forget that there was a time when spending the rest of your life with this person was the most important thing in the world.

People emerging from a fractured marriage often tend to rewrite family history in their mind, deleting the positive about their ex and magnifying the negative. The ex that you now have in your mind may be a dark, even dreadful figure with little resemblance to the person you once held in your arms.

There's a mountain of complicated emotions at the end of a marriage. You're not going to lift the mountain; that's not what you're after. What you're after is a little peace, and the best way to get it is by trading eyeballs with your ex. When you do, you'll find that buried under the mountain of emotions is a vulnerable human being just like you.

Although it may be hard to believe, your ex really is from the same planet and species as the rest of us—which means that she has most of the same basic longings and desires that you do. Also, most human behavior is motivated by positive intention, and, yes, your ex is a human being. Pause for a minute. Allow yourself to see your ex as someone who is fumbling around in this world attempting to feel good about herself—just like you. When you realize that, then maybe you'll begin to hear, behind her crazy and upsetting behavior, the things she is really longing for or worried about. And surely you can respond to her at that level.

One of my favorite stories about coming to this kind of understanding was told to me by a client, Bill, who had sought therapy to help him deal with his problems with his ex-wife, Sarah. Those problems, frustrating and exhausting in the extreme, were centered on Sarah's pattern of constantly canceling her visits with the kids or changing the times of the visits. Her behavior gave rise to numerous angry exchanges between the two; many of the exchanges proceeded in the context of court battles, as both parents spent their children's college education money on attorneys. In Bill's eyes, Sarah was nothing but a "neglectful mother," as he called her. Even as he and I began to work together on his anger with her, their battles raged on.

Then, one day, Bill showed up at my office surprisingly brighter in mood. He was noticeably happier, less burdened, more at peace. I remarked on the change and asked Bill to explain it. This is what he told me:

He had gone to a personal growth weekend in which a group of people had come together to try to improve their lives. At one point during the weekend, a woman stood up and began to speak about how she felt torn apart by the conflicting demands of her ex-husband, her new husband, and her children. She wept as she spoke of working hard to make sure her children maintained a good relationship with their dad and feeling stymied at every turn. It seemed that whenever she was willing to be flexible with her ex-husband about the schedule or vacations or other issues, her new husband would berate her, reminding her that she owed her ex nothing and that he had made her life miserable. By the same token, when she surrendered to her new husband's request that she accompany him on weekend business trips, she felt she was betraying her children when she canceled their time together, and that she was betraying her new husband when she didn't.

Bill sat in the room and looked at me with his eyes wide and his mouth hanging open. "I can't believe it," he said at last, "but I never stopped to think about the fact that Sarah has a new family and someone else's demands to contend with." He still hated what he saw as the coldness with which Sarah called to cancel visits, as if she didn't care about his time, his schedule, his life—or the children's. He hated the way she would become furious and hang up the phone when he would refuse to accept her request to change the schedule for a particular week. But something had softened in him. He had traded eyeballs with his ex, had seen her life as she saw it. In doing so, he began to see that, although Sarah's methods left much to be desired, her constant cancellations were her way of trying to meet the demands of a new life. As a result of having traded eyeballs, Bill could no longer see Sarah as nothing but the "neglectful mother" he had complained of when we began treatment.

Trading eyeballs can also help you to understand your ex's emotional limitations. Some divorced parents find themselves in continual distress because their ex displays mood swings, rigid behavior, explosiveness, or chronic selfishness, yet they haven't accepted the obvious: If such behavior is chronic and extreme it may mean that your ex actually has a bona fide psychological disorder that explains what appears to be unreasonable behavior on its surface. In trying to see the world through your ex's eyes you may come to accept that he or she is disabled by a genuine disorder. Not that this excuses such frustrating behavior. It just means you may feel a bit less distress once you accept the nature of the problem.

Trading Eyeballs with Your Ex

Trading eyeballs will be easier if you ask yourself the following questions:

- What positive things is your ex trying to get for herself with this frustrating behavior?

- What pain, fear, or concern might be behind the way she acts?

- If you had to make your ex's argument for why she is acting this way, how would that argument sound?

- What demands or stresses may be bearing down on your ex to produce her behavior or position?

- Have you ever acted in a similarly irrational or upsetting way with anyone? If so, what were your reasons?

- What tools is she missing in her emotional toolbox, without which she is limited to these frustrating reactions?

Whatever your dilemma is with your ex-spouse, it never hurts to ask yourself how she views the problem or what she is seeking for herself through the behavior you find so frustrating. In fact, the only risk in trading eyeballs with your ex is that he or she may seem more human to you.

> *If we could read the secret history of our enemies, we would find sorrow and suffering enough to dispel all hostility.*
>
> —Henry Wadsworth Longfellow,
> renowned 19th-century poet

Strategy 6: Consider Forgiveness

Stephen stood in my office, all six feet six inches of him, strong and powerful in appearance, and wept as he recounted the moment two years ago when he had discovered his wife with another man. He had been separated from her since that time but found himself daily rehearsing the details of his discovery. And each day, Stephen would fill with fresh rage that only masked the other emotions her infidelity had aroused—his forlorn sadness at having been set aside for another man, his embarrassment that his wife's choice had somehow disclosed to the world the ways in which he had always felt he was less than lovable. Two years after the event, a weeping Stephen was still indignantly demanding, "How could she do that to me? I can't believe she could do that to me!"

For Stephen, as for many people, the idea of forgiving an ex-partner who has caused pain is about as appealing as the prospect of root canal. It feels impossible. You've been hurt. Someone has done you profound harm. How can you forgive it? Why should you forgive it?

Because forgiving will make you free! Forgiveness is one of the most powerful strategies there is for carving a path toward peace with your ex. It is, of course, based on respect for and understanding of others, yet forgiveness is also a wonderful way of caring for yourself and regaining your own life.

There are many reasons to forgive those who have caused us pain. To many people, forgiveness is a moral precept—even a religious requirement. But the act of forgiveness I am speaking about here is also a strategic imperative, a means to an end, the end in this case being your peace of mind. Its purpose is to free you of your anger and pain so that you can move forward, regain your life and act in an affirming way toward your ex, despite the ways in which he or she may be imperfect, or frail, or disrespectful toward you.

That doesn't make forgiveness any easier to achieve. In fact, resistance to the idea of forgiving someone who has hurt you is so standard a response as to be almost universal—at least at first. Unfortunately, that standard response usually arises from misconceptions about what it really means to forgive someone[3].

MISCONCEPTIONS ABOUT FORGIVING

One: Forgiving someone means condoning the offending person's hurtful behavior, implying approval or at least acceptance. Indignation, on the other hand, is assumed to be a way to keep the offending ex-partner in his or her place, always communicating that their actions were wrong.

In fact, however, forgiveness does not mean condoning or accepting the behavior that has hurt or mistreated us. We can forgive someone and still hold the belief that his or her hurtful behavior was inappropriate, immoral, or just plain wrong.

> *The weak can never forgive. Forgiveness is an attribute of the strong.*
>
> —Mohandas Gandhi, Indian civil rights leader

Two: You can't forgive a person who is not sorry for what he did.

Yes, you can. The forgiveness I am talking about here involves a change in your own heart and mind and does not require the other person to view his behavior in any particular way; in fact, it requires no action on the other person's part at all. Forgiveness is a way for you to get free. It is not about changing the other person.

Three: If we forgive someone, we have to be that person's chum.

Wrong again. The forgiveness I am discussing is a private event in your heart and mind and does not require that you have a more involved relationship with the other person.

HOW TO FORGIVE

Forgiveness requires that you accept the feelings that flow from your having been injured. Something has happened that has hurt, or embarrassed, or offended you. You need to accept that—gently and nonjudgmentally. In other words, the first step in forgiveness is wrapping your arms around yourself and your experience and not trying to pretend that you have no feelings about what happened.

Forgiveness involves accepting what has been. Simple as it sounds, it isn't so easy to absorb the reality that the upsetting thing or things that your ex has done are genuinely part of the past; there is nothing that you can do—absolutely nothing—to make that history different. Of course, you can still hang on to the *wish* that your history with your ex had been different, but it is important to accept that no wish can change history.

Forgiveness means deciding to refocus on the human side of your ex—that is, on the side that is no different from you. It does not mean ignoring or denying your ex's upsetting behavior. It does mean, however, that you must look behind that behavior to find the frightened or struggling human being behind the upsetting actions. You must remind yourself that, like you—like all of us—your ex is an imperfect traveler in a confusing world. He or she will make mistakes along the path to self-protection and happiness. We all want happiness. We are all trying to fulfill our needs, achieve our dreams, avoid suffering. We have all been lonely or sad at some point. As we bumble along, we are all learning—and making mistakes—about life.

That's why this last step to forgiveness requires that you refocus on the positive, even benevolent intention behind the behavior that hurt or offended you, reminding yourself that all human actions are meant to achieve something positive or healthy. True, we don't always succeed, and a lot of rotten results flow from positive and healthy intentions. But most of the ways in which we hurt or offend those around us are attempts to protect ourselves, to gain a sense of control, or to recoup feelings of self-esteem or security. The problem is that sometimes the methods we choose for getting these wonderful things can fracture our relationships with those we love and leave them with scars.

Stephen and his wife are a perfect example of this. When I met his wife, I learned that during their marriage she had always felt that Stephen was controlling her life. She felt she had no life of her own within the marriage, nor did she have any career outside the marriage. Her husband made all the decisions; her role, in which she felt trapped, was to raise the toddlers. Her affair with another man was a grab for feelings of freedom and excitement; it was a way of saying "I can have my own life." Who among us has not wanted freedom and excitement and a feeling of control over our lives? They're all wonderful, healthy things, yet the way Stephen's wife chose to get them was hurtful, morally wrong, devastating to her husband, and something that split her family in two.

For Stephen to forgive his wife, he had to look past her hurtful behavior and see the woman who felt powerless in her marriage and no longer in control of her life. He had to see the turmoil and pain she caused not as evidence of a fundamentally evil person but as the behavior of a person who lacked certain life skills. It is the difference between seeing someone as evil and seeing her as missing tools in her toolbox. It means choosing to "see the light instead of the lamp shade," in the wonderful phrase of Dr. Gerald Jampolsky.[4] In her unskillful attempt to get something positive for herself, Stephen's wife had indeed caused pain to others—to him and to their children. Only when Stephen thought deeply about this issue and chose to view his ex as unskillful rather than evil could he gradually let go of his anger.

Notice that this model of forgiveness does not suggest that you run out, shake your ex-partner's hand, and say "I forgive you." There are times when this would be the worst thing to do. For example, your ex may not believe that there is anything he needs to be forgiven for or that he has done anything wrong. At such times, an announcement of forgiveness can backfire.

In fact, while reaching out and speaking of forgiveness can at times be wonderfully healing and yield a powerful unity between people, the most essential part of forgiveness involves no words or actions. It's a strategy for your heart and head.

Remember also that forgiveness does not mean passivity in the face of mistreatment; it does not mean tolerating intolerable behavior. You have not given up your capacity for assertive self-protection, your ability to complain, or your request for different behavior on your ex's part. You have simply chosen to forgive the behavior through deep understanding and to free yourself.

When you do choose forgiveness, your entire way of behaving in the other person's presence will change. Freed from the compulsion to be judgmental, liberated from the need to be in "fighting mode," you can focus more clearly on the light behind the lamp shade, and anything that blocks or distorts the light becomes just an unfortunate distraction. The great surprise of forgiveness is that when your ex experiences the change in your behavior, his or her behavior may also begin to change.

The visualization exercise that follows can be a powerful tool toward helping you achieve forgiveness of your ex. The best way to do the visualization is with the aid of a counselor. Failing that, have a close friend read it for you. Or, if you have a tape recorder, have the friend record the words on tape—even record them yourself—and listen later in a relaxed environment. One caution: Do not listen to the tape while driving, it tends to be quite relaxing.

THE VIEW FROM THE OAK TREE: A VISUALIZATION FOR FORGIVENESS

Find a place where you can sit calmly and quietly with few distractions. Settle into a comfortable chair and spend a few minutes paying attention to your breathing. Close your eyes and turn your attention inward. Notice your breath as it leaves and enters your nose. Notice your stomach rise and fall with each breath. Each time you breathe out, feel yourself releasing any tension that lies anywhere in your body. Each time you breathe in, imagine yourself taking in serenity and peace. Each time you exhale, breath out any tension you feel. Pay attention to your breathing so that as thoughts and distractions enter your mind, you simply acknowledge them and allow them to float by, as if they were leaves on a flowing river. Gently bring your wandering mind back to your breath and let it be your anchor. Continue this process for a few moments.

Now create a picture in your mind. Imagine that you are entering a secluded and very beautiful garden. The garden is luxuriant with greenery. The grass is soft and thick like a rich carpet. You hear the gurgling sound of clear water rippling over rocks in a nearby brook. The brook leads to a wide, shimmering pond. As you enter this garden you notice a large, tall oak tree. You have heard about this tree before. It is astoundingly beautiful, but what makes it special—or so you have heard—is that when people sit beneath its branches, they feel absolutely safe and secure in the universe. They feel no need to defend themselves or to attack others; they feel able simply to be themselves. Under this tree, people feel perfectly loved. You have heard that because this tree gives people a sense of profound security and serenity, they feel able to speak with a deep honesty they find completely refreshing.

You decide to climb this special tree so you can get a glimpse of the garden from above. As you sit high up in the tree, you notice your ex entering the garden accompanied by a gray-haired person who has the appearance of wisdom. They walk together toward the oak tree, then sit down together beside the shimmering pond in front of the tree. As your ex and this companion gaze into the pond, its surface seems to become a movie screen. On it, scenes from your past are playing.

The first scene on the pond is of a time when your ex acted in a hurtful or insensitive way toward you. As the scene comes into focus, you notice that your ex is watching the action with great seriousness. As you watch from your perch in the oak tree, as you see the scene in the pond unfold, you remember the feelings of anger that your ex's behavior inspired in you. You remember the hurt behind the anger, the sense of having been set aside, or betrayed, or diminished by your ex. At the end of the scene your ex's gray-haired companion inquires about the scene, asking your ex: "What was life like for you then? What led you to act that way?"

Your ex begins to respond, and you're aware that because he or she is sitting under the oak tree, the response is given with a clarity, an honesty, and a centeredness that you have never heard before. Under this tree, your ex-partner is able to be the light behind the lamp shade. Gone is the urge to be defensive. Instead, your ex is able to speak about the fragile feelings behind the hurtful or insensitive behavior: the sense of loss, the fear, the pain, the desire to regain control, or self-esteem, or the feeling of being loved. As you listen, you begin to be reminded of the ways in which you and your ex are fellow travelers through the same human condition. Neither of you is perfect; each of you is trying to make your way; both of you at times hurt others in the process, usually when you are feeling frightened.

Now you notice that the wise companion is leaning toward your ex, about to speak. You listen in. "When you acted in that hurtful way shown in the pond," the gray-haired person says to your ex, "you wanted to find happiness. You wanted to feel loved. You wanted to feel in control of your life. You were in pain and you did not want to suffer anymore. Like all of us, you were learning and making mistakes as you went along."

The surface of the pond now clears, and a new scene appears. This one recalls a happy time in your relationship with your ex, a time when you felt a deep love for each other, a sense of unity together. Notice all the details in the pond scene: the softness in your smiles, the sense of mutual comfort even though everything wasn't perfect. It was a time, even if for a few moments or hours, when you both felt at home with one another, when laughter and happiness reigned. As your ex and the wise companion watch this scene unfold, you notice a warm smile on your ex's face. When the scene finishes, the wise companion inquires: "What was that like for you? What brought you happiness in that scene?"

Again, your ex replies with an honesty, clarity, and sense of peace that you have not experienced before, telling of all the things about you that your ex loved, about all the ways in which you had fun together, about how very much your ex wanted the two of you to spend the rest of your lives together.

Now you again see the wise companion leaning over to your ex. Again, you listen. "Always remember," the companion tells your ex, "that this happiness, however brief, was part of who you were when you were together. Don't let the pain you have been through erase the reality of any happy memories that you have."

From up in the oak tree you continue to watch as your ex gazes at the changing scenes on the pond and reviews several more uncomfortable or hurtful times in your relationship together. At the end of each unhappy scene you hear your ex speak honestly from the heart about his or her true feelings at the time, and you hear the wise companion's comment: "When you acted in that hurtful way, you wanted to find happiness. You wanted to feel loved. You wanted to feel in control of your life. You were in pain and you did not want to suffer anymore. Just like all of us, you are learning and making mistakes as you go along."

Now watch as your ex views more happy peaceful times between the two of you. Listen to him or her speak about those times; hear the wise companion's reminder that "this happiness, however brief, was part of who you were when you were together. Don't let the pain you have been through erase the reality of any happy memories that you have."

As you sit in the oak tree watching your ex, feel your heart softening. You have a sense that you are seeing your ex somewhat differently, that you have glimpsed his or her true nature, have realized how that true nature was often hidden behind anger or fear. You see the light behind the lamp shade. And despite your differences, you feel a small sense of unity and understanding with this fellow traveler, someone who, like you, occasionally lacks important tools for coping with life's challenges, someone who, like you, is growing and learning along the way.

Your ex and the gray-haired companion stand up and begin to walk away from the tree. As you watch them leave, you find yourself whispering the following to your ex: "I know that you want to find happiness. I know that, just like me, you want to feel loved. I know that you want to feel in control of your life. I know that you have been in pain and that you do not want to suffer anymore. I know that, just like all of us, you are learning and making mistakes as you go along."

Climb down from the tree now, and remind yourself as you do that you and your ex will each forget your true natures at times. You'll forget that you're perfectly whole, that you have nothing to fear, that there's no reason to hurt others. There will be times that you will do things that upset or hurt one another. But you now know that there is always a place you can return to where the hidden light in your ex and in yourself is evident, a place where you can see the light behind the lamp shade.

Strategy 7: Make Lemonade

The phrase has become almost a cliché: "When life hands you lemons, make lemonade." Perhaps all it asks of you is to remind yourself that when life brings you unhappiness, you should try to think happy thoughts and do happy things to pull yourself out of the doldrums.

As a strategy for your head, however, there is a far more profound way to "make lemonade," and this way can be positively life-transforming. It asks that you not simply stop feeling blue, but that you use your unhappiness as an opportunity to make changes in yourself. Ram Dass[5] tells a story that illustrates this perfectly.

During the 1980s, there was one particular member of the U.S.

cabinet whose policies, in Ram Dass's view, caused suffering around the globe. Every night, when the cabinet member appeared on the nightly news discussing his policies, Ram Dass would find himself filled with anger and frustration. He decided to use his ill will toward the cabinet member as a vehicle for personal and spiritual growth.

Ram Dass found a large picture of the cabinet member and placed it on the table he used for daily prayer and meditation. Each day, when he approached the table, there was the photograph, prompting Ram Dass to pray for the cabinet member and to meditate on why he himself had become so trapped by resentment about this man. Through such prayer and meditation, Ram Dass hoped he might evolve as a person, one less likely to be trapped by such resentments again. In a very real sense, Ram Dass *used* this cabinet member who disgusted him as a vehicle to grow as a person. It was as if the cabinet member was "given" to Ram Dass to help him move closer to the god that he believed in.

See your life as a wisdom school with you as a student and your ex as dean of the faculty.

The idea here is simple, yet its application requires discipline and compassion for yourself. It isn't easy to accept repeatedly foolish or hurtful behavior on your ex's part as an opportunity to grow as a person. Can you bring yourself to view your ex-partner's habit of pushing your buttons as an opportunity to learn more self-control? Might your ex-partner's repeated lateness in picking up the children offer you a chance to cultivate patience? When your children look sad because your ex has again failed to arrive for their scheduled time together, is it possible to use this as an opportunity for teaching your kids how to deal with painful moments in life? Can you shift from saying "What a rotten hand I've been dealt with my ex!" to "What an interesting class I enrolled in when we divorced."

Of course, you want an end to the frustration, discomfort, or hurt created by your ex. But if nothing seems to be changing, can you turn your pain to a purpose and use it as an opportunity to make some lemonade?

If you can, the results can be as delicious, soothing, and bittersweet as the drink itself.

Remember:

✓ Working hard to return your mind to the present moment when you are in distress can be a quick shortcut to relief.

✓ Frustration with a challenging ex often makes us forget the ways in which our life is blessed.

✓ Honesty about your contributions to some of the pain between you and your ex takes courage.

✓ Viewing the world through your ex-partner's eyes positions you to respond more effectively to the problems you are having.

✓ You can choose forgiveness while still objecting to your ex-partner's behavior.

✓ Turning frustrations into opportunities for growth can offer a wonderful kind of freedom.

Real Life

My ex was always fragile. He would become almost immobile and depressed at the slightest setback. Now that we have separated, my eleven-year-old daughter is telling me stories of rotten food in the refrigerator, an unclean house, and frequently seeing her dad tearful during visits. Kids shouldn't have to deal with this. He won't go for counseling. How is working on my own head going to solve a problem that's really in his head?

Part of every problem starts in our own head. Obviously, you have to make sure your daughter is safe and that her basic needs are being met. Do what you need to do to make sure she's all right when in her father's care—express your worries directly to your ex, offer to help him find counseling or medical care, check with people who might know how he's really doing, speak with Child Protective Services if there are indications of serious neglect or abuse. But once you've done that, check to see if you have a mental demand that your ex *must* be happy or energetic and consider how you might rephrase this as a preference, e.g., "I would prefer that my daughter experience her father as happy, but I recognize I can't control this and that it doesn't have to mean disaster for myself or my child—it may just mean some unfortunate unhappiness for my child." When you find yourself lost in ruminations about your ex-partner's depressive life and its effects on your children, quickly find a bit of beauty close to you and inventory your own blessings. Try to mentally get inside your ex's life and seek some understanding of how he has arrived at this sadness, reminding yourself how difficult it can be to free oneself from a depression. If you can, reassure your daughter with the fact that you have seen him emerge from depression before, that it will take time for her dad to heal, and that it is not her responsibility to make him better.

PART TWO

Whose Problem Is This?

CHAPTER SIX

Recognizing Unnecessary Burdens

An important aspect of self-mastery is knowing which burdens—which problems with your ex—belong on your shoulders and which do not. Once you know the difference, you can take charge of choosing whether to take on the burden or remain uninvolved.

Complexity and Confusion

There's no question that having children complicates relations between ex-partners, relations that are complex enough to begin with. Concerns about children escalate the tensions and add to the number of players involved in a separation.

Even when you have the nagging suspicion that something isn't your problem, if it has anything to do with your children, your instinct always is to protect, defend, or speak for them. Or perhaps you're accustomed to taking care of an ex-spouse who has always been dependent on you. Or maybe it just seems like the path of least resistance is to handle problems yourself and not involve anyone else. Whatever the reason, it's all too easy to become confused about which balls you need to pick up and dribble and which need to be passed to your ex, to your children, or to someone else altogether.

Does This Problem Belong on Your Shoulders?

You've got problems. Your ex is habitually late to pick up and drop off your daughter for weekend visits. He called Friday morning to say he wouldn't pick her up till after supper that evening, and chances are he'll be late returning her home on Sunday, meaning that on Sunday night she'll have to rush to finish up homework and get ready for school the next day—not to mention what his tardiness does to *your* ability to have a life. Now the phone is ringing, and it's your ex, early on a Saturday morning when you're trying to relax, and he's complaining because the minute your daughter got into the car last night, she began insisting that her father allow her to attend a dance on Saturday night—something you hadn't even heard about. Your ex is upset because he seldom gets to spend much time with your daughter now that she is a teenager, and he had made plans for the two of them to attend a play together. He pleads with you on the phone to help persuade your teenager.

What should you do? What action, if any, should you take? Should you offer to help your ex with the dilemma? There's no question that helping would mean disrupting your own life on what you had hoped would be a quiet weekend. On the other hand, this is your daughter; she needs help or discipline or a long talk or all of the above. Is there ever a time when it makes sense *not* to jump in and help your children with a problem they are having with their other parent? And why can't your ex ever get it together to be on time?

Here's a perfect example of a child unknowingly worsening the misunderstandings and mistaken assumptions that already plague a relationship between ex-spouses. In fact, this case involves a teenager, which probably makes matters far worse. As in this example, teenagers tend to add their own two cents, their own demands, and their own misunderstandings to an already brittle connection between their parents.

Parents often feel guilty because they have separated; they fear they have harmed or injured their children by breaking up their home. Feeling guilty, separated parents may be quick to assume responsibility for solving every family dilemma, even when the dilemma does not directly involve or affect them. It's only natural to want to rescue your children when they come home upset about something their other parent has done; it's only human to allow your ex to shoulder you with his or her problem because solving it will benefit your children. But in letting yourself become involved, you may not only be creating unnecessary distress for yourself, you may also be preventing others from learning to resolve their problems on their own. In short, assuming responsibility for burdens that belong on someone else's agenda doesn't do anybody any good—not you, nor your ex, nor your children.

Refusing to take responsibility for solving an unnecessary burden can actually empower your ex and your children.

DEVELOPING ANTENNAE

It's essential to develop antennae that can sense when a particular family problem does not necessarily belong on your shoulders.[1] Sensors that can lock on to what I call *unnecessary burdens* are critical for moving toward greater contentment in a troubled relationship.

Developing these antennae does not mean doing nothing about the problem or pretending it doesn't exist. It means knowing that the principal responsibility for solving it is not yours. You can still care about the dilemma, you can offer assistance or suggestions, and of course you're free to worry and fret and become upset about what is happening. You may even *choose* to help, but what defines a burden as unnecessary is that ultimately the dilemma lies in someone else's lap. It's someone else's responsibility, and it's up to that someone else to find and execute a resolution of the dilemma.

In fact, when you have learned to accept that a particular burden is unnecessary, you can often be more helpful in solving it if you assume the posture of an available, understanding person who is not overinvolved. You will certainly find relief and satisfaction when you allow problems you do not own to remain where they belong— and when you can trust others to solve them.

Deciding who owns the problem means figuring out who is most responsible for finding a solution.

You can grow these burden-sensing antennae by asking yourself four questions about every problem that arises in your relationship with your ex.

1. Is someone other than you expressing the concern or making the complaint?

When unhappiness bubbles up over some conflict or event, someone has to speak out about it first. When you find yourself in the middle of an uncomfortable or distressing dilemma involving your ex-partner, look around to see who is the primary person complaining. Is it you, your ex, one of your children, or someone else?

In the case of your ex's habitual lateness in picking up and returning your daughter, you are the primary person with the concern. Your answer to this first question is, therefore, no. But as for the complaining phone call early Saturday morning about your daughter's desire to go to the dance versus your ex's demand that she attend the play, your answer to the question is yes—someone other than you is making the primary complaint. You didn't complain about this dilemma at all. Even though you may feel bad for your ex, even if you agree with him about what your daughter should do on Saturday night, *it isn't your problem*. Making it your problem is taking on an unnecessary burden—bad for you, bad for your ex's parenting skills, and a bad example for your daughter.

2. Is someone other than you feeling most of the emotions about the problem?

As to your ex's habitual lateness, the answer is no—assuming that your daughter doesn't care about the time of arrival, and further assuming that your ex believes his tardiness is no big deal. No, it is you who feels most of the emotion over this pattern of behavior; you're the one who is inconvenienced, and you're the one who is annoyed, frustrated, and angry.

In the tug-of-war over how your daughter will spend Saturday night, however, it is your ex who feels most of the emotion; after all, he's the one raging on the phone.

3. Is it another person's life—not yours—that will most improve if the problem goes away?

Again, in the case of the forever late ex-partner, the answer is no. Assuming your daughter enjoys being with her father, it is your life and no one else's that will most improve if your ex-spouse finally decides to show up on time. When your ex is on the phone asking you to persuade your daughter not to attend the dance, it is your ex's life, not your own, that will improve most if this conflict and his unhappiness with your daughter are resolved.

4. Does the problem lie mainly between two or more other people?

Your antennae should not be sending you any warnings in the first case because the problem lies between you and your ex, i.e., *his* lateness, *your* annoyance. But in the second case, the dilemma is fundamentally between your ex and your daughter. As the ex-wife, you are simply the concerned recipient of the complaint; you're still essentially an outsider to the dilemma.

LISTENING TO YOUR ANTENNAE

As a general rule, if you answer yes to two out of these four questions, the dilemma is likely an unnecessary burden. If so, that's a signal to you that you have the freedom to decide whether you want to help directly or remain detached and let others seek a solution.

SUMMER PLANS

Judy had just booked a cabin at the shore for herself, her new husband, and her kids for their summer week together. When the phone rang, it was Judy's ex-husband—a man who has often chosen to schedule visits that conflict with her plans—saying that he had made plane reservations to fly the children to Disneyland with him but had mistakenly booked the trip for her summer week. He pleaded with Judy to switch weeks with him. Is this a problem Judy should own or an unnecessary burden?

Raise your antennae and apply the four questions:

1. Is someone other than Judy making the main complaint?
Yes, obviously, her ex-husband is bringing the concern to her.

2. Is someone other than Judy feeling most of the emotion about the problem?
Again, yes. It is her ex who is most upset about the dilemma.

3. Is it another person's life that will most improve if the problem goes away?
Yes. Judy herself does not have a scheduling dilemma; her ex does.

4. Does the problem lie mainly between two or more people other than Judy?

No, the problem lies between Judy and her ex.

Following our general rule of thumb—more than two of the four questions were answered yes—Judy realizes that she is confronting an unnecessary burden. While she can freely *choose* to change her vacation schedule, she is not obligated to do so, and she can choose to say, with regrets, that she cannot help. Either way, there is no reason for guilt.

"WHAT SHOULD I DO WITH THEM?"

When Jeremy's ex-wife, Susan, calls in the middle of her long weekend with the children and complains that the boys are out of control as usual, Jeremy immediately recognizes her pleading question—"What should I do with them?"—as an unnecessary burden. Susan, not Jeremy, is expressing the concern; Susan, not Jeremy, is feeling most of the emotion about the problem; and it is Susan's life that would most improve if this problem went away. Finally, the problem lies mainly between two or more people other than Jeremy, i.e., Susan and her boys.

Like Judy, Jeremy can decide to help his ex with suggestions or by speaking with his sons, but he reminds himself that he is also absolutely free to stay out of this dilemma. After all, Susan is their parent too; she has a responsibility to learn what to do with the boys when they're out of control.

YOUR EX'S BEHAVIOR, YOUR PROBLEM

When the problem you face is your ex's behavior, it would seem at first glance that it is her burden. But our four questions may reveal otherwise.

Philip came to my office describing the terrible tension he always felt in the presence of his ex. His stomach would actually tighten and his body would grow rigid with the strain. Whenever she came to his door, or whenever he had a phone conversation with her, she would begin to complain about him to his face, building up to a fury and ending by calling him names, then hanging up on him or walking away. When she drove up the driveway to drop off the children or if they were scheduled to attend a school function together, Philip found himself filled with anxiety.

Is this problem an unnecessary burden for Philip? The answers to the four questions make it clear that it is not. As the person who came to my office, Philip is obviously the one with the complaint. Certainly it is Philip who is most emotionally upset. Only Philip's life will obviously improve if his ex begins to behave more reasonably. And Philip is a central player in the dilemma, so the problem doesn't lie mainly between two other people. Moreover, only he is motivated to seek a solution because history would suggest that his ex thinks she's acting quite sensibly. Consequently, seeking a solution is his responsibility. We might agree with Philip that his ex has a problem with her temper, but he's the one who has to cope with her outbursts or solve the problem.

CHILDREN AT THE CENTER

What about problems where the child is at the center? Karen could see the pain in fourteen-year-old Deborah's eyes as she complained about how her father and stepmother had taken away her telephone privileges during her last week of summer vacation because she had used bad language. Karen knew how hard it had been on Deborah not to be able to talk to her boyfriend for an entire week; she concluded that the punishment seemed a bit harsh for the crime.

However, this was an unnecessary burden for Karen. Karen is not the person with the primary complaint. She is not the person most upset about the dilemma. It is her daughter, Deborah's, life, not Karen's, that would improve most if the problem were resolved. And clearly, this dilemma belongs to Deborah, her father, and her stepmother; it does not directly affect Karen at all.

Karen can surely listen to her daughter with understanding. She may even offer suggestions. But she does not have to feel that it is her parental responsibility to rescue Deborah; she need not make the requested phone call to her ex. Indeed, she *should not* feel that responsibility.

Finally, if Karen needs to assuage her worry over her child's unhappiness or her own guilt about refusing to interfere, she should remember that sometimes, in fact, our best efforts to help our kids cause us unintentionally to rob them of opportunities for developing important life skills.

Remember:

✓ All problems between you and your ex do not necessarily belong on your shoulders.

✓ Learning to spot unnecessary burdens does not mean you are abandoning your responsibilities as a parent or co-parent.

✓ Asking the four simple questions in this chapter helps determine whether a particular dilemma should be considered an unnecessary burden.

✓ Once you have decided that a particular dilemma with your ex can justifiably be considered an unnecessary burden, you are in a position to decide whether and how you will help your ex or your children.

Real Life

My fourteen-year-old calls me, swearing on the phone about how rotten his stepmother is for not letting him watch wrestling on TV. He's yelling that she's not his mother and wanting me to jump into the mess. He keeps me on the phone for so long that I miss the ending to my favorite Friday night show and I end up ticked off too. Who owns this one?

Both you and your son have a problem, but they are distinct from one another. The dilemma that he called about is in fact an unnecessary burden for you: It is your son who is making the complaint, it is he who is most upset, it is his life that would most improve if the problem went away, and the conflict lies primarily between him and his stepmother. You're stuck with the problem of having missed the ending to your show—an entirely different problem.

As for the unnecessary burden of your son's dilemma, please remember that you can still choose to get in the middle—although it will likely be unwise—and you can certainly coach your son on how to solve his own challenges at his dad's home.

You're saying that when my child is upset and in a mess with her mother, it isn't my job to help her? Sorry, but I view all of my daughter's problems as my own.

Our natural instincts tell us to protect our children at every turn, therefore it is natural and instinctive to resist the idea of walking away when a child is "upset and in a mess." But no one is saying that you should walk away from an unnecessary burden. Defining it as unnecessary only means that you have decided that most of the responsibility lies with others. Remember that allowing your child to retain responsibility for some of her problems is a wonderful opportunity to teach her lasting life lessons.

There's no way I'll ever compete with all the stuff my son's mother buys him. Her new husband is loaded, and they've made it their business to shower my son with things I'll never be able to afford. I think *she's* the one with the problem because she doesn't know how spoiling Jason will eventually backfire.

I understand why you would say that your ex has a problem, but remember that in doing so you mean something very different from what this chapter is focused on. You're saying that she's insensitive or manipulative and, therefore, has a problem. According to the four-question model we are using here, however, you are the one with the primary responsibility for seeking a solution: you are the one bothered by her indulgence of your son; You are the one who's complaining and upset. True, you might answer yes to question three by saying that it is your son's life that would improve if the problem went away, but your antennae should also be telling you that this problem does not involve two or more people other than yourself—again, her indulgence, your disgust, and that's it. After all, your son doesn't have a problem with the indulgence: He thinks it's wonderful! Three nos, one yes, and this is not an unnecessary burden. Finding a solution—such as accepting the differences between you and your ex, or countering the overindulgence with some understanding of what's really important in life—is your responsibility.

CHAPTER SEVEN

Unnecessary Burdens and Your Ex

Connie's ex, Barry, was ticked off because the soccer team she had chosen for their son held its practice sessions on a night he had to work. Barry complained that since their son lived mainly with Connie, it was really important that he be able to attend the games.

To Connie, Barry's ranting was more amusing than annoying. The fact was that he never helped set up activities for their son; when she asked about his schedule before she picked the team—an important first step for all co-parents—he told her it was none of her business, yet now he was barking at her when she made arrangements that conflicted with that schedule.

Obviously, this is an unnecessary burden for Connie. To three of our four questions, she can easily answer yes: Barry is the initial complainer, he is the one most emotionally upset about the problem, and his life would most improve if the problem went away.

How should Connie go about making this clear?

How should Tom approach a similar issue? His ex-wife, Laura, is scheduled to see the kids on Thursday nights, but rather than driving over to pick them up, she keeps insisting that Tom deliver the children to her. The reason? Laura simply does not want to see Tom's new partner. Not only has the new partner moved in, but, adding insult to injury, she has grown very close to the children. In fact, Laura finds the idea of running into the new partner so distasteful she has actually missed some Thursday evenings rather than come to Tom's house.

Using our questions as a guideline, it is surely Laura who owns this problem. She is the initial and primary complainer, the person most upset about the issue, the one whose life will improve most if the problem goes away, and a central figure in the problem, along with Tom's current partner.

How can Connie and Tom and all the Connies and Toms of the world give these problems back to their owners? What do you say and how should you behave as you leave the job of solving these problems to their rightful owner, your ex-partner? The answer involves seven steps:

1. Make the perceptual shift: Identify the person on whose shoulders this burden belongs.

2. Trade eyeballs again: See this problem through your ex-partner's eyes.

3. Avoid the guilt trap: If you're going to help, do so because it's right.

4. Pause for breath: Allow yourself to go slowly.

5. Decide: Do you *want* to help?

6. Don't "just say no": Effect change.

7. Avoid being rigid: Help out now and again.

1. Make the Perceptual Shift: Recognition Is Half the Battle

The first step is simply admitting *to* yourself and asserting *for* yourself that you don't own the problem. It's not that you're uninvolved. On the contrary, Connie is pretty sick and tired of her ex's claim that she messed up his schedule; amused or annoyed, his complaints waste her time, and that's an involving issue. But the dilemma over the soccer team is Barry's dilemma and, therefore, ultimately Barry's responsibility.

Tom, too, has a complaint—he is insulted and hurt by the incessant phone calls in which his ex puts his current partner down—but he is not the one with the primary complaint, and the problem is an unnecessary burden for him.

For Connie and Tom, as for you, the perceptual shift is basic to everything else. Look at yourself in the mirror and tell yourself the following:

"This problem rests on my ex-partner's shoulders. I do not own this problem, and I can freely decide whether or not to help with it."

2. Trade Eyeballs Again:
View the Problem Through Your Ex-Partner's Eyes

Once you do make that perceptual shift, and before you decide whether to help with the problem or not, step back for a wider view of the problem. All you've done, after all, is recognize that the problem is not yours; you haven't changed the emotional atmosphere, and emotional atmosphere is what must change if you're to find the personal peace you seek.

So do what was suggested in Chapter 5: trade eyeballs with your ex. Put yourself in his or her shoes and try to understand the dilemma from that point of view. It doesn't mean you're assuming responsibility, but it will help you respond in a way that doesn't elicit defensiveness or counterattacks.

Tom, for example, could consider how emotionally challenging it must be for his ex to accept the fact that her children are learning to love another parental figure—his new partner. He could remind himself that his ex-wife always had difficulty feeling secure in intimacy; understandably, she must be finding it especially difficult now to see her kids becoming close with his new partner.

Similarly, Connie might reflect on how she would feel if she were suddenly unable to attend activities important to her child; no doubt she would feel frustrated and angry too. It might help her realize that although Barry is being unreasonable, he is also a human being who wants to stay connected to his son.

Before deciding whether to help, try to gain as full an understanding of your ex's dilemma as possible.

---

3. Avoid the Guilt Trap

If you are going to decide to help out on a problem you do not own, let it be because you feel it is the right thing to do, not because you are caught in the guilt trap. It's a trap that tends to snare more women than men simply because our society puts so much pressure on women to live up to certain standards of motherhood. One mom I knew would drop everything the minute her ex called to claim he was busy with one of his many projects and could not drive the kids home after their appointed time with him. She would just hop in her car and drive to her ex-husband's to bring the kids back—although the court order specified that it was *his* responsibility to do so. In her eyes, leaving her ex-husband in a position of responsibility for solving the problem would mean that she was somehow failing as a mom. A small but distinct voice inside her said *mothers* were supposed to take care of that.

There's a flip side to the guilt trap; I call it the it's-not-in-my-contract phenomenon, and it afflicts many men who still hold to the old-fashioned view that mothers *are* supposed to take care of child-related dilemmas while the fathers tend to other, more important things. Because many men have been trained to think this way, separated dads need to make a special effort to redefine themselves as co-equal parents for whom tasks like changing diapers or attending a child's Halloween parade are as valuable as traditional "Ward

Cleaver tasks" like earning the family's daily bread and changing the oil in the car.

The fact is you *are* co-equal parents. Even if your ex may have acted as a secondary caretaker for the children while you were together, he or she must be treated as a fully responsible parent now that you live apart. The ex who has been less of a hands-on parent will not learn to deal with child-rearing problems unless and until he or she takes responsibility for such problems. By handing over the responsibility to your ex-partner, you actually communicate your belief that he or she can learn to solve problems. There should therefore be no guilt in handing over that responsibility, and as for the person to whom it's been handed, it *is* in their contract—their contract as a parent.

Man or woman, if you have been in a relationship in which you have been manipulated through the use of guilt, it can be particularly difficult to let go of a problem that actually belongs in your ex-partner's lap. You may have spent years learning to jump at the slightest hint that you're not being who you should be, that you're not quite the parent or spouse that he expects. And here you are, separated, and your ex may still attempt to control you with guilt-inducing messages!

Frank and Christine illustrate precisely this point. Under their arrangement, Frank was the primary custodian for their children, with Christine having custody at certain appointed times. Thursday was her weekly night with the kids; she was supposed to pick them up at 4:30 PM from their childcare setting, keep them overnight, and return them to childcare the next morning. Christine, however, was a busy woman who was late for almost everything, and two or three times a month, Frank would get a call from the child-care worker at 5:00 PM, just as the site was closing, telling him that no one had come to get the children. At about the same time, his beeper would go off with a frantic call from Christine: she was stuck in a business meeting on the other side of town, and she'd never make it to get the kids on time. Instead, could they reschedule so she could see the kids another night that week? The implication, of course, was that Frank would certainly go and pick up the kids for her because he was their primary custodian and it was therefore his responsibility.

As indignant as her actions made him—these frantic reschedulings made a hash of Frank's own busy professional life and sent him into a frenzy of anger at Christine—her tone of voice would also take him right back to times during their marriage when she would imply that he was somehow inadequate. Rather than seeing the issue as her failure of responsibility, Frank was caught in the guilt trap: Christine needed "rescuing," and the situation needed "fixing," and it was all up to him as primary custodian. An exaggerated sense that it was his responsibility always to say "yes" when his children were involved in any way had landed Frank in the guilt trap. It wasn't until he and I had worked together for some time that he could break free, feel less like a puppet dancing around on the emotional strings that his ex was pulling, and begin to treat Christine as a fully functioning and responsible parent.

So look hard at what appears to be a sincere desire to help the other person; make sure it isn't guilt that's driving you. Then, whether you decide to give or withhold help, your choice will be flowing from rational considerations rather than from irrational demands on yourself.

4. Pause for Breath:
Allow Yourself to Go Slowly

Many people evidence a physical response when confronting an unnecessary burden. The stomach tightens; the muscles in the back of the neck grow taut. These are the body's signals that something is awry. They are also a reminder to slow down: You don't have to respond this minute; you can pause for breath.

The first time Christine called Frank to bail her out and pick up the kids up at day care, he didn't mind helping out. But as time went on, he began to resent her demands even as he continued to give in to them. His anger grew greater each time she called. In our work together, I encouraged Frank to respond to Christine's demands by not responding—that is, to allow himself to slow down, often just by asking for time to consider her request. He learned to say, "Christine, I'll give you a call back in ten minutes after I decide if I can do this." That little bit of breathing time allowed him to make a clear, centered decision about whether he wanted to help with her problem or pass the ball back to her.

The pause for breath is a way of empowering yourself. Rather than allowing your ex to pressure you into an action you may resent, you simply ask for time. "Give me a little time to think about it, and I'll get back to you," or "I'll call you in a half hour and let you know." There's nothing wrong with explaining your delay, either: "I know you're asking for an answer now, but I sometimes make bad decisions when I rush them. I'll call you in a half hour." When you're feeling particularly pressured, an even more assertive answer may be called for: "If you must know right now if I'll help you, the answer is no. If you can wait until tomorrow and let me call you back, the answer may be yes."[2]

Another important point about the pause for breath: Asserting that you need time to think also reminds your ex that you have the right to decide to refuse his or her request, even if you eventually call back and decide to help out.

5. Decide: Do You *Want* to Help?

Recognizing that a burden is unnecessary removes a significant weight from your shoulders. Avoiding the guilt trap gets you out of the lose-lose bind of solving a problem that isn't yours or reproaching yourself for handing it back to your ex. Taking some time before you respond establishes your right to decide. Once you've done all that, you still must determine whether you *want* to help out your ex—not whether you should, must, or will, but whether you want to. Then, and only then, should you answer your ex's request for help.

Remember, the name of the game is finding personal peace in all this custody chaos. If helping out on a burden that doesn't belong to you will advance your personal peace, you probably want to undertake it. If it won't bring peace, consider passing the ball back to your ex.

6. Don't "Just Say No": Effect Change

Of course, you can simply say: "Forget it, pal, this is your problem," or "Leave me alone, sweetie, you're stuck with this one." Those methods of saying no will work wonders if your goal is to see your ex turn red and grow fangs—hardly a surefire path to personal peace.

Rather, the challenge, is to communicate to your ex that you do not intend to take responsibility for solving his or her dilemma while at the same time avoiding attacks or criticism. That means treading gently. It means that when you pass the ball back, make it an easy lob and empathize. It means remembering that you are trying to change years of conditioning—much of it by you.

THE CONSEQUENCES OF DEPENDENCY

Mary came to the session exasperated, wondering out loud why her ex-husband had called her, for the third month in a row, asking for advice about how to manage his money. With obvious frustration, she recalled years of her husband's poor financial decisions during their marriage, decisions that had often plunged the family into significant debt. Back then, she had always rescued the situation—whether it was a credit card he had overused or a bill he had not budgeted for—but she had made no secret of her anger, and she had consistently lectured him about what he should do differently in the future.

So when she came to see me and wondered out loud, with some amazement, why he was still asking her help despite their divorce, the answer seemed obvious.

"You taught him to ask for your help," I told her. "You spent years demonstrating that you were there to rescue him, and he learned the lesson well."

The revelation proved a shock to Mary. It shocked her into understanding that if her rescuing behavior continued, it would lock Mary and her ex in this same dependency dance for a long time. Little by little, Mary began to act on this new understanding; she began to treat her ex as a separate person responsible for resolving his own dilemmas—and quite capable of doing so if she would only let him. She went beyond that too, to express understanding proactively, even to offer him other resources—the name of a good financial planner, for example.

The lesson that Mary finally learned is an important one. Our own quick willingness to come to the rescue very often actually disempowers the other person; it reinforces a dependency that may end by overwhelming us. That's why it's so important to recognize your own historical role in having conditioned your ex's dependency. It's important to examine how you may have taught your ex to place problems in your lap despite the fact that those problems did not belong to you.

This was true for Frank and Christine. Over the years, Frank had made it perfectly clear by his actions that if Christine called him in the middle of a business meeting on a Thursday afternoon, if she were upset enough, if she could make him worried enough about the kids, he would, in fact, do just what she asked. By assuming the burden and taking on what was really her problem, he had actually deprived her of the chance to learn responsibility. He had never made it really clear that, after all, these were her children as much as his.

Sometimes ex-partners assume you will rescue them because you have taught them you can be relied on to do just that.

WHEN YOU PASS THE BALL BACK, EMPATHIZE

Empathize, empathize, empathize. That's the key to breaking the conditioning pattern and passing the ball back. Find some way of communicating that you recognize your ex is in the midst of a dilemma and that you understand it is difficult. You may have to swallow a bit of pride, but it can go a long way toward improving the outcome of the discussion. You might say, "That's difficult," or "You're in a tough spot," or "This must be hard for you." Anything that communicates some semblance of understanding can help soften what you're actually doing, i.e., passing the ball back to the other person's court, giving the responsibility back where it belongs.

Actually, empathy isn't enough. It helps to go beyond empathy to express faith in your ex's ability to resolve the dilemma. Yes, you understand that your ex-partner is in the midst of a dilemma, but while you are unwilling to take responsibility for the problem, you're sure your ex can solve it.

Here's how Frank went about it—the result of many weeks of counseling. During that work together, we discovered that Frank identified himself as the primarily active parent for the children seven days a week, twenty-four hours a day—even when they were with their mother. We began to work on a redefinition of his role so that he could view himself as the active, responsible parent only during those times that he was scheduled to be with the children, while viewing their mother as the active, primarily responsible parent when *she* was scheduled to be with them.

This elicited another important conclusion: Frank decided that Christine's punctuality problem was an issue that she owned; for him, it was an unnecessary burden. The next time Christine called him, frantic about being late because of a business meeting and implying that he should get the children, he was ready with a different response. "Christine," Frank said, "it must be hard to have to juggle a crazy work schedule with having to get the kids. I understand, because I've made a decision that I have to begin to protect the professional time that I schedule for the days when the children are with you. I need to do this so that my boss knows I am reliable. This means that on Thursdays, if you have a sudden conflict with getting the children, I will have to trust that you can find a way to take care of that yourself. Let me give you the names of a couple of the babysitters that I use, and I'll give you the number for the child-care place so that you can contact the director yourself when you're going to be late. Just remember, her place closes every day at 5:00 PM"

This response has all the right components: understanding of and empathy with Christine's dilemma, a very clear "no" answer, help, and the expression of faith that she can manage this. Although Christine grumbled and complained and continued to try to make Frank feel guilty, she gradually began to make her own arrangements and called Frank for help far less frequently. He had effectively passed the ball back to her. He had ended that long process of conditioning her to rely on him whenever there was a glitch in her schedule.

CHOOSE YOUR WORDS CAREFULLY

There are many different words you can use to pass the ball back, although there is no guarantee that even the gentlest, kindest words won't stir your ex's anger. Frank might have used a variety of alternatives: "This is a tough one . . . Have you tried arranging for backup child care during your time with them . . . ? That has really helped me . . . What other ideas have you had?" Such comments subtly communicate that you are setting a limit; they're helpful while also making it clear that you're unwilling to take the burden onto your exhausted shoulders.

As you begin to pass the ball back to your child's other parent, remember that the way you phrase your response, the words you choose, the attitude that you present, even your tone of voice can determine the kind of response you'll receive from your ex.

Keep in mind, for example, that your ex believes that you *should* pick up the ball on this dilemma. You've been doing so all along; there's every reason for her to believe sincerely that it is your problem. After all, your ex doesn't know yet that you have made a private decision not to take on the responsibility. By saying no and giving an unanticipated response, you're injecting an element of surprise that can make your ex defensive. That, in turn, can make a discussion deteriorate into an argument.

Don't add fuel to the fire by sounding parental; avoid lecturing or advice-giving. You don't want to come across as a know-it-all who's finally figured out the truth in life. You simply want to communicate—gently but firmly—that this is a problem you're unwilling to take on and that you believe your ex can handle. There is a world of difference between "Forget it, that's your problem!" and "I understand that this is a tough one for you, but I'm not able to help out this time." The former is like issuing a challenge; the latter sounds like a decision, not an attack.

In a very real sense, the trick is to say no while sounding a little bit like you're saying yes. Try for a palatable no—not "I just can't do it. It's up to you to handle it," but rather "I'm sorry, I'm not free to get the kids early from your house, but I'll be glad to give you my sitter's number so you can see if she can help you with the bind you're in."

Try:

✓ Reflecting on any times that your ex implied that something was your responsibility and you felt, somewhere deep inside, that you were being unfairly shouldered with a responsibility that did not belong to you. Close your eyes and watch an imaginary movie that shows your ex making the same request, but in this movie you can direct the action. Pay particular attention to the actor who is yourself. Coach yourself on the importance of listening to the warning messages from your own body. Remind yourself that you must be clear about whether or not you should be taking this particular problem onto your shoulders. Encourage yourself to perform the same scene again, only this time with an entirely new attitude: acting assertively, recognizing that you can decide to help but do not have to, and being willing to say no with confidence if a no is preferred. Coach yourself on trying to relax, recognizing that you do not have to give your ex a quick response but can pause and decide what is best. Sit back and watch the movie run again, acted in an entirely different way, and enjoy what you see.

WHEN YOUR EX HAS A PROBLEM WITH THE KIDS

Sometimes the problem is between your ex and the kids. Whose shoulders should this one fall on? As you listen to complaints from both your ex and your kids, you may pick up a subtle implication that somehow it should be yours.

That was the message Peter got from his ex-wife, Yolanda. The two came to see me once a week for co-parenting counseling. One week, Yolanda came in looking particularly exasperated and worn out after a weekend with her son. She reported that seven-year-old Jason had been "a little monster" the previous weekend. In fact, she said, he had been growing more and more monstrous during their last several weekends together. Indeed, it had gotten so bad that she was afraid to take him out in public. He seemed to delight in provoking her, challenging her in front of others, and throwing tantrums.

As she spoke, it became clear that Yolanda wanted Peter to do something about Jason's behavior; there was a subtle message that somehow he was responsible for the problem—or at least, for fixing it. Peter seemed dumbfounded. He claimed he had seldom, if ever, experienced such behavior at his home, and he implied that Yolanda "must be doing something wrong." "You have always let him run wild anyway," Peter said, "so why should you expect respect now?" To me he said that he was "sick and tired" of having to fix his ex's failures to discipline the boy, and he was equally "sick and tired" of her implication that he was somehow responsible.

Clearly the responsibility for this problem lies on Yolanda's shoulders.

Tasha's story was different, but it was also a case of an ex-partner trying to saddle her with his problem. Two months prior to her coming to my office, Tasha's nine-year-old daughter, Jennifer, had seen her father kissing one of the neighbors down the street. The daughter told Tasha what she had seen, and this led to a family confrontation in which it was revealed that Duane had been having an extended affair with this woman. Tasha told him to leave home.

Tasha was devastated by Duane's infidelity and by the breakup of the marriage, yet I was impressed with her ability to keep her resentment to herself and not infect her child with it.

Duane, however, complained that their daughter seemed to want to have nothing to do with him. She was sullen when she visited him in his new digs, he said; she seldom spoke and instead stayed glued to the television. Seemingly forgetting his own infidelity as a factor, he claimed that Tasha had somehow poisoned Jennifer's attitude toward him and demanded that she should straighten everything out.

For her part, Tasha kept hearing stories from Jennifer about how her father would yell at her to start acting "like she used to." It was frustrating, but for this mother, this was essentially an unnecessary burden. The burden here fell not on her shoulders, but on those of her ex.

Both examples highlight how difficult it can be to choose to stay out of the middle when your children are directly involved—and when what the adults decide to do will directly affect the children. How easy it is in such situations for the parent to feel pulled into the problem. How difficult it is to turn your back.

Nevertheless, even in such situations, you must remind yourself that you are not turning your back, that the problem is between your child and your ex, and that it is your ex's responsibility, not yours, to fix. Seeing it through your ex's eyes, giving yourself time to respond, you can then decide if you *want* to help or if you want to remain outside the situation.

If you decide that you want to help, you must do so by offering assistance, not by assuming responsibility. You might offer your ex thoughts about what has worked for you in the past in similar situations; you might suggest an approach. Whatever you decide, you must tread carefully in giving your response, remembering that you are in the highly sensitive area of your ex-partner's feelings about himself or herself as a parent.

Put it the way Peter did to Yolanda: "I know it can be hard when Jason gets crazy that way. Sometimes it has worked for me to remind him that he has a choice between behaving and losing Nintendo for the night." Or try Tasha's approach: "Duane, I feel bad that Jennifer is ignoring you these days. That must hurt, and it sounds like she has a lot of feelings that are hard for her too. Maybe you should sit down with her and ask what our family mess has been like for her." Helpful suggestions that gently pass the ball back and firmly keep the problem off both speakers' shoulders.

There are occasions, however—depending on the nature of the problem or the nature of your relationship with your ex—when you may just want to firmly tell him or her that it is a dilemma that you can't help with because it is between parent and child. Period. That is a difficult judgment call, but it is essential to remember that you neither neglect your child nor act unfairly toward your ex if you say that you want to keep the problem where it belongs. A firm response can be particularly important if your relationship with your ex has been tinged with guilt or if you have a tendency, as so many of us do, to jump in and try to fix any problem between our child and anyone else in the universe. Besides, even a firm response can communicate trust, which is essential for putting an end to custody chaos and ensuring your personal peace.

Refusing to take problems onto your shoulders can communicate trust in your ex's capacity to work through the difficulties.

---

7. Avoid Being Rigid: Help Out Once in a While

Treat others as you would wish to be treated yourself. It's pretty ancient wisdom, but it can work wonders in moving your relationship onto a more cooperative footing. So every now and again, there's no harm in giving the help that's needed. Just make sure you understand the difference between jumping to the rescue out of guilt and deciding to help when you know it's actually not your problem. The difference is your own freedom.

Once Frank became clear about the difference in his relationship with Christine, he could decide to help her without any strings: "I see you're in a tight spot, and I think I can help you out this time." The response implies both that he will help her and that he knows he does not have to.

Remember:

✓ After identifying an unnecessary burden, determine whether you want to help your ex with his dilemma.

✓ Work hard to view the problem through your ex-partner's eyes.

✓ Choose to help only if you believe it is right or fair, not out of guilt.

✓ Give yourself the luxury of a pause or delay to decide whether you want to help.

✓ If you decide you don't want to help, express understanding while communicating that you won't take the problem on your shoulders.

✓ Avoid being rigid with your ex: Helping him out occasionally may sow seeds of cooperation.

Real Life

When my ex calls and is freaking out about how the boys are out of control and pleading for me to step in, part of me wants to get involved because she has such rotten judgment about how to control them. Is there anything wrong with my deciding to offer ideas or even yelling at the boys to behave at their mom's home?

No, there is nothing wrong with deciding to help out. If you were under the same roof, you might help out or even put in your two cents by reprimanding the boys personally. But because this is an unnecessary burden, you should tread carefully. Repeatedly jumping in and bringing order to your ex-wife's household reinforces her image in your kids' eyes as someone who is incapable and who has no control over them. Instead, deal with the boys *when they are at your home* about their behavior with their mother. When they get out of control at her house, simply offer her ideas about how you typically bring them under control; try to stay out of the middle.

PART THREE

Nudging Your Ex to Change

CHAPTER EIGHT

Sow Respect, Reap Peace

As this chapter unfolds, I'll suggest a number of choices you have for ways to behave, ways to think about your relationship with your ex, and points to remember in dealing with your ex. But they all come down to one basic choice—the choice to act with respect and civility whatever the immediate response from your ex. In making such a choice you will be nudging your ex to change by first changing yourself.

The best reason to choose to give respect when there's no guarantee you'll get respect in return is because you see respect, even with an adversary, as the highest, best way to live your own life. By choosing respect, you take an activist, assertive stance for making peace more alive in your relationship with your children's other parent, and you consciously choose to be a still point in a relationship that often feels like a storm. You're emphasizing openness and dialogue, lessening the need for defensiveness on your ex's part. You thus maximize your chances of a decent relationship with your ex. At the very least, you can be sure that choosing bitter and hostile conduct will provoke a response in kind. Fire poison darts, and chances are good that poison darts will return your way.

Whatsoever a man soweth, that shall he also reap.

—Galatians 6:7

What Doesn't Work

You already know the things that don't work. You probably already know that keeping up a brave front—smiling and pretending nothing is wrong—only brings on ulcers; it doesn't bring on change.

Getting even doesn't work, either. Maybe you feel better for a second, but all you've achieved is the next step in the payback cycle of disrespect. Getting even is a feeble attempt at self-protection in response to a perceived attack.

Walking away doesn't work. Hanging up on your ex or shutting the door in his or her face should only be the very last of last resorts—and then only for self-protection.

Doing nothing doesn't work. Sometimes, it is true, inaction can be a short-term tactic for appeasing your ex in a situation in which you have no power. In the long run, however, inertia becomes impotence, sapping your sense of effectiveness.

Trying respect and civility once, however, is also insufficient. In a long history of acrimony, one sparrow of courtesy does not a spring of peace make. For one thing, it lets you off the hook. "I tried being nice, and it didn't work," you might claim, thus giving yourself permission never to be "nice" again. More to the point, however, peace is not a one-time trial, and respect is a path, not a single act. It takes time and commitment.

Respect must be a choice for a life path, not just a strategy. In fact, even without the potential benefit in return, the choice for respect, as a personal decision, is a personal triumph. Whether your ex changes behavior or not, your own moral compass will tell you you're on the right path. The decision has been not just for the relationship but for your life, and nothing your ex does or fails to do can diminish or in any way affect your choice for how you want to be in this world.

Giving What You Want to Receive

It's interesting how many of the principles we have discussed so far have their earliest roots in the great spiritual traditions, and this one is no exception. In the New Testament, we are told that "whatever you wish that men would do to you, do so to them."[1] Gandhi gave the idea an activist's twist when he said: "Be the change you want to see." The meaning is the same: If you want others to live a certain way, you must choose to live that way yourself.

For parents struggling with an ex, it means that if you want your ex to act more respectfully toward you, you must be sure you are consistently respectful toward your ex. If you want your ex to control his or her temper when you are negotiating something, be sure that you carefully control yours. If you wish your ex would not say hurtful things about your family when the two of you are together, be sure to speak respectfully about theirs.

And remember that as you try to improve things between you and your ex, you may have to fake goodwill. You may not feel respect. You may not feel appreciation. But sometimes the behavior has to happen before the feelings flow. Choosing to "act" respectfully over and over will gradually make such behavior feel more natural.

On one level, giving what you yourself want to receive is simply the right thing to do. But it also offers critical advantages. Think of it, in the image so eloquently developed by Stephen Covey,[2] as a kind of investment, i.e., as if you are making a deposit of respect to a bank account from which you will eventually want to withdraw respect. With interest. In other words, when you invest in the Golden Rule, it can return platinum profits.

Try:

  ✓ Considering your relationship with your ex as a soup that you both must eat. Whatever bitter ingredients your ex may add, decide to add only those things that will make it taste more tolerable for both of you.

✓ Making a list of the specific ways you wish your ex would be-have toward you. Then ask yourself if you are consistently acting in those ways yourself. If not, begin little by little to model the exact behavior that you yourself long for—such as being on time for commitments, speaking in a respectful fash-ion, and the like.

Living Your Life According to Your Own Moral Compass

One measure of that return on your investment is simply the gratification that comes when you act according to your own moral compass, the fulfillment you achieve when your actions and behav-ior define something about your life and assert what you want to be for others. The alternative would be to yield to your ex's bad con-duct and imitate it. It's easy to do. "Well, she acts ridiculous when-ever she comes over, so I certainly won't be nice to her," you might think, or "Why should I be flexible about his time with the kids when he is always rigid and unreasonable with me?"

> *You cannot make yourself feel something you do not feel, but you can make yourself do right in spite of your feelings.*
> —Pearl Buck, author of *The Good Earth*

Returning tit for tat so entwines your own path in life with your ex's that you eventually lose yourself; you allow your conduct to be dictated by someone else—in this case, by an ex who is driving you crazy. It makes no sense. Deviating from what you want your life to be never does make sense. The choice for civility and respect should spring from your own moral compass telling you it is the right way to be, rather than because you want to change your ex. Being the change you want to see is essential for your own peace—it brings you home.

MOM AND DAD AT THE BLACKBOARD

Respect and civility with your ex are also essential tools for teaching your children—the second measure of return on your investment. In fact, such conduct towards your ex models a way of acting in adult relationships that will give your kids a better shot at success in their own relationships, both as children and later in life. Imagine, as you begin a difficult exchange with your ex, that you are standing in front of a classroom at one end of the blackboard, chalk in hand, while your ex stands on the other side of the blackboard, also with chalk in hand. Your children are the students sitting at the desks and scribbling in their life notebooks as they learn, for better or for worse, the lessons that you teach.

The way the two of you choose to work this issue through, either rationally or in an angry or insulting way, will determine what your children scribble in their life notebooks and what they do in their own future relationships. To see the two of you acting civilly toward one another, even to see at least *one* of you acting civilly, can be a wonderful learning experience. Keep in mind that your children are participating observers in your family drama and what they observe can shape how they participate in their own relationships. That should be a reminder about how you should conduct yourself.

The blackboard can be anywhere. If you and your ex scream or put one another down at the doorstep as you exchange the children, or in phone calls as the two of you make arrangements for custody exchanges, or at events where both of you are in attendance, your children will write that in their notebooks. In time, they will likely behave the same with their own spouses, boyfriends, or girlfriends. If they see you being respectful in any or all of these situations— flexible, polite, even-tempered—they are far more likely to act in those ways with others when they grow up. As has often been said, a good example is the best sermon you can preach.

Here's a case where it doesn't really take two to make a positive impact. If your ex has decided that his or her hostility cannot be abandoned, leaving you as the only parent teaching a healthy lesson on the blackboard, your children can still benefit from the one positive lesson; while they learn disrespectful behavior from your ex, they are also scribbling down your model of civility. So even if the respectful behavior they see is a solo act, you are doing right by your children—not to mention the fact that by behaving in a way that is consistent with your own values, you will undoubtedly sleep better at night.

> *Live so that when your children think of fairness,*
> *caring, and integrity, they think of you.*
> —H. Jackson Brown, Jr., author of *Life's Little Instruction Book*

Try:

✓ Imagining the following: You and your ex are having coffee with your now twenty-year-old child, and you ask your child the following: "After we separated, what did your mom (or dad) and I do in our relationship that you appreciated?" What do you hope to hear? Start doing it with your ex now.

DOUSING A FIRE

A third important advantage of using this tool is that it can help slow down the cycle of animosity between your and your ex. Responding to your ex's unreasonable behavior with unreasonable behavior of your own perpetuates anger and hurt. Fighting fire with fire, after all, usually only leads to more fire. A different kind of behavior can douse the fire.

Catherine was sick and tired of her ex calling and leaving a message saying that he would not bring the children home that night as planned but would instead take them to school the next day. While I agreed that her ex's behavior was disrespectful and frustrating, I asked Catherine to look more closely at her own response to his be-havior: She sent complaining notes to her ex via the children's knapsacks. She tended to schedule doctors' appointments during his times with the children. Other seemingly small actions were in the same spiteful vein.

When Catherine finally accepted the fact that her approach to the problem was only making things more difficult for *herself*, she de-cided to try "killing" her ex with kindness. It took hard work to act respectfully toward someone for whom she felt little respect; she had to force herself to be fair-minded and to speak in reasonable tones. And while the hard work did not transform her ex overnight, he did gradually begin to act more reasonably toward her. The tone of their exchanges softened a bit. The two of them reached the point where they could discuss issues more calmly and rationally. Even-tually, he came to understand that his cavalier treatment of the cus-tody agreement disrupted her life, and he began asking permission to keep the children for the additional night, rather than just doing it on his own.

It was simple, and it was also hard at the same time: Catherine gave her ex what she herself wanted, and it began to come back to her little by little, her investment yielding a like return with interest. And as her children watched her counter disrespect with respect, they scribbled this lesson in their life notebooks and took it forward with them into their own futures.

Redefine Your Relationship with Your Ex in Business Terms

Jack and Jennifer had been close friends for a long time when they decided to turn their joint passion for gardening into a busi-ness. Their plan was to grow a large showcase garden of flowers so beautiful that that it would catch the eye of anyone passing by.

The process of working together taught them a lot. They learned that Jennifer was particularly skilled at the business end of the busi-ness as well as at "reading" the plants. She had a sense of the best products and could negotiate well with suppliers. She also had an instinct for what the plants needed—which flowers needed more fertilizer, or a special type of feeding, or simply more water. It was almost as if the plants talked to Jennifer, and the information she "heard" from them was critical in helping Jack decide how to use his time in the garden during the day.

For his part, Jack had a knack for tilling the soil efficiently and effectively; even under hot sun. By day's end, everything that needed to be done was done, and the garden looked fresh and new. In this way, the two friends worked together successfully for several years, achieving their dream of growing unique and beautiful flowers that people came from miles around to look at.

Then, inexplicably, cracks appeared in their close relationship. They began to argue over the composition of the garden, began to carp about the work each one did, began to disagree about plans and results. Suddenly, nothing was the same anymore. Jack and Jennifer had difficulty being together without barking at one another. They gradually began to work more and more independently, Jennifer reading the plants but keeping the information to herself and ordering supplies without talking to Jack, Jack going off for his day of work and planning his tasks without consulting Jennifer.

The flowers soon began to wither and turn brown. The showcase garden took on an almost haggard look, as if reflecting the frayed relationship of its owners. The crowds dwindled. Business declined. "Our investment is slipping through our fingers," Jack thought to himself. "Our work is passing away before our eyes," thought Jennifer.

And then, one day, Jack ran into Jennifer near the field, and the two seemed to be thinking the same thing at the same time: If they could find a way to work together as business partners despite the fact that their relationship as it used to be was gone, maybe the flowers would come back to life and be beautiful again. They began to discuss the garden as a business, and to think of themselves as business partners. They agreed that Jack should continue to work the field and Jennifer continue to read the flowers. It would be her responsibility to give Jack her sense of what was needed and to or-der the supplies. It would be Jack's responsibility to do the field-work needed to execute the garden plan. And, they agreed, in their dealings with one another, they would both "stick to business."

Of course, the crowds began to gather once more. The petals on the wilted flowers once more lifted toward the sun. Once more, the stalks on the plants seemed strong and sturdy. And although the old friendship between Jack and Jennifer seemed gone forever, their new business partnership allowed them to appreciate together what they had created together.

The example illustrates how to turn a personal relationship into a purely business relationship. Think of any business, from the local gas station to the giant corporation turning out thousands of wid-gets every hour. There are workers in those businesses who can't stand each other. Even those who get along probably don't socialize with one another outside of work. But when they come together in the work environment, a place where they are committed to certain responsibilities, they stay focused, concentrate on the task at hand, and get the job done—whether they are the best of friends or sworn adversaries. The gas still gets pumped. The widgets still get made—all toward the greater good of the company.

To redefine your relationship with your ex in business terms, think of your children as your garden. Even though you and your spouse have separated, the children continue to need the unique gifts that each of can provide them. They cannot truly flourish—that is, they cannot lead truly happy lives—if the givers of those gifts let their relationship become toxic or explode in hostility. So you must find a way to work together with your spouse in ways that keep the focus on the garden you're responsible for—your chil-dren.

In later chapters, I'll go into specifics about how you can make the business-relationship metaphor work in your relationship with your ex. For now I ask you only to consider applying tried-and-true business practices to the task of working together as parents while living apart as individuals. Scheduled conversations about how the children are doing, orderly exchanges of information about health and education matters, agendas for meetings together, agreeing to disagree at times without putting one another down, negotiating in good faith, writing letters when a particular issue is too hot to discuss personally, and similar methods suit the relationship between ex-spouses precisely because they are meant to take strong emotions out of the process. They help keep powerful feelings of resentment or sadness from creeping into the essential task of working cooperatively together to nurture your mutual investment—your little ones, the beautiful flowers you are preparing for the world.

Try:

✓ Saying to yourself before each of your next several meetings with your ex: "I am now going to meet with my business associate." Act as you would with a business partner with whom you have disagreements.

Establish Boundaries

Emotional boundaries exist. When we're under the same roof with a partner or spouse, the boundaries might be as simple as a rule that when one person is in the bathroom, the other person doesn't walk in. Or perhaps it's the unwritten understanding that one spouse doesn't open the other spouse's mail. Maybe it's a separate room in the house that's the "personal space" of one or the other of you, into which no one may go unasked. When two people live together, however, the boundaries also tend to be somewhat porous. After all, people who live together share a bed, may share a checkbook, probably share a range of household tasks and share confidences about one another's emotional struggles.

Once you separate, however, there's an adjustment period in which each gets used to what the other person will and will not tolerate. New boundaries gradually build up as you communicate to one another the things that are now off limits. You may not want unannounced visits to the children by your ex because you have met someone, you're beginning to have a personal life, and your new partner may be at the house. Your ex may not want you entering her house when she's not there even though it used to be your house also. One woman I counseled found it distressing that her ex would just show up at the house and come in without knocking. Another man was annoyed that his ex-wife would come to the home they used to live in together to do her laundry because her new apartment lacked a washer and dryer. Situations like these beg for the setting of new boundaries—for new relationship rules—so that both ex-partners can have their own psychological and physical space. Where the boundaries between ex-partners are concerned, they need to be regarded with the same caution as the boundaries between nations.

Boundaries are important because they represent ways in which we make ourselves feel safe and shore up our separate identity. They also can contribute to an atmosphere of respect because they help everyone understand what they should and shouldn't do. It's paramount that you allow yourself to set limits—to demarcate those areas of your life that are open to your ex and those that must stay closed.

You may decide that you don't want your ex staying in your home for more than a few minutes at transition times or that you don't want her coming in at all. You may decide that you are no longer going to answer the phone before 7:00 A.M. when your ex usually makes annoying attempts to speak with you about money matters. You may even come to a point where celebrating a child's birthday together with your ex is just too uncomfortable for you; you've decided you must insist on separate celebrations.

Whatever the boundaries are going to be, be clear in your own mind—before any discussion with your ex—about the boundaries that are important to you and about why this is so. Remember that when one person in a relationship sets boundaries, it can be experienced by the other person as a rejection or a distancing. Sometimes, this can yield an angry response. A boundary can also be misinterpreted as an attempt by you to limit your ex–partner's access to his children. Consequently, while you should assertively attempt to establish healthy boundaries between you and your ex, it's important to communicate about this issue in a sensitive manner that does not fan the flames of conflict. In upcoming chapters I will outline specific ways to speak about such difficult matters to decrease the likelihood of an angry response.

It is also critical to remember that one way to sow seeds of cooperation with your ex is to respect *her* boundaries. Pay attention to the signals from her about where you should tread lightly—or not at all—and behave accordingly. The less intrusive you are in your ex's life, the more likely you are to reap respect in return.

Choose Your Battles Carefully

The principle here is quite simple: Learn to become clear about which issues between you and your ex are really important, and let go of those that are not. Decision-making in the child-rearing arena typically gives rise to scores of things to complain about, to be frustrated about, and to be angry about. Intact families have an opportunity to work out their differences day by day by day; separated parents enjoy no such leisure. Communications tend to be sparse and can be difficult when ex-partners are separated by time and by miles, and they can regress to all-out war when the relationship is already brittle.

Letting go of certain issues with your ex can be a powerful way to regain control in your life.

Before opening up a discussion with your ex about a thorny problem, pause and ask yourself: Is this particular "battle" worth fighting? If you complain or argue about everything that bothers you, your relationship with your ex will soon become a front in an ongoing war, with each of you feeling vulnerable to attack at any time, with both of you forever on the defensive. You can take control of this vicious cycle by deciding that certain matters just aren't worth pursuing—only some very important issues are worth the unpleasantness, the *agita*, the potential emotional damage to yourself and your children. This can help keep the degree of conflict to a minimum.

> **The art of being wise is the art of knowing what to overlook.**
> —William James, American philosopher and psychologist

Maxine was ticked off at her ex for not giving her the children's medical insurance cards, for showing up late for visits, and for consistently being two days late with the support checks. The relationship had seemed like a continuous battle to her. But one day she made the decision that she could live with the other problems if she could just resolve the issue of the medical insurance cards; in fact, she decided that bringing up the other problems again would probably cause her more long-term heartache than simply putting them out of her mind. It was difficult for her to let go of these issues, but in doing so she made her life a bit easier; it gave her ex fewer complaints to fight, and the number and frequency of their arguments diminished as a result.

Be Proactive Rather than Reactive with Your Ex

Mr. Reactive saw himself as a puppet on the strings that his ex-partner was pulling, dancing about without any self-direction. During every exchange of the children, his ex would berate him about various matters in front of the kids, and at some point she would say just the right words to make him hit the roof. This happened over and over and over again, and he alternated between screaming at his ex, feeling depressed and hopeless, and simply being caught off guard by her comments.

Mr. Proactive started out with pretty much the same dilemma as Mr. Reactive, but after his ex had effectively pushed his buttons for six or seven months, he decided that whenever his ex said something insulting to him, he would simply respond "I'm sorry you feel that way." He made a list of the topics he would not bring up with her, because he knew they tended to unleash a new barrage of insults. And he decided that when her verbal abuse crossed a certain line—when she began to disparage his parents or curse at him about old marital history—he would simply let her know that he was going to hang up the phone and that he would be open to talking on another occasion when she was calmer. Finally, he decided that there were certain issues that he would communicate with her about only via a businesslike letter, so that she would have a chance to digest the information and not feel that she had to react.

The difference between these fathers is enormous. The reactive father lets himself be bounced about by circumstances, feels helpless and victimized, and continually goes back for more, simply taking what's thrown at him and then reacting uncontrollably in the moment.

The proactive dad, by contrast, has slipped out of the passenger seat into the driver's seat; he has *planned* how he will respond to a difficult and challenging relationship. He has abandoned the role of passive victim and determined that the one thing he has control over is the way *he* responds to his ex, and he is zeroing in on this. He has no way of knowing whether his new attitude will make a difference in his ex's behavior. Even if it doesn't, he at least feels more in control; he is at least living his life his way.

Being proactive means planning for difficult circumstances, rehearsing how you can respond, brainstorming solutions and trying different options that might make the exchange go better with your ex. It means seeing yourself as having choices. The proactive person is never helpless; there's always something he or she can do. This does not mean pretending that there are simple solutions. It means identifying what you can control and doing what you can within that arena to make a difference.

Being proactive also means viewing the dilemmas with your ex as a problem to be solved rather than as an unalterable catastrophe. There are no guarantees that your problem with your ex can be solved, but having a positive attitude goes a long way toward setting the stage for a better relationship. At least you are taking action. Moreover, you are acting on your own beliefs and attitudes—the places where you have the most influence.

Scientists in a laboratory tend to be highly invested in the project at hand. But when their initial experiments fail to work, they don't cry, feel victimized, or run off to a therapist. They look upon the failed experiment as a problem to be solved, and that means going back to the drawing board, devising new ways to put together the right ingredients till they find the solution. They brainstorm options, try them out, modify them, and see what works.

Although relationships are much more complex and emotion-laden than laboratory experiments, you can be proactive in the same way in relationships. You can step back and think about what's going wrong with your ex, brainstorm different approaches, and try different ways of influencing him to make your relationship more satisfying, or at least less painful. You won't be able to be as emotionally detached as you would be with a laboratory experiment, but you will be able to feel more in control of your life.[3] Being proactive is empowering.

Marlene told me about her own experimentation with a particularly difficult issue with her ex: "At first, I'd give him a call about this issue, then I started meeting with him over coffee to see if that would work, and ultimately I found that he just did better when he received a letter about a complaint I had. Somehow that made him feel safer, and he wouldn't act like such a caged animal whenever I complained." Marlene's proactive creativity ultimately hit on something that made things go better with her ex.

Try:

 ✓ Creating a proactive game plan for dealing with your ex. Put
   the plan on paper; commit to it. You might use each of the
   suggestions in this chapter as a topic heading for items in your
   plan.

Find Things to Appreciate— And Show Gratitude

Looking for things to appreciate in your ex is a tough assignment
if your relationship is filled with anger or resentment, as so many
broken relationships are. Remember, however, that we're focusing
on the things that you can do to lay the foundation for a more cooperative, less hostile relationship.

And the truth is that annoyances tend to be more evident than
joys. Think about your own parenting experience: Like most of us,
you're probably much more attuned to what your children are doing wrong than the things they do right. Part of this has to do with
the way our brains are neurologically organized; negative information is given greater weight than positive information because the
negative can be a potential threat to well-being. We often do the
same in our adult relationships. Unfortunately, however, relationships don't work well when positive behavior goes relatively unno-
ticed while negative behavior is pounced on.

In addition, the pain and anger separated parents may feel toward one another can blind them to the things that deserve to be
appreciated even in a pain-in-the-neck ex–spouse. One of the most
tragic events in separated families is the rewriting of family history:
In the service of recouping self-esteem after a failed marriage most
couples begin to mentally review the marriage and to highlight and
amplify parts of history that either support their decision to leave—
"See, there's another time he lied!"—or that make the rejection feel
less personal—"If she didn't need to drink so much, she wouldn't
have left us . . . it was the booze." Thus a new mental image of the

ex is born, an image made up of selective, ego-serving memories rather than the full picture of the person who once was a lover. Pain and anger can make you forget there ever was anything good about your ex, and they obscure the good he or she does now. That's why it's particularly important to watch how your anger or pain may cause you to distort the full reality of your ex; don't let them screen out the things your ex may be doing that are worth your notice—and your appreciation.

Appreciation doesn't mean giving up your pain or anger; you can still stay mad at the dumb or hurtful things your ex-spouse gets up to. The point, however, is to take note of the good, accept it, and express gratitude for it.

Gratitude softens conflict.

In fact, you should look hard for things to appreciate in your ex, and you should make it a point regularly to note and express appreciation for something he or she is doing right. It may be something significant—perhaps your ex has agreed to attend a school meeting for you. It may be about the smallest of matters—maybe this week, unlike most weeks, your ex remembered to bring back the asthma medication, or perhaps he remembered to call you in advance of a schedule change, or maybe you liked the pair of pants she bought your child during her last shopping trip, or maybe you just like the way he is combing your kid's hair. If you remember that appreciation can be about the tiniest matters, I promise that you *will* find something to appreciate if you look.

And then all it takes is the simplest expression of appreciation. The phrase "I want you to know that I appreciated that" can go a very long way toward softening the angry tone of a relationship. And, yes, it is important to do this even when disagreements or complaints remain unresolved. Remember that what goes around really does come around. We really do reap what we sow. Expressing appreciation can, in time, bring appreciation back your way.

Commit Small Kindnesses

It's really only a small step from finding things to appreciate and expressing gratitude to becoming proactive and doing something nice for your ex. How hard is it really to offer your former spouse extra time with the children? Or, while you're making copies of your child's artwork, to make an extra copy for your ex? Or to drive the kids back yourself—even though the usual arrangement is for your ex to pick them up? Or to help the kids buy your ex a birthday present—and maybe even to send a card yourself?

Yet small kindnesses can make a big difference—not in ending the difficulties between you and your ex, but in making the relationship more harmonious so that you can deal with the difficulties rationally, peacefully, without rancor. Finding an opportunity to do good for someone for whom you feel animosity can be transformative. It might well transform your ex; it will certainly transform your distress at the chaos of your custody situation into something closer to personal peace. Besides, it is the right way to live.

Be Flexible

You're about to have a conversation with your ex about where and when he intends to take the children for their summer vacation. Take a deep breath and surrender any rigid positions you may have developed about the issue. Instead, try to take the view that you have *preferences*—not positions, not even options to offer, just preferences. Preferences indicate that you are flexible, that the issue is negotiable, that there are no absolute "shoulds" or "musts" lurking between your ears. When you're flexible, you won't miss the reasonable solution or fair compromise that might meet both of your interests.

Construction engineers look for flexible materials because such materials are far stronger than rigid materials that may crack or splinter under pressure. It's the same with people. Rigidity can feel powerful, at least for a few minutes, when your self-esteem has

been diminished by the problems with your ex. Scrambling to protect our egos, we refuse to give in because we think yielding is surrender; we think it makes us look weak or is evidence of colluding
with the enemy. In fact, however, flexibility is a sign of great
strength. It is a sign of confidence to be attentive to new ideas, and
it takes courage to admit that a person you may disdain has come
up with a reasonable idea.

**A flexible tree bends in the wind and rights itself; a rigid
tree snaps. It's the same with people.**

One separated father once said to me: "I regularly give in or compromise on small issues so that when I bring up the big ones, I've
earned some chips that I can cash in." Openness and flexibility are
even better than yielding, but the approach is equally valid; in this
case, it led to positive progress in the man's relationship with his
child's mother.

Be Willing to Say You're Sorry

We sometimes underestimate the power of an apology. We tend
to forget that we are all imperfect human beings who make mistakes and occasionally regret the way we behave. Being willing to
say "I'm sorry"—regardless of your ex-partner's response—can
make you feel good about your own honesty. It can also add a positive dimension to the dance that you and your ex are doing together.

Think the Unthinkable

As you learned earlier, the thoughts you allow yourself to have
about your ex have a powerful effect on how you feel in the relationship. However, the power of your thoughts may go well beyond an effect on your own feelings. Some research even argues

that the tone of your thoughts about those around you may have an effect on the positive or negative quality of what happens in the minds of others! You don't have to accept such ideas, however, to acknowledge that when you are thinking angry, retaliatory, toxic thoughts about another person and you then are in that person's presence, your body posture, voice tone, and facial expressions will somehow communicate your disdain. The other person will likely respond with tension, defensiveness, or outright aggression. When you are mentally focusing on the other person's good qualities or about things that you appreciate, these thoughts will be obvious in your posture, face, and voice, more likely leading to a gentler response in the other person.

A good strategy for improving the tone of the relationship between you and your ex is to discipline yourself to mentally focus on aspects of your ex that conjure up positive feelings for you. It may take some work—it may seem impossible—but purposely rehearse in your mind images of things you appreciate, respect, or admire about your ex. Bring to mind memories that make you feel good or that make you laugh, and do so not just while you are talking to your ex, but during times you are apart. It may help to say such affirming things to yourself as "Despite John's antics, I know that deep down he is a good, loving father" or "Even though we have many differences, I know that Deborah would do anything for our children." You will then be much more likely to create an atmosphere of acceptance and emotional safety for your difficult ex that will dampen the chances of frustrating behavior on his part.

The Commitment Letter

Another simple tool that can go a long way is to inventory the behavior that you'd like to see in your ex and write a sincere letter promising to work hard to model that behavior to her. If you'd like to be treated with civility by your ex, write that you promise to treat her with civility at all times. If you'd like to see her be flexible about arrangements, make a written commitment to be flexible. The letter can be brief, but the tone is critical: a genuine statement of what your ex can expect from you with the implication that you hope the same will come your way. Here's an example:

Dear Sheila,

We've had some really hard times and I think both of us have made some mistakes. I know that you are very angry at me about the separation and I carry my own resentments. I just wanted you to know that I intend to work hard to shield the kids from our feelings about each other. I will work hard to treat you with respect when we see each other because, despite our differences, you deserve that as the mother of our children. In my household, you will always be spoken of with respect and I will do nothing to interfere with your relationship with the kids. And when we have differences, I will work hard to pay attention to your side of the story so we can resolve things in a way that feels fair to both of us.

I hope that you will consider returning these things to me in kind, but my commitment to act in these ways toward you will in no way depend on whether or not you do; you can expect these things from me because I want to make things easier for the kids.

Sincerely,
Sam

Sowing Seeds for your Kids

Please remember that as you cultivate respect and cooperation with your ex, you not only make your own life easier, you also bring more peace into the lives of your children. Toward this end, remember some of the basics with your kids that can help you avoid "poisoning the waters" with your ex:

- Speak respectfully about your ex with your children.

- Don't ask your children to keep secrets from their other parent.

- Speak directly with your ex—don't use your children as messengers.

- Don't interrogate your kids about their time with your ex.

- Don't let the children make decisions about seeing or not seeing your ex.

- Talk about your divorce in a way that doesn't blame anyone.

- Keep adult issues—financial support, court rulings, etc.—between the adults.

- Don't criticize your ex's parenting style with the kids—teach them with your own.

"PEACEFUL" DOESN'T EQUAL "PASSIVE"

Before you take any action with your ex, there's one very important element of the cooperative mindset that you'll need to cultivate. *Acting with respect and civility and orienting yourself toward cooperation do not mean being docile or passive, nor does it mean surrendering your own needs and desires.* It is critical that you affirm for yourself your right to complain about matters that are important to you, to set boundaries around your personal and physical space that help you feel safe and secure, and to take forceful action when necessary to protect your rights and those of your children. Deciding to do everything you can to sow seeds of cooperation and peace between you and your ex does not mean becoming a wet noodle; it does mean acting from strength while attempting to minimize the animosity and discomfort between you and your ex-spouse.

You can be both assertive and respectful.

You can aim for peace and still make it clear that your ex is not welcome in your house when you're not there. You can give respect and still decide in certain instances that you will not change your plans because your ex has come up with yet another scheduling dilemma. You can offer civility and still decide that you need to hang up the phone when you are being called names. You can remain courteous while insisting that your ex give you the insurance cards for the children. You can be oriented toward peace even if you decide you need to contact the authorities regarding your personal safety.

I hope that none of these things will ever be necessary for you. I offer them only as examples of how important it is not to confuse a decision to sow the seeds of peace with passivity. Peace is not submission, and it is certainly not weakness. It takes enormous power to transform an enemy into a friend, a power that comes from treating others as we wish to be treated, even if the other is acting like a jerk.

Remember:

✓ Act with your ex in the manner that you want your ex to act with you.

✓ Focus on how *you* are choosing to act with your ex so that you teach your children the most positive lessons possible.

✓ Define your relationship with your ex as similar to a business contract. Work together with civility to protect your "investment."

✓ Give yourself permission to establish healthy personal boundaries between you and your ex-partner.

✓ Carefully choose the battles you pursue with your ex and let go of those that are of lower priority.

✓ Choose to be proactive; plan how you will relate to your ex rather than allowing yourself to be tossed about by old habits and patterns.

✓ Notice small things your ex does that you can appreciate; communicate your appreciation.

✓ Replace rigid positions on issues with preferences—and be flexible.

✓ Apologize when you should.

✓ Think positively about your ex despite your frustrations.

✓ Avoid poisoning the waters with your kids.

✓ Don't confuse cooperation with passivity.

Real Life

Why should I consider making myself into a little peace-loving softie when all I get back from my ex is rotten disrespect? My six-year-old son told me last week that my ex looked at a photo of me and said, "That one must have broken the camera." He did that in front of my son! I'm supposed to be nice to this guy?

When your child grows up and finds himself working with a colleague who treats him with disrespect, will you want him to hurl insults at his co-worker or behave in a civil yet assertive fashion? Choosing to be civil doesn't mean you can't make forceful complaints. It just means you have decided to seek higher ground.

Expressing gratitude seems like a nice idea, but I'll be honest: I can't think of a thing that that jerk does that I appreciate.

Remember that after a separation—particularly when the relationship with the ex is a conflicted one—the mind tends to amplify all that is wrong and upsetting and to minimize anything positive. As you make your list of things you appreciate, remember to think very small. "Thanks for braiding Jenny's hair," "Thanks for remembering the diaper bag," or "Jonathan seems to love that park you take him to" can go a long way.

How long do I have to keep this up? How long do I have to keep acting reasonably in the face of her foolishness?

For as long as you think that acting reasonably represents living a good life. Remember, sowing seeds of cooperation and respect often reaps wonderful benefits, but your efforts may need to be sustained over many months. And indeed, your ex may never actually change. That is why it's important to decide that the main reason you are acting with civility is because your moral compass directs you that way—and because you want your children to copy good lessons from the blackboard.

CHAPTER NINE

Conversations about Hot Topics: Before You Say a Word

The topics of conversation between divorced parents can range from the momentous to the mundane—from visitation rights and financial support to who gets to go to the senior play and who should attend the 7 A.M. track meet. But major or minor, every topic of discussion is consequential when you're discussing it with someone who drives you crazy.

Emotions between ex-spouses are often raw. One or both of you may be struggling to regain a sense of self-worth after a painful parting. One or both may be feeling marginalized as a parent. One or both of you may be filled with guilt, with worry, with fear of losing control over your life. You may be feeling you must right the past by getting back at your ex in the present. Such feelings only make you more vulnerable—ready to be injured all over again by a former partner's critical comment, by harsh behavior, by the slightest hint of disdain or rejection.

> *Relationships that do not end peacefully do not end at all.*
>
> —Merrit Malloy, poet

The possibility of such injury or attack—the threat of it—can impel you and your ex to prepare for a fight before any fight has occurred, digging in your heels and raising your swords before a word has been uttered. The tendency is to construct a superficial shield for protection, an external rampart for keeping yourself emotionally safe and regaining power. Thus armed, you go to meet your adversary, and even the most trivial concern becomes a hot topic. The sparks it emits can all too easily burst into flame. The conversation becomes a confrontation, resistance turns to intimidation, feelings of inadequacy fuel aggression, and the discussion falls apart at the seams.

It doesn't have to be this way. It shouldn't be this way. But how do you keep a conversation alive and transform a dysfunctional argument into a true meeting of the minds that advances your child's well-being and produces harmony all around? The truth is you can do more with a conversation on a hot topic than keep the discussion cool; you can actually use the exchange with your ex, however rocky or difficult, as a vehicle for evolving as a person and for crystallizing who you are and what you stand for.

Learning to Talk All Over Again

The process of communicating in a hot-topic conversation—and the tools for managing the process—divide naturally into three stages:

- before the conversation—how to prepare, mentally and in practical terms, for a discussion of a hot topic.

- beginning the conversation—how to take the lead and increase the chances of a satisfactory outcome.

- responding—how to deal with your ex becoming resistant, angry, contentious, even combative during the conversation.

For each of these stages, I'll offer strategy options and tactical tools for you to choose from. You won't use all the tools at once—

there are some you might never use at all—and you won't use them in any prescribed sequence. But they'll add to the tools in your toolbox for conversations about hot topics so you can make the right choices to suit the circumstances, your own purposes, your ex-partner's, and the topic itself.

After all, you and your ex will be having these conversations for many years to come. Getting through them successfully, in a way that achieves a conclusion, produces harmony, and keeps you grounded in your own values is essential.

Keep in mind that while these tools will significantly increase the chances that you will feel good about your next hot-topic conversation with your former partner, there can be no guarantees that your ex will choose to act reasonably. For this reason, make that result only the third of three wishes. There are two more important wishes: that the conversation proceeds in a way that protects your children and enhances their lives, and that you become more of the person you want to be. When you choose to view the hot-topic conversation as an opportunity to practice listening, compassion, self-respect, flexibility, and assertiveness—as a chance to grow—rather than as a battle you must win, you can't help but triumph, regardless of the dance your ex does in response.

Preparing For The Conversation: Planning a Strategy, Preparing Your Mind

A conversation with your ex about child-related issues must be approached as a negotiation—that is, as a meeting in which you and your ex confer in order to reach agreement. Because it involves your children, it is a very delicate negotiation. Because you and your ex have a long history of failed, often contentious conversations, it will likely be a difficult negotiation. No negotiator ever goes into a negotiating session equipped only with hope and good intentions. Even for the most skilled and experienced practitioner of the negotiating art—the worldly diplomat flying from capital to capital to secure a peace treaty, or the savvy union leader bent on crafting the best deal for his membership—serious preparation is required: goal-setting, strategic planning, tactical guidelines, and a plan of action.

You too need a strategy going into the conversation. You need a plan for having your say—clearly, calmly, respectfully. You need a script with which to rehearse the plan and alternate words in your head that help you adjust when the negotiating deviates from the idealized script of your best-case scenario—as negotiating invariably does. And you need to be prepared to listen with compassion.

In other words, you need to prepare both mentally and in practical and concrete ways for a conversation on a hot topic. You prepare mentally by determining the mindset you will maintain and the goals you want to achieve. You prepare in practical ways by deciding what you will and will not do during the conversation.

Careful preparation can mean the difference between a disastrous conversation and an amicable resolution.

PREPARING MENTALLY: REFLECT ON IT

Who do you want to be? What kind of a person do you hope to become independent of your ex? What do you stand for? What do you believe people should be to one another, even when they are in conflict? If you were trying to model a good, moral, compassionate life for your children, how would you converse with your ex? What would you want them to scribble in their life notebooks if they sat in on the conversation? If you laid the groundwork for the conversation you are about to have with your ex by choosing respect, as discussed in the preceding chapter, then you are ahead of the game. You can carry forward your view of what constitutes right behavior in the conversation itself, using it as an opportunity to become the person you want to be and live the beliefs you hold.

That means that step one in preparing for a hot-topic conversation is reflection. How *should* people behave when they're in conflict? How would the person you wish to become behave in this upcoming conversation? How would that person respond to resistance or anger—your ex's and your own? How would you like to see your children behave in future years when they have differences with someone?

Write it down if that will be helpful to you. Create the picture in your mind. Crystallize your understanding by visualizing the person you believe you are or intend to become. Come to as complete an understanding as possible of who you want to be, how that person behaves, how you want to live. You'll need as much clarity as you can muster because it's a sure bet that the upcoming conversation will severely test your picture of yourself. A range of forces will try to pull you away from the person you want to be; your ex's responses to you will likely drag you off-center. The clearer you are ahead of time as to just who you are as a person, the more effectively you'll be able to come home to your own moral compass—to recenter yourself—if and when the conversation gets out of hand.

As you go through this process of reflection, keep in mind that you are not trying for perfection. If that is the goal, the slightest deviation in your conversation with your ex will constitute failure. When the goal is unattainable, the temptation is to kick yourself the moment you fall short of it. Learning to remain respectful and civil in the face of attack takes practice, practice, and more practice. Make your own personal growth the goal and you transcend the conflict with your ex in a way that gives you complete freedom and ultimate power.

Know who you want to be before the conversation begins.

SET GOALS

An essential component of knowing who you are and how you want to behave is to set practical goals. In doing so, keep in mind above all that you are not trying to achieve a victory but to achieve "yes." You are not out to win but to come to a harmony in which there are no losers. When the outcome is one that satisfies or at least seems fair to both you and your ex, that is a triumph, because the real winners are your children and your own sense of yourself.

To clarify your goals for the coming conversation, write down clear, concise answers to these four questions, what master negotiators sometimes refer to as the "four keys":

1. What outcome do I want?

2. What would I settle for?

3. What am I willing to give up?

4. What will I absolutely not do?

In articulating these points, the aim is not just clarity but also a sense of security about what is important to you. As you write down your answers, note next to each why this counts. Make a speech to yourself about why your desires are reasonable and not crazy and list reasonable arguments against what you want. If you're unable to reach a point of feeling genuinely secure about your wishes, you probably shouldn't have the conversation yet. Either you're wishing for something that's unreasonable, or you're too frightened of your ex's responses to be centered and calm in advance.

If you're unable to feel secure about your wishes, delay the conversation.

Of course, becoming secure in your desires does not mean being rigidly attached to your own particular vision of what's best. You can be secure in your conviction that it is important to you to spend significant time with the children at the holidays while also being open to different suggestions about how best to fulfill that conviction. Remember that many roads lead to Rome.

TRADE EYEBALLS WITH YOUR EX—YET AGAIN

Among those roads is the one your ex is walking. That is why mental preparation for a conversation on a hot topic should include imagining how your ex might be perceiving the situation. After all, you're about to ask your ex for something or complain to him about something. Doesn't it make sense to remember that your ex also may have requests or complaints, preferences and needs that at some point he will make known to you? Trading eyeballs with your ex helps you anticipate resistance, craft proposals that are less likely to get rejected, and better understand what your ex may be struggling with.

> *You never really understand a person until you consider things from his point of view—until you climb into his skin and walk around in it.*
>
> —Harper Lee, acclaimed novelist

And when you do imagine how your ex perceives the situation, remember to imagine him in the life he now leads. Sure, nobody knows better than you how he looked at things during the years of your marriage. But he leads a different life now, and he very likely has a different angle on life. After all, you do.

Try:

✓ Seeing the proposals you are making through your ex's eyes by arguing with yourself about why they make no sense from her perspective. As you reflect in this way, use what you discover to craft new ideas that might better meet both your needs.

CONSIDER THE OPTIONS

Once you've imagined how your ex-partner might be perceiving life these days, you can go on to imagine some optional outcomes that might satisfy the two of you. Generating as many solutions to your problem as possible—before the conversation—will give you more freedom to move and maneuver when you're in the throes of the conversation—especially if you encounter resistance.

For example, you are concerned that you do not have enough access to school information. What are the options? How can you get the information you need? You mentally list the possibilities:

- Your ex agrees to regularly photocopy school records and announcements and send them to you.

- The school agrees to double-copy all documentation so that your ex doesn't have to be part of the loop.

- You decide to be present at all quarterly school conferences to get the information verbally from the teachers—that is, if your ex refuses to go along with your other proposals.

Think of this option-designing process as something like the initial steps in brainstorming: don't censor or judge the potential solutions you come up with; just list the greatest number of solutions possible. If you then encounter resistance from your ex, you have other ideas to fall back on. "It sounds like that approach doesn't work for you," you might say. "How about this one?"

There is one exception to the no-censoring rule for brainstorming solutions. Anything you come up with must have a chance of being mutually satisfying. It must offer the win-win potential to leave you both feeling that the agreement is basically fair. If what you want is significantly more time with the children during the holidays, but you know it is important to your ex to have Christmas Eve at her mother's home, a proposed solution might be that she could have the children at Christmas Eve every year, but that you would alternate, year by year, which of you would have the children on Christmas Eve day or on Christmas Day itself. It would make no sense to include on your list a proposal that cuts out Christmas Eve for your ex—unless you just want to see those angry veins in her neck again!

CREATE A WON'T-DO LIST

At the same time you are brainstorming mutually satisfying options, define your won't-do list. What are the options on the list that you feel would compromise who you are as a person or would force you to neglect important needs of your children? These "solutions" would be absolutely unacceptable to you; they are therefore not solutions at all.

Suppose the hot topic is the Christmas holiday. You know in advance that your ex, who hates the fact that she only sees the kids on alternate weekends, is going to push hard to have the children both Christmas Eve night and Christmas Day every year, leaving you with only the remaining hours on Christmas evening. This will be her way of making things more "even." But your won't-do list says that you will not agree to any plan that limits your time with the children to less than ten hours during the holidays. This still allows you considerable flexibility; you might even decide to give up Christmas Day entirely, as long as you end up with a full ten-hour stretch of holiday with your children that includes Christmas evening. The won't-do list thus serves as a mental alarm; if your ex begins to push you into a corner about the scheduling issue, it goes off with a shrill alert. It's telling you that you need to look to another option, and that's how you respond to your ex: "Well, Mag-

gie, I understand that you're uncomfortable with what I'm proposing, but your plan leaves me with too little time with the children.
So, we'll have to keep working to come up with another option."
The won't-do list should not be an excuse for inflexibility, but it
should clarify those essential issues that you surrender only at the
risk of your own well-being or that of your children.

WHEN YOU TAKE AWAY, GIVE

There are times when your need to set limits or refuse a request
from your ex sets you up for a defensive retaliation. Preparing in
advance to offer alternatives that you are comfortable with can go a
long way toward softening your ex's anger.

For example, instead of insisting that there must be "no more
showing up to this house unannounced!" rehearse saying: "I'm uncomfortable not knowing when you might stop for a visit. . . . I have
no problems with you having time with the kids outside of the
schedule if you will simply call ahead." Rather than "I'm going
back to the court order . . . Tuesday nights with the kids are out,"
try substituting, "I'm worried about the kids at school because even
though we talked about this, you bring them back too late Tuesday
nights. . . . I want to go back to the written plan with no weeknight
visits, but if you want, you can keep them longer on Sundays . . . I
know you want as much time with them as possible."

KEEP YOUR EXPECTATIONS REALISTIC

Round out your work of preparation by dropping your expectations. Don't just lower them; get rid of them! In particular, don't expect respect. If your relationship with your ex has been an angry
one, if you have often asked yourself why he won't treat you better,
remember that it is often our own expectations that create our pain
in life. If, time and again, despite the evidence of the past, you continue to expect that *this time*, your ex will act in a way you consider

reasonable and decent, then no wonder you are disappointed yet again.

Instead, as part of your mental preparation, remind yourself of the ways in which he may act like a jerk the minute you start talking to one another. Think back to the kinds of foolish, hurtful, or disrespectful things that he has sent your way in the past; chances are, he'll be lobbing them at you in this conversation as well. Remind yourself that when they do occur, your ex is acting in a way that he believes makes sense; after all, he thinks he's right. Demanding that he act differently will only waste energy.

It's the old saw about telling a custard pie it should taste like an apple pie; it simply can't. Same with your ex. Yes, you would prefer him to behave differently. You wish he would. If he does, you'll be thrilled. But don't expect him to.

It's entirely possible that your best efforts may provoke reciprocal respect from your ex-spouse. Be grateful if they do. But remember that your ex's behavior—good or bad—is not something you can control. What you *can* control is your expectation, and when you drop the expectation of respect, your ex's disrespect will not have the power to hurt you. You won't be as angry—and you'll be better able to get the result you seek.

Not expecting respect does not mean accepting abuse. It is still important to be clear about what you will and won't tolerate and to have a line that you will not allow your ex to cross. Dropping expectations is an exercise in realism, not in welcoming mistreatment. You still have the right to complain when your ex acts unreasonably or disrespectfully. It just means you'll be less fragile and less likely to throw in the towel or say something you regret when the old behavior kicks in.

You should still prefer respect. You should still want it. You can still greet it with a smile when it happens, but if it doesn't happen, you won't be thrown into a crisis that knocks you off of your center.

Don't expect respect.

HANDLING THE LOGISTICS

Logistics is the way you manage the details of an operation. Arranging the details of your hot-topic conversation in advance can mean fewer distractions while you're talking. You'll want to plan the place, set an agenda, rehearse the words, and calm and center yourself so you can be completely prepared to achieve what you came for. You might even start by issuing a carefully considered invitation.

"YOU ARE CORDIALLY INVITED . . ."

Sometimes the way we propose a conversation can be as important as the conversation itself. The proposal forms the framework; it's the why of the conversation. It can be helpful to both you and your ex to let her know that you have some concerns about a particular issue and you want to hear her side of the story. An invitation is a good way to avoid surprising your ex or catching her off guard—tactics that all too often can be taken as deliberate attacks or cunning maneuvers.

How do you word such an invitation? Plainly and honestly: "Laurie, I've got some concerns about the way you and I have been dealing with the visitation schedule. I'd like to have a chance to hear your opinions. Would you be willing to sit down sometime and talk through some of the problems we've been having with these visits?" Or, maybe like this: "Chuck, I've been noticing that every time we meet at the door on Sundays, we end up having an argument and I walk away feeling rotten. My guess is that you don't feel great afterward, either. I'd like this craziness to stop. Would you be willing to sit down with me so we can come up with some ideas about how we can make things work better between us?"

FIND NEUTRAL TURF

Speaking spontaneously can work fine with issues that are not emotionally loaded. But when it's a hot topic and conflict looms on the horizon, choosing a place ahead of time assures that you'll meet on neutral turf—specifically, turf that excludes the children or at least offers them a separate place to go to so they can remain insulated from any open hostility. If there is a history of domestic violence, you may prefer to not meet in person at all. In any case, choosing a public location like a restaurant can create an added degree of security. The watchful eyes of strangers can help keep both of you under control.

SET AN AGENDA

Agreeing in advance on an agenda helps both you and your ex stay on track instead of veering off onto emotionally charged tangents. Judy and Bob had come up with a plan for a half-hour phone conversation on the first Sunday evening of every month. At the end of each call, they agreed on the general focus of the next one. That left them both with a month to come up with items they wished to discuss. Then at the next call, they would first create the agenda and then check off the items on their lists one by one. They also had a rule that either one could interrupt the other if they felt the discussion was going off the agenda. The idea was to cover the list before getting into new concerns—a good rule of thumb for all ex-spouses.

Stay on track instead of veering off onto emotionally charged tangents.

REHEARSE THE WORDS

Once you know what the agenda is going to be, you can begin to plan the words. Most of us feel anxious before a conversation in which we will probably be complaining about the other person—and may then have to deal with the person's anger or frustration. We worry that we will trip over our words, say things we don't really mean, lose control. That's why it's helpful to rehearse in advance the types of things you want to say to your ex and how you want to say them. Write them down, playact them.

Even better, try rehearsing the words with a trusted friend—someone with no ax to grind, with no partisan stance on the issue—who will serve as a sounding board. The friend, in effect, takes the role of your ex and throws the curveballs you know you can expect—only this time, you can hear yourself respond. When you do this, you're practicing to be the person that you want to be when you're conversing with your ex; you're practicing sticking to your own moral compass—and you're doing it out loud.

At the same time, it's helpful to decide on the things that you won't say, even if you feel a strong impulse to do so. In that negotiation about the holiday schedule, for example, it would make sense to refrain from comments about your ex's family that might inflame the conversation. Work hard to resist the temptation; it will pay off handsomely in the end.

> *The real art of conversation is not only to say the right thing in the right place but to leave unsaid the wrong thing at the tempting moment.*
>
> —Dorothy Nevill, noted English writer and collector

To plan your words, visualize yourself in conversation with your ex. See her face, imagine both her happy and angry expressions, hear in your mind some challenging responses or "curveballs" that you may have to deal with. Then rehearse your own responses. Imagine a worst-case and a best-case scenario. In your mind's eye, see yourself surviving the worst-case scenario, realizing that, even though the conversation didn't go the way you wanted, there will be other conversations. Then watch yourself accepting the best-case scenario with dignified equanimity. Such visualization can provide a strong foundation for the responses you will give in the actual conversation, however it goes—best case, worst case, or something in between.

Visualize the person you want to be; rehearse the conversation. . . .

GET CALM, GET CENTERED

Finally, it's important to calm and center yourself in advance of your hot-topic conversation. If you are like most people, you will feel anxious—even frightened—as you approach the time when you are actually going to discuss difficult issues with your ex. Unfortunately, anxiety makes us do things that we often regret afterward. It clouds our thinking. It can make us react defensively, saying and doing things that we wouldn't say or do if we felt safer, things that can damage the relationship with our ex even further. Anxiety can also make us say "yes" to things to which our heart says "no." Starting the hot-topic conversation in a calm and centered state will let you think more clearly and feel more in control throughout the conversation.

How do you *get* calm and centered? There's no great mystery to it; at the most basic level, involving the simplest exercises, you don't have to go anywhere or buy anything or even move very far at all. Try these steps:

1. Sit in a comfortable chair and close your eyes.

2. Breathe deeply for five to ten minutes.

3. Slowly and progressively tense and loosen your muscles, one muscle group at a time, from head to toe. As you release each group, imagine the muscles growing heavy, then beginning to warm.

4. Visualize calming mental imagery, including images of peaceful settings that you enjoy.

5. Meditate quietly in this way for ten to fifteen minutes to help yourself fully relax.

Any library or bookstore offers numerous resources for practicing relaxation. The important thing is to find something that works for you in reducing your level of anxiety so that you can be as clear-minded and in control as possible. Practicing twice daily is recommended, certainly at the start.

Once you've learned to relax through meditation, taking a few minutes to center yourself in advance of conversations with your ex can go a long way toward making you feel better about the conversation—both while you're having it and afterward. It goes a long way in other aspects of your life as well.

SHOULD YOUR CHILDREN BE PRESENT?

Allowing your children in the vicinity as you and your ex have a discussion can offer them a wonderful learning opportunity—*if* the two of you are able to control yourselves and remain rational and if the topic isn't a volatile one or one that will cause them unnecessary anxiety. After all, intact families don't shuttle their children off to separate rooms whenever the parents discuss a concern or thrash out a complaint. The children of divorced parents can occasionally benefit from watching their parents try to work through an issue— so long as the topic is not an upsetting one for children and so long as what the children see is two grown-ups working to reach agreement.

If the issue to be discussed is a volatile one, however, or if it is on such issues as support payments or legal arrangements, that's no place for kids. And certainly, if there is any chance that anger or hostility might erupt, keep the children out of it; if they're present and the anger or hostility unexpectedly occurs, end the conversation immediately or at least send the children to another part of the house. The last thing you want to do is cause unnecessary anxiety, and exposure to open animosity can be very disturbing for children. If your children do witness hostility between you and your ex, decide as parents to apologize mutually to your children, let them hear from each of you that you view your angry behavior as a mistake, and offer them a chance to watch the two of you talking calmly about a benign issue. If your ex remains hostile, apologize and set the good example on your own.

Remember:
In advance of a conversation with your ex about a hot topic . . .

- ✓ Set goals

- ✓ Trade eyeballs with your ex

- ✓ Consider the options

- ✓ Create a "won't-do list"

- ✓ If you must take something, give something

- ✓ Keep your expectations realistic

- ✓ Issue a cordial invitation

- ✓ Find neutral turf

- ✓ Set an agenda

- ✓ Rehearse the words

- ✓ Get calm and centered

Real Life

Preparation is a great idea but most of the blowups we have just happen. There we are with the kids at the doorstep and she's there, fangs out and ready to bite about something I didn't expect.

Careful preparation and rehearsal for conversations that you *can* predict will help you stay in control and be effective at times when her fangs appear unexpectedly. And remember that taking the high road sometimes involves strategic delay: "Karen, you're obviously very upset about this and I haven't had any time to think about it. . . . Let me think, and I'll call you Tuesday night with some ideas, because I can tell this is important to you . . . this just isn't a good time for me."

CHAPTER TEN

The Hot-Topic Conversation: Saying What You Came to Say

"Well begun is half done," goes the proverb. The point is to begin well.

By now you've worked hard at sowing seeds of respect and co-operation. You've prepared your mind for the conversation and are clear on what you want to say and how to say it. You're sitting down to talk. How do you begin? What are the words? This chapter offers concrete suggestions that will increase the chances that your hot-topic conversation will be successful.[1]

Start by setting the stage—perhaps with ground rules. Then ease into the conversation, speaking in an affirmative manner before you even broach the hot topic, and speaking in rational, simple terms once the hot-topic issue has been raised.

When the conversation is rolling, it's important to avoid the hard edges of argument and contention. Soften those edges with the kind of proactive initiatives I'll outline below to replace bitterness and bite with a businesslike approach.

AVOID SURPRISES

Giving your ex a cue or a warning that you intend to raise a difficult or touchy issue can avoid the defensiveness that is often sparked by surprise. This is especially true if you haven't given an invitation in advance for the discussion. Remember that while you knew you were going to bring the issue up, your ex may be completely unaware that complaints are coming his way. When you give the cue, be sure you're clear about what you want to discuss, offer a guess about how your ex will feel, and express hope for a good discussion.[2] It might sound like this: "Gus, I need to talk with you about something that is a bit touchy and that might upset you . . . I hope that we can talk about it in a calm way . . . I intend to work hard to find a plan that is fair to you too." This allows your ex to get both feet on the ground before you begin, while you diffuse his anger both by mentioning it in advance and by setting a positive tone.

START WITH AFFIRMATION

The best negotiators in the world know that before you make a complaint or ask people to do something differently, it is helpful to "soften them up." The best way to do this is to say something affirming about the other person, to offer a compliment or meaningful praise. Think of your own experiences. A neighbor telling you your garden is magnificent will find you considerably more receptive to his complaint that your dog barks too much. The supervisor who praises your work has a much better chance of getting you to work extra hours than the sourpuss boss who just gives orders. In a hot-topic conversation with your ex, try starting with a congratulation. "You're so good at being a Little League coach—much better than I could ever be. And Eric loves having you there." All it takes is a brief comment—something that communicates that, whatever the problems between you, there are things about the other person that you appreciate and admire.

Appreciation is even more effective if you choose to express it vis-à-vis the topic at hand—support payments, for example: "Sally, before we talk about my concerns about the support, I want you to know that I do notice all the things that you buy the kids in addition to the weekly payments that you send me, like the school clothes and the computer games that help Alec with his math . . . and I know that you do these things even though money is tight for you too."

Another way to set a cooperative tone is to begin with a statement of empathy regarding the other person's needs or feelings— something like this: "I want you to know that I understand how tight money is for you these days, and I recognize that when I show up asking for help with unexpected expenses it places more pressure on you and your family." You can even take the empathy a bit further, beyond understanding, to commitment: "Before we begin talking about whether I should move to Baltimore, I want you to know that it's clear to me how important the children are to you and how central you are in their lives. I'm committed to finding a way to handle this problem that keeps the children close to both of us."

Appreciation and empathy serve to help your ex relax, rather than making her feel she'd better get ready to defend herself. Setting the stage right can go a long way toward improving the ultimate outcome of your discussion.

Find a way to affirm your ex, even if doing so feels unnatural.

SUGGEST GROUND RULES

Propose ground rules—procedural guidelines that can help govern how you talk and listen and thus make things go more smoothly. If this sounds artificial, consider that free-flowing conversations are prone to angry digressions. A mutually agreed-upon structure, by contrast, can help keep the proceedings respectful. Simple guidelines are best. For example, you might agree on the following: No interrupting the other person. Commit to speaking calmly and respectfully to each other. Avoid tangents and stick with the agenda. Stay away from old history and focus on now and tomorrow.

You may feel that suggesting ground rules is too formal or is perhaps out of sync with the way you relate to your ex. Maybe you're afraid your ex will think the whole thing is a dumb idea. But if your ex decides not to follow the guidelines, or if you decide not to bring up the idea, you can improve the quality of the conversation by sticking with them yourself. You will at least have taken a step toward a higher standard of discourse.

BEGIN WITH A NO-BRAINER

It's time to plunge into the hot topic. Do it with a no-brainer. Chances are the hot topic has a lot of subtopics. Start with one you know will be easy to reach agreement on. If you're getting together to discuss how to exchange school information on the kids *and* your complaints about how your ex feeds the children when they're with him, start with school information first; it's likely to be less emotional. If there really isn't a pertinent, easy topic, pick one out of the air just to set the proper tone: "Am I right, Susan, that this year Jennifer will be with you on Halloween and with me on Thanksgiving?" At least you're starting off with something you both agree on and can feel relaxed about.

TOXIC TALK CAN BE POISON

Certain approaches to talking and certain types of language virtually guarantee that your ex will get defensive and want to strike back. I call this "toxic talk." If you start out intending to omit toxic talk from what you say, you'll be way ahead of the game.

There are eight major talk toxins:

1. "You" language.
It's full of accusations: "You're never on time with the kids;" "You feed them nothing but Twinkies!" "You always want to argue

with me in front of the kids." Such statements have a way of making your ex deaf to your complaints and requests.

2. Character slams.

Broad references to your ex's character: "You're irresponsible," "You're mean," "You're self-centered." Why attack the character when what you want to change is the behavior that frustrates you? You can't control what you see as your ex's inherent laziness; what you must influence is his current inability to get the children's insurance card to you on time. So what if she's irresponsible? The point is that she is almost always late picking up the children. You find him insensitive? Your *complaint* is that he uses vulgar language with you when dropping the children off. The difference isn't only in the way you talk but in the response it elicits. Labeling your ex as irresponsible, lazy, or insensitive provokes self-defensiveness. Offering a respectful complaint about specific behavior will make him feel less under attack; maybe he'll listen instead of shutting down in anger.

3. Using the past as a weapon.

Digressing from the present is another way of broadening your attack and making your ex defensive. And it is oh-so-easy to do. After all, the two of you once shared an intimate relationship. You have exchanged vows, created children together, shaped and lived a life as a couple. This is well-charted territory—as opposed to the vexing hot topic you're supposed to be discussing. Resist the temptation to say things like: "You were never on time for anything in the entire fifteen years that we were together," or, "It's like that time at your sister's wedding when you called me a bitch in front of the bartender." Your ex can't very well give serious consideration to making the changes you want in the present if you divert his attention to unchangeable aspects of the past—not to mention the fact that reverting to history invites your ex to dig into his memories of *your* past foolishness.

4. "Always" or "never" language.

Absolutes are virtually always untrue. No one is 100 percent anything. Comments like "You were always in the ozone when it came to the kids," or "You never once took your mind off yourself" simply compel your ex to bark back. Besides, if you're convinced that your ex always or never does something, why would he bother to change? For every rule that you can generate about your ex there are almost certainly some exceptions. Keep them in mind.

5. "Should" language.

Nothing is more guaranteed to make people feel under attack than being told they should or should not do something. Replacing "shoulds" with preferences or wishes can go a long way toward softening a difficult discussion. Instead of "You should have the support checks at the house on time," try "I need you to pay the support on time," or: "I wish you would pay the support on time," or, more directly: "I'm here to ask you to have the support check at the house on the date we agreed." The simple omission of the word "should" tends to lower the tension, reduce the pressure, and dampen the defensiveness.

6. Threats.

Although most of us would say that we never threaten people, it is surprisingly easy to do so. Comments like "You'd better give me back the lawn mower—it was mine!" or "If you don't start paying on time, you can forget about seeing the kids for your family reunion" are the sort of "or-else" comments that constitute threatening approaches. You aren't threatening bodily harm, but you are certainly delivering ultimatums. In doing so, you force your ex into a corner and virtually ensure he will want to come out fighting.

7. Giving advice.

When your ex tells you she needs more money for day care, hearing from you that she needs to budget better is a ticket to an angry conversation. Expressing understanding about your ex's dilemma is far more likely to resolve the day-care issue—and keep the conversation civilized.

8. Invalidation.

When you respond to your ex by telling him that what he has just said is ridiculous, or that he misunderstands the situation, or that he knows nothing about the subject at hand, what you're really telling him is that you haven't heard or understood a word he's been saying—in which case you can hardly expect him to hear and understand you. Calling another person's feelings into question, invalidating their convictions, or belittling their abilities is a sure bet for provoking defensiveness and shutting down a conversation.

Words matter.

LISTEN ATTENTIVELY

The antivenom to toxic talk is attentive listening, perhaps the most neglected tool in human conversations and the most powerful way to keep the peace and enhance harmony. The reason is simple: We all want to feel that what we have said has been heard. Make your ex feel that way, and you greatly increase your chances that he will listen in turn to what you have to say.

Attentive listening requires more than just paying attention. You also must show the other person that you're paying attention, and you must reflect back what you think you've heard. The goal is to let the other person know she is being heard and to make sure you have accurately understood what she said.

Seek first to understand, then to be understood.
—Stephen Covey, author of *The 7 Habits of Highly Effective People*

In a respectful way, Jack has complained to Sue, his ex, that he ends up frustrated every Tuesday night when she takes the children for the agreed-upon four-hour visit to her home, then calls up insisting that they stay overnight. The agreement, after all, stipulates that they are to be returned to Jack's house. He states his complaint and asks Sue to stick to the agreement.

Sue: "Well, yeah, Jack, but you've got them all the time, and I hardly ever get to see them. You know I have to leave town often on weekends for business, and Tuesday nights are the only nights that I can guarantee a free evening. I just miss them."

While Sue is saying this, Jack is listening attentively. He leans forward to show Sue that what she's saying is important to him. He nods his head to make sure she knows he gets it. He waits for her to finish. Then he speaks. "Okay, Sue, I think I've got it. So you feel that, because of your business schedule, you don't see the kids enough and you miss them. When you keep them on Tuesday nights, you're trying to make up for lost time. Did I get it right?"

Jack is not necessarily agreeing with Sue. He is simply letting her know that he listened; he is checking to make certain he understood. But he hasn't understood. "No, Jack," Sue immediately replies, "that's not it at all. I don't think it's my business schedule that's screwing things up. I think it's this ridiculous court agreement that your lawyer jammed down my throat. It simply ignores the fact that I am most available for the kids during the week." Now Jack knows that her struggle is not about a busy schedule but about a mismatch between the custody plan and her work demands. At the least, they're both getting their points across—something that can avoid a long list of potential misunderstandings.

Or suppose Sue becomes enraged. Suppose she attacks Jack: "You're a pathetic excuse for a father, and you took my kids from me. I'm not about to bend over backward to make your schedule nice and neat!" Although there may be no perfect response to such insulting language, Jack still has the option of simply responding that he hears what she's saying: "You're ticked off at me because I was given custody and you don't want to make my life easier . . . is that it?" It may not erase his ex-wife's beef, but it will create less emotional fire than hurling a counter-insult.

Listening attentively to your ex, even when he is angry, also means taking the focus off your own point of view and off the old history between the two of you. Both typically scream for your attention like a nagging toothache. But if you're really going to listen to your ex, you must focus in a disciplined way on the words and feelings he offers just at that moment—with no history and no barking back. Just listen.

In videotapes of divorced couples "handling" confrontations, you see people blaming each other, using put-downs, even calling one another names. No one is listening to anyone. It's a classic case of the very human tendency to seek power and safety in the middle of an inherently uncomfortable situation by assuming an attacking posture. But pointing an accusing finger—as toxic talk does—only invites counteraccusations; the so-called power you feel it gives you is fleeting and fragile.

Attentive listening, by contrast, is choosing to be receptive and open rather than reactive and closed. Among other things, that means acknowledging that you actually don't know it all, that you could be wrong, and that you might indeed have missed something that is important to your ex. When you make the choice, when you listen truly attentively to your ex, you actually put yourself in a position of enormous personal power.

COMPLAINING WITH ALL DUE RESPECT

Instead of toxic talk, use respectful complaining to reduce defensiveness in your ex. The technique is simple enough; it relies on what communications experts call I-statements. Just state what it is your ex does that concerns you, then use the first person singular to specify how that behavior makes you feel and what you would prefer your ex do differently in the future. Like this:

"When you're late with the support payments (the thing that

concerns you), it becomes difficult to make ends meet and I feel frustrated and worried for the kids (how it makes you feel). I'm here to ask you to please make the children's support payments on time starting this week (what you're asking your ex to do differently)."

Here's another: "When you put me down in front of the children, I feel worried because of what it teaches our kids. I'm here to ask you to speak with me respectfully, especially when the kids are there." Or: "When you call my home three and four times a day to speak with the kids, I feel angry and invaded, and I want to ask you please to call no more than once daily."

What I-statements do is make the problem your issue. By emphasizing what *you* feel and what *you'd* like changed, rather than making moralistic proclamations about your ex, you take the issue out of the realm of attack and convert it to a request for change. Your conversation doesn't need to be an assault. It can be an opportunity to behave with respect and concern for the children you both cherish.

EXPRESS WORRIES, NOT DEMANDS

Imagine your ex saying to you: "I want you to start feeding the kids more healthy food on the weekends. All they're eating with you is junk."

Now, imagine instead that she says: "I'm worried about how much weight the kids are gaining. If they keep eating fast food and don't get more fruits and vegetables, I'm afraid they're going to have health problems down the line."

The second statement, presented as concern for the children rather than as a demand that you change your way, elicits a less angry response and invites further conversation. When an expression of worry on your part sparks your ex-partner's concern for the children, it allows the two of you to remember that you share a common goal. All of which begs the question: If you can't come up with a way to express your complaint in a child-focused way, ask yourself if the issue is worth bringing up at all.

PROBLEM-SOLVE IN A BUSINESSLIKE MANNER

Once you have raised a concern or expressed a worry, pursue it in a businesslike way. Imagine that you are at a business meeting, with a colleague with whom you have some differences, and behave accordingly. It can be helpful at times to imagine that a third party—someone you highly respect—is sitting in the room with you and observing. Maybe it's Jesus, your rabbi, a particular political leader, or a thinker whose philosophy you admire. If that person were there now, listening in on your conversation with your ex, how would he or she suggest you conduct yourself?

One way to ensure a businesslike environment is to use formal problem-solving techniques. Such techniques, guiding you logically and systematically through your discussion, can generate creative and quite unanticipated options for reaching resolution. Here's how formal problem-solving works:

First, specify clearly both the nature and dimensions of the problem between you and your ex. Second, brainstorm a variety of potential solutions. The brainstorming process should aim at volume—think of as many solutions as you can, as fast as you can, without either of you criticizing solutions mentioned or even thinking about whether they make sense. Where brainstorming is concerned, the more "far out" the solutions offered, the better. You'd be surprised at how creative your ideas can be when you take the fetters off your mind. Third, assess the solutions one at a time to eliminate those that obviously won't work or that one of you finds too objectionable. Finally, evaluate the solutions that remain to find the one—or ones—that best respond to your interests and concerns.

Consider suggesting such an approach to the thorny issue you have with your ex. Even if she dismisses the idea, you can use it in the privacy of your own mind to aid in the creative pursuit of a solution.

THINK INTERESTS, NOT POSITIONS

Most human conflict arises when people take positions about the way they want things to be instead of expressing the interests and concerns that underlie those positions. Once we have staked out a position and issued a demand—such as wanting the kids for Memorial Day, or refusing to "go to the trouble" of copying school information—it's hard to backtrack. It's hard to keep in mind that what really counts is not the particular position but a deeper interest—having more time with the kids on holidays, or getting more help with the practical aspects of co-parenting. The fact is there are many ways to create more holiday time with the kids; there's only one way to have the kids for Memorial Day. Presenting a fixed position creates disharmony at best, conflict at worst. The bottom line, of course, is that if nobody's interests and concerns are met the problem is not solved at all.

Brian had a busy business life and was satisfied to see his children every other weekend and on the Wednesday night of the off-week. He never wanted to be the primary caregiver or custodian; it was enough for him to be a dad on this limited schedule. But when he heard that Ann, his ex-wife, was relocating three hours away, he became furious. He applied to the judge to either stop her move by court order or grant him custody. Brian and Ann barked back and forth and filed court papers. Then, on the advice of their minister and in hopes of avoiding litigation, the two sat down for a cup of coffee.

They began their talk by staking out their positions yet again. Brian insisted on his either-or statement: Either give up your relocation or give up custody. Just as harshly, Ann asserted that Brian had no right to control her life or stop her from living where she wanted to live. But then, as Ann related the story in my office, a shift occurred between them. They stopped barking and began to hear what the other was truly interested in. Between the lines, Ann heard a man worried about losing touch with the day-to-day details of his children's lives. Yes, Brian had a busy life and was not really interested in custody, but he hated the idea of being completely out of touch.

Once Ann had seen through to this more basic interest, she too could loosen up and move away from her rigid position. She made Brian an offer—just a few very simple things: once she moved away, she would send him a monthly calendar of school events; she would videotape any event that he could not personally attend; she would accept all charges for phone calls from his home; and she would drive the children one way for each of his weekend visits. That was all it took. Brian relaxed and agreed; his basic interest was being attended to, and he could drop his rigid position on custody.

The moral of this story is simple: When you're discussing difficult issues with your ex, look beyond the position that he takes and try to hear the essential interests underlying his position. And pay attention to the interests beneath your own fervent positions. Do that, and you open yourself to new perspectives; you can offer solutions that respond to your ex's interests while giving each of you room to let go of disagreeable positions.

Here's another example. During litigation in family court, Peter decided that he should have his children every weekend because Pam, his ex, was with them all during the school week. "It's only fair," Peter contended, staking out his position early in the discussion. "It's the only plan I can live with." Pam was furious. How dare he try to change the custody arrangement at this late date? He always did insist on his own way in everything—no matter who got hurt.

The toxic talk flew back and forth, until Peter suddenly decided to listen to the basic interest Pam was expressing behind her anger. All she wanted, he saw, was to have some leisure time with the children herself—time when she was not simply giving baths and helping with homework. Since her interest was a guarantee of some leisure time with the kids, and his interest was more time with the kids, couldn't they compromise and find a mutually satisfying option? Instead of "every weekend or nothing," his original rigid position, Peter suggested that he see the children one week on the weekend, and another week Monday through Wednesday. He would get more time, Pam would get more leisure, they would both give up the barking and litigation, and they would be responding to one another's needs—to their children's benefit. A true "win-win" for both parents.

Listen for the interest being expressed—albeit silently— behind what your ex is saying. Beyond the rigid position, what is your ex-partner really seeking? What are you really seeking?

SLOW DOWN

Whatever the shape of your hot-topic conversation, its pace should be slow. The stakes are too high to rush to judgment. There's no need to make a decision right now, or today, or even tomorrow. Making a decision when we feel anxious or nervous often leads to premature closure; it's a decision made solely for the sake of ending the discussion, not on the basis of what works or will most benefit your children or yourselves.

Going slowly means giving yourself permission to think about the issue. To an ex-spouse pressuring you for a decision *now*, try this: "Jack, this plan might work for me, but it has some downsides, and I want to think it through. Let me live with it for a couple of days. I'll call you Wednesday night to tell you whether I'm comfortable with it." You've let him know that you will respond, you've given him a deadline, and you've made it clear that the issue is too important for a quick fix; you need time to consider the proposal.

FIND SOMETHING TO AGREE ON

One good way to keep the conversation on a positive track is to be vigilant for anything your ex says that you can agree with—and letting her know that you do. It reminds her that you're not in an endless battle together and thus may help her relax and open up to the suggestions you're making. It can also make each of you feel less hopeless. And it can work with even the smallest areas of agreement; it takes so little energy: "Okay Cindy, we agree that it makes sense for you to know when the soccer games take place. I'll make sure you get the schedule."

A strategy I frequently use when mediating with couples is to stop every half hour and ask them to list all their points of agreement. Couples are often surprised to find that there are many things they see the same way, and that they are in dispute about only a few items. You can do the same by interrupting your conversations at regular intervals to note something that you agree on: "So, Judy, at this point, we both feel that the kids should spend significant time with each of us. We agree that we should be sharing information about school with each other. And we agree that it would be helpful for us both to be at pediatrician appointments when possible." It doesn't matter what the points of agreement are, or whether they're big or little. The point is to remind yourselves that you *can* agree. As for finding and identifying things that you and your ex agree about, it's easy—if you are willing to look hard enough.

PAT YOURSELF ON THE BACK

And while you're looking, don't forget to praise yourself for being willing to take the courageous step of having this conversation with your ex. Applaud yourself for offering constructive solutions in a challenging situation. Remember that in choosing to try to work through your difficulties with your ex-partner, civilly and rationally, you are teaching your children an invaluable life lesson.

Remember:
During a conversation with your ex about a hot topic . . .
   ✓ Avoid surprises.

   ✓ Use affirmation.

✓ Suggest ground rules.

✓ Start with an easy topic.

✓ Avoid toxic talk.

✓ Listen attentively.

✓ Offer complaints respectfully.

✓ Express worries, not demands.

✓ Behave as if meeting with a business associate.

✓ Think interests, not positions.

✓ Slow down, find something to agree on, be kind to each other—and yourself.

Real Life

Give me an I-statement and a respectful complaint for this one: Twice I've seen my ex arrive with my eight-year-old daughter sitting in the front seat of a car with a passenger-side airbag, something that could injure or kill her in an accident. He has no brains when it comes to safety.

Okay, here goes: "Chris, first, I wanted you to know that I appreciate how you've been getting Christie home on time on Sundays. It is making things a lot easier for me. Thanks. I've also got a concern, however, and my guess is that you may be bothered by what I have to say. When you pull in the driveway and I see that Christie is sitting in the front seat of your car, I get really frightened. I've heard on the news that some kids can get really hurt if there's an accident and the airbag comes out. I know you're concerned about her safety too, and my guess was that you just weren't aware of the risk. I can also see how, after not seeing her for a week, you would want to sit close with her and be able to talk. But would you mind having her sit in back where she's safer?"

Some of the words you use don't fit the way we talk to each other. They sound like something a professional would say and I can imagine my ex laughing at me.

I use language that comes naturally to me. It will be your task to translate the core ideas into language that comes naturally to you. Where you might say "Jane, I appreciate how you braid Jenny's hair before our weekends together," someone else might say "Hey, neat braids, thanks!"

When I'm in the middle of talking to her, her back gets up, she gets real defensive, and then, as usual, she starts acting like a wacko, yelling at me, putting me down. Any shortcuts for getting her to chill out?

Given how brittle your ex sounds, I suggest putting your energy into minimizing the chances of a blowup rather than trying to calm her down once it's blown. Everybody becomes defensive if they feel they're being criticized or attacked, and your ex may have some personality problems that make her particularly likely to feel this way. But all you can control is yourself, so turn your attention inward and look at the content of what you say to her. With a volatile personality like your ex's, it's particularly important to express appreciation, seek points of agreement and note them verbally, and avoid toxic talk. I-statements will be critical because they are less likely to be perceived as critical attacks. Proposing in advance the idea of breaks when things get hot may be most useful if your ex tends to get volcanic.

CHAPTER ELEVEN

Responding in a Hot-Topic Conversation: How to Answer Resistance and Opposition

You've prepared diligently for your hot-topic conversation. You've begun well. Calm and centered, you listen attentively for the interests behind your ex's position, present complaints not demands, suggest ground rules and a problem-solving plan.

But your ex isn't buying it. No matter how sweetly reasonable you feel you're being, you meet only resistance, opposition, even insult. Your ex decides to act like a jerk. What's going on?

In his helpful book on how to brush off hostility and its stresses,[1] Dr. Richard Driscoll makes the point that children repeat the old saying, "Sticks and stones can break my bones but names will never hurt me," precisely because they know that "names" *do* hurt; they know that verbal insults can be incredibly powerful. Angry, hurtful words are aimed at shaking our confidence and self-esteem; caught off guard by your complaint, your ex hurls his verbal spears as a way to reestablish a feeling of control, power, or competence—by diminishing yours. You can easily find yourself angrily striking back in self-defense.

Between ex-spouses, angry verbal attacks and counterattacks are often rapid-fire reactions to feeling surprised, hurt, threatened, or embarrassed. The anger expressed in a hot conversation is almost never about the topic under discussion; it is instead a cover for other emotions—often, far more tender emotions. But unless one party decides to stop the music of verbal sparring, both of you can end up in a draining dance of mutual hurt and reactive anger.

> *The test of a man or woman's breeding is how*
> *they behave in a quarrel.*
> —George Bernard Shaw, British playwright

There are three strategic responses to attack: calming yourself, attempting to disarm your attacker and render him or her at least neutral, and countering the attack. For each strategic response, the tactics we use—the ways in which we go about delivering these responses—can make all the difference.

Strategy 1: Button Your Lips and Stay Calm

Whenever we feel we're being attacked or even opposed, the almost automatic first response is to defend ourselves. That means, in essence, barking back at the person barking at us. And that, in turn, means that all the helpful tools discussed in the preceding chapter—listening attentively, complaining respectfully—go right out the window. A barking-back reaction, driven by emotion, is almost guaranteed to make you say ineffective or stupid things that only fan the flames of hostility.

What's more, barking back lends significance to the insult or criticism; in a sense, it rewards the insulting or critical behavior on the part of your ex. Stepping around the insult by simply not responding at all is its own response to that behavior—and it can be an effective way to stay on track in a heated conversation.

Remind yourself of your moral compass; even if your ex veers onto a disrespectful course, you can still choose to stay oriented toward peace and respect. Your ex can never take away your side of the blackboard. You've always got your own chalk.

TACTIC: THE CAREFULLY PLACED SILENCE

A few seconds or minutes of pause can allow you to collect your thoughts. Now, maybe the exchange won't spiral out of control. Now, maybe you can counter with an effective, nontoxic response.

I call such a pause the "carefully placed silence." It can be a powerful tool for avoiding a fight; by leaving your ex exposed just as he or she is trying to overpower you, carefully placed silence can, almost literally, disarm your ex. To make it especially effective, follow the silence with a question: "Why don't you tell me what you would suggest? I'll just sit and listen a bit."

Stay calm during your carefully placed silence. We all make better decisions and think more clearly when our anxiety level is low, and it can be hard to avoid anxiety in confrontations. You already have a history of discomfort with the person confronting you—a failed marriage, a separation, a divorce; a little bit of opposition can easily make you nervous and agitated. Relax. Ironic as it sounds, *discipline yourself to relax*. Breathe deeply. Focus on your breath for a few seconds; watch it move in and out. Use any tool that works to bring yourself back to a state of calm and self-control. You will only regret impulsive reactions; you will only be unhappy with decisions you make under conditions of anxiety.

> *When angry, count ten before you speak; if very angry, an hundred.*
>
> —Thomas Jefferson

While you are silent, if only for a few seconds, you can privately talk to yourself in ways that further calm you. Talk to your lizard brain—the part of you that wants to blast back—and say such things as the following:

"I will stay calm and peaceful."

"This will pass—it always does."

"I know in my heart that I am a good person, despite what she is saying."

"He is just angry—it's not the end of the world."

"There are things I appreciate about her, even though she's acting like a gorilla."

"He is only firing words, not bullets."

TACTIC: USE YOUR INNER TOTO[2]

Do you remember the moment in *The Wizard of Oz* when Dorothy and friends stood trembling before the wizard, pleading for his help, only to be met with bursts of fire, steam, and the angry rejection of the one they thought could save them? Puffs of smoke, a mean face on the wizard, all in response to a request that came from the best place in Dorothy's heart. And then a wonderful and surprising thing happens: Toto snoops around and finds a curtain that he pulls back to reveal a small, embarrassed man pushing buttons and turning cranks in an effort to make others see him as powerful and invincible. That's who the angry wizard really was—a very frightened, insecure man. The fury, the smoke, the flames were just a shield he erected to make himself powerful in a foreign land.

When your ex becomes angry or resistant, use a few moments of silence to mentally peak behind the curtain for a glimpse of the more tender feelings that are likely fueling her irrational response. Use your inner Toto—the higher part of yourself that knows there is always more to anger than meets the eye—to peak at what may be making your ex feel she has to look powerful by acting with anger or resistance. Did your comments send a message that she may be incompetent in some way? Did your request or complaint threaten something important to her? Is it possible that, because your ex feels she has little control in many things that happen between the two of you, this issue is offering her a chance to finally feel effective by thwarting your efforts?

The goal here is to focus less on your ex's anger or resistance and more on the essential feelings behind the curtain. This will allow you to respond with clarity, compassion, and, if necessary, firm resolve—not with the smoke and fire that you will later regret.

TACTIC: CREATE A MENTAL SHIELD

Do you need more concrete tools for switching into a relaxation mode? It's all in the mind. You can also choose to build a figurative mental shield [3] during your carefully placed silence, which protects you from the barbs being sent your way. Here's how:

The first step is to master the relaxation response learned on page 152.

Then let your mind go to work. Imagine a point of light ahead of you and expand it into a window of light. Use this mental window of light as a shield you can hold up to protect yourself against hostility and insults. Be playful with the mental image; feel free to make your window of light into a screen, steel bars, protective angels, flames, or any other means of protection that can insulate you from your ex-partner's intense or hurtful reactions.

Now visualize your ex-partner's angry words striking the shield and falling harmless to the ground. If you know that you remain connected to your ex in emotionally destructive ways—he knows just how to push your buttons, manipulate you, make you feel guilty—try visualizing the connections as vines, tentacles, or ropes reaching out from your ex and taking hold of you. Cut them. Mentally practice picking up a sword or knife and severing these connections. Free yourself from these clinging bonds and you won't need to react to your ex-partner's antics.

This mental shielding technique requires daily practice in advance of your conversation with your ex. If, during the hot-topic discussion, your anxiety begins to rise, simply begin to concentrate on your breath as a way to center yourself before imagining your shield. Since breathing is natural, your ex won't even know you are doing this.

TACTIC: GO TO YOUR CORNERS

Even in boxing, where people are paid to do violence to one another in front of cheering crowds, the contenders are often sent to their corners for infractions of one kind or another. No matter what, each round is finite so there are consistent breaks in the action. The same principle can be applied during your hot-topic conversation with your ex.

The most sophisticated research we have to date on verbal fights between couples[4] offers convincing evidence that blood pressure and heart pace rise along with anger and threats, making it very difficult—if not impossible—to apply the kinds of skills this book advocates: I-statements, reflection and empathy, mental shielding, and all the other respectful practices we've discussed. Sitting still and assuming the carefully placed silence are hard to do in the throes of anger. The reason is as simple as it is ancient: Our lizard brains[5] are trying to take good care of us by firing up our bodies for defense and counterattack.

The pulse races, the heart thumps, our muscles tense, a flush steals up the face, sweat breaks out—it's all a resurfacing of primitive self-protective responses that worked when we were fighting off tigers in our caves. Yet these responses are precisely what lead us to counter our ex-partner's foolishness with our own verbal violence.

Interestingly, men tend to evidence these responses faster than women. They also take longer to calm down, probably because men spent more time confronting angry tigers as they foraged for food, while women stayed in the cave keeping the newborns fed and healthy. Regardless of this gender difference, however, both men and women are quite capable of the "fly-off-the-handle" retorts that most people later regret and that only teach children bad life lessons. When it comes to dealing with a difficult ex, our lizard brains are outdated models; in most situations, they just make things worse.

A break away from the discussion—physically separating and going back to your corners—is the most effective thing you can do when you feel the lizard brain kick in. Formally propose a twenty-minute break in the discussion and find a space in which you can try one of the relaxation exercises discussed earlier. Or head for the nearest restroom and collect yourself, even if your ex wants to keep arguing. The suggested time of twenty minutes is usually enough time for cooler heads to prevail; that's about how long it takes for your heart rate to return to normal.

If you are on the phone, going to your corners is even easier. Just offer the suggestion: "Jim, things are getting too angry for me right now and I don't want to say something I'll regret. Let's hang up for half an hour and I promise to call you back then so we can keep working on this."

During your time-out, some form of brisk exercise followed by purposeful relaxation—deep breathing, meditation, even prayer—will work best toward returning you to a centered state.

Although it may seem hard to imagine with *your* ex, some couples actually agree in advance that they will signal each other when one or the other becomes really angry or feels threatened. Others agree to speak in fifteen-minute segments about especially difficult issues. Either of these prearranged agreements can be a wonderful way of mutually committing to civility.

The conversation going south . . .

. . . is no excuse for defaulting to the lizard brain. In fact, as you feel tensions going up and the discussion going down, that is more than ever the moment to center yourself and return to your moral compass. Letting yourself respond with the same anger that is coming your way is a primitive reaction. Rise above it. **Stay calm by staying yourself.**

Strategy 2: Disarm Your Ex

Imagine yourself in battle. You are driving an armored tank. Coming toward you is the enemy is his armored tank. You are both prepared to fire. You face off, cannon to cannon. Then you lower your tank's weapon, open your hatch, climb out, walk toward your opponent, and place a bouquet of flowers on the tank's gun. At that point, it would be pretty hard for even the most hardened enemy to fire on you.

That's exactly the point of this strategy: hand verbal flowers to an attacking ex-partner. Instead of taking up arms yourself, try to get her to lay down her verbal weapons. Doing so puts you in a safer place and keeps alive the possibility of finding common ground—or at least an acceptable place to meet—in the midst of intense emotion.

The goal is a response that will reduce the intensity in the room. Lowering the intensity gets you closer to your goal of resolution by taking you away from mutual destruction. After all, remind yourself that after this conversation ends, you still have five, ten, fifteen years of co-parenting with your ex. That's not necessarily a happy thought, but it is the reality you must deal with.

> *A soft word turns away wrath, but a harsh word stirs up anger.*
>
> —Proverbs 15:1

You can also try to disarm your ex by reflecting back the energy that's been aimed at you. This idea has its origins in the martial arts, where the principle is to use your opponent's energy to reach a state of harmony, rather than trying to oppose that energy with your own. Instead of striking directly, martial arts practitioners roll with the attack—they actually try to become one with their attacker—to reach a winning position. Of course, we are not interested here in winning but in reaching acceptable solutions. Still, the idea of using the other person's opposing energy can be useful.

Once you see that your partner is opposing what you have to say, resist the impulse to fight back directly. Center yourself and engage with your ex's energy by reflecting her own feelings back to her. Let her know that you understand what bugs her; it will most likely disarm her by sapping her anger of its strength.

Diane has proposed that Ralph, her ex, eliminate his Tuesday night visits with their daughter, Jennifer, because Jennifer has Girl Scout meetings on Tuesdays. Ralph is ticked off, and he is expressing his anger by blasting Diane. There's no point in screaming back at Ralph. Instead, this is how Diane answers: "I know it's really important to you to have as much time with Jennifer as possible, and I can see you're mad that I'd suggest any change in your schedule." This response doesn't solve the problem, but by showing Ralph that she understands his angry energy, Diane deflates its power. Although it takes practice, poise, and restraint, offering back to your ex a reflection of what you think he is feeling—"I can see this really upsets you" or "You're ticked off because my idea seems unfair"—can be a powerful way to reduce his angry energy. And remember, expressing understanding or empathy doesn't mean you are surrendering what's important to you or agreeing with your ex. It's just another tool in your toolbox for keeping things sane.

Soft words are hard arguments.
—Thomas Fuller, 18th century author

If you can't come up with an empathic reflection of what your ex is feeling, neutral yet sincere statements can act as fillers; they give you a way to respond without attacking, while you collect yourself and decide on your next move: "I'm sorry you feel that way" or "Thanks for telling me that" or "We may have to agree to disagree on this one" or "We obviously have different needs here."[6] All can work. Then, follow the neutral statement with a carefully placed silence if you suspect that further comment will just reinforce your ex's aggressive behavior.

Fighting fire with fire creates more fire.

TACTICS: ASK A QUESTION, CONCEDE A POINT

When in doubt, ask. It's a good strategy for just about anything in life, and it's a great way to respond to resistance on your ex's part. Unsure what her real concerns are? Ask her. Amazed at her anger? Probe to understand its source. Obviously, this can be difficult in an angry exchange, but it can be a very effective way to disarm an angry person who is verbally attacking you. For example, let's say you've just let your ex know that you would like to change the parenting schedule with the children. His response is to become red in the face and to shout angrily. Any number of counterresponses on your part might escalate the conflict. But try saying this: "Rob, tell me more about why my idea won't work for you and your wife." Or: "Kathy, I didn't know that this idea would upset you this much. . . . What bugs you the most?"

If your ex is resisting the schedule change because it's hard for him to arrange a new schedule around his work commitments, you might say the following: "Tell me more about your job schedule so I can understand why this won't work for you." Of course, you may still want to advocate for your proposed plan, but your questioning will have slowed things down, given time for gathering your energies, and likely softened the exchange. And, in discovering more about why your ex is resistant to your idea, you will be better positioned to work toward a plan that meets both of your needs.

Someone once said that the three words that guarantee marital bliss are "You're right, dear." Well, you and your spouse failed to find marital bliss, but the three magic words can work just as well when you are ex-spouses. Although it may be hard to admit, there will be times when your ex is actually right—or at least has a good point. Conceding the fact can go a long way toward finding harmony in your current relationship. "I agree," or "I think you're right," or even "I'm sorry" can gnaw at your ego's needs to defend itself and are the kinds of phrases that make you feel vulnerable, but, in fact, you gain power and strength when you're able to say them. You defuse your ex's attack and actually put yourself in control of the situation. Often it is our intense need to be right in a conversation that guarantees a long spat.

Concession and apology aren't so hard: "I'm sorry, Susan. You're right. That holiday plan can't work with your family's schedule. Let's think of other ideas." Or: "I know I just said something that upset you and I'm sorry. . . . Let's start over." You can put a final flourish on your apology by thanking your ex for the complaint or objection. It may sound strange, but it can soften an angry conversation: "Thanks for letting me know it won't work for you. What ideas do you have?"

TACTIC: STAY FOCUSED

What are you here for? Your focus, remember, is not to win an argument or to blast your ex but to reach an agreement. Stay on that focus. Your original solution is proving unworkable? Drop it. Move on. Your ex is lecturing you again? Or bringing up old issues, the same kinds of things that led you to split up in the first place? Issues like these are emotional potholes; they jolt you off your planned route—if you let them.

Remember that firm commitment you made to keep a businesslike focus on the task at hand? When you find that your ex is angrily digressing to matters that have little bearing on the problem that you've brought to the table, speak up: "Those are things that we really can't solve right now. But we *can* resolve the schedule problem that we came here to discuss, and I'd like to stay focused on that." Keep bringing the conversation back to the issue at hand.

Sometimes, of course, the issue at hand is a point of intractable disagreement. Many conversations go down the tubes because people don't know when to let go of a disagreement. So occasionally, when it seems that you and your ex are spiraling into endless conflict, it can be helpful to suggest "Let's come back to this one" or "Why don't we sleep on that one?" Move on to a no-brainer as a temporary way to cool tension. It keeps the focus on the ultimate purpose of gaining agreement while providing time for you and your ex to regroup before returning to the difficult topic.

TACTIC: SPEAK YOUR EX-PARTNER'S LANGUAGE

Staying focused and businesslike need not mean sticking to a prearranged script. How you phrase a response can be as important as what you say. The creative use of metaphors[7] and analogies can show you're attuned to your ex's perspective on the issue and can be a disarming way to respond to resistance. The more your point can fit her perspective, the clearer it will be. If your ex becomes furious over a complaint you've lodged, rephrase it in language that fits his or her life. For example, if your ex is a businesswoman accustomed to emphasizing teamwork on the job, try putting it this way: "The way you're reacting to this problem is the same as if you went to work, had a co-worker raise an issue, and proceeded to yell at him for five minutes. Obviously, nothing would get resolved and the business would suffer. Please speak with me in the same respectful way you would with a co-worker." If your ex is a train conductor for a local railroad and you feel like he's listening to absolutely nothing you're saying, you might say the following: "I came to you with a concern, and you've yelled for the last five minutes. It's as if you were driving your train at work, saw a deer on the tracks, and didn't even slow down to see if the deer would move out of your way. I feel like you're just running over me rather than listening. Please slow down and at least consider my concern here." Notice that in each of these examples the speaker doesn't just use an analogy or a metaphor to make a point—there is also a positive and clearly stated request for the ex to act differently.

TACTIC: POKE FUN AT YOURSELF

Irony is as powerful as metaphor. One of the most effective responses to a verbal attack is to admit that you are a goofball, that you made a bad suggestion, that your idea is simply unworkable. By injecting some levity into a tense situation, you can actually help get the conversation back on track. For example, after your ex gets through blasting your proposal for the holiday schedule with the kids, offer him this: "Well, as usual, Dick, I'm gifted at coming up with ideas that make you unhappy. What ideas do you have that will give each of us enough time with the kids?" Again, irony—and by that I mean self-irony—can slow the pace, defuse the tension, and remind you both that the point of all this talk is the well-being of your children.

TACTIC: SUGGEST AN EXPERIMENT

There is no law that says that you and your ex must be locked into eternal agreements together. Sometimes, even when a plan sounds reasonable, we may find ourselves reluctant to embrace it because it feels like committing to something forever. If your ex feels that way about your plan, or if you feel that way about his, suggest a trial period in which you give the plan an opportunity to succeed or fail: "Mike, I know you don't like the idea of shifting your weeknight visits, but it also sounds like you think Rachel should be in Girl Scouts. What if we agreed to shifting your weeknight time with her for one month and seeing how it works for all of us? Then we can sit down and talk about it again." Your ex may feel a lot more comfortable agreeing to something if he knows it is simply an experiment, with a deadline set for reevaluation, rather than a final conclusion to your discussion.

Strategy 3: Make a Bold Move

There are times, of course, when you cannot stay silent or remain neutral—times when empathy, carefully chosen words, even concession on your part still engender hostility. You simply must try something with more impact to stop your ex's angry dance. If you respond to anger with anger, you only continue the spiral of attack and counterattack. Nothing is achieved. Everyone loses, especially the children.

Other response tactics let you make your point while recouping the situation. You can say what you feel, but it must be said without feeding into your ex's resentment and without poisoning relations even further.

TACTIC: NAME THE GAME

When you find yourself the victim of an ongoing dysfunctional game your ex is playing, just name the game[8]—that is, let her know you're aware of what she is trying to do.

Tim, a single, disabled dad of twin four-year-olds, tended always to give in to his ex-wife's demands for last-minute changes in her visitation schedule, demands invariably accompanied by subtle threats that she would not pay support if he didn't yield. Although the schedule changes caused Tim to miss important physical therapy sessions, the idea of losing even one support check was especially frightening. So for a long time, he went along with the game of threaten-and-surrender.

But eventually Tim mustered the courage to let his ex know he was on to her: "Fran, I know you hate the current schedule, but it sounds as if you might be trying to get me to change the kids' schedule by threatening to cut off their support. The schedule and support are two different issues, and I'd like you to keep them separate."

The effect was immediate. Fran's game was up, and now she knew it. Tim had punctured its power. The schedule and support problems remained, but by calling Fran on the carpet, Tim at least got her to act more reasonably.

TACTIC: REPEAT YOURSELF

If the issue that you're discussing is one you feel very strongly about and you're not able to find a way to compromise with your ex, first express some understanding for his feelings, and then repeat clearly and firmly what it is that you want from him.

Caroline was always nervous about impending conversations with her ex, Jeremy, because he tended to steamroll her in conversations. The problem was a persistent one: Jeremy invariably brought their daughter Betsy back to Caroline's so late on school nights that Betsy was exhausted in the morning, so much so that her teachers had raised the matter with Caroline. When Caroline raised the issue with Jeremy, however, he, as always, grew red in the face, and with the veins in his neck popping out, began screaming that Betsy was his daughter too and "I can do what I want with her."

I coached Caroline on the use of creative repetition, and for her next meeting with Jeremy, she agreed to try it. When the issue of the late-night returns came up, as it always did, and Jeremy began his usual strident bulldozing, Caroline looked him straight in the eye and said, "You sound angry, Jeremy, because it feels to you like I'm questioning your judgment as a parent. I know that you only want to share time with Betsy, and I respect that, but I expect that you will return her at 8:30, as we have agreed." Jeremy then became even angrier; in response, Caroline calmly repeated what she had said—almost word for word. Again Jeremy yelled; again Caroline repeated that she understood but wanted Betsy home by 8:30. It took four repetitions, with Caroline looking Jeremy directly in the eye each time, remaining firm and calm. She then decided simply to change the subject and trust that her resolve had had an impact. It had. The next week, Jeremy brought Betsy home at 8:40.

Thanks to the coaching, Caroline understood that if she kept waiting for Jeremy to concede to her expectation, he would likely have dug his heels in even more deeply, and they would have been locked in an insoluble dispute. Instead, she simply asserted herself repeatedly, resolutely, respectfully, and then moved on. The repetition ensured that the words would be remembered; the moving on gave Jeremy the chance to decide to do as she asked—and to save face.

TACTIC: OFFER A CHOICE

It works with children as an effective form of discipline. "You can either have the ice cream now or dessert after dinner. You cannot have both. Please choose." With adults, offering a choice can be an effective way of asserting what you will and will not tolerate when all else has failed; it can help you gain the outcome you seek while maximizing your sense of control over your life.

Stuart had felt for years that his own life schedule dangled like a puppet on strings pulled by his ex-wife, Joan. On their weekly transition days, she was routinely thirty to forty minutes late arriving to pick up the children. Although Stuart was concerned about the frustration and disappointment this caused for the kids, he was most concerned about his boss's recent comments about his tardiness. He complained angrily to Joan for more than a year; then he tried a different tactic—a choice:

"Joan, I came here to again ask you to pick the children up on time so that I can get to my weekend shift on time. You don't seem willing to listen to what I'm saying about this, so here's what you can expect. If you pick up the children at the hour that we have agreed, they will be waiting at the house for you. If you arrive late, I will have taken them to the baby-sitter's house or to my mother's on my way to work. You can then pick them up at one of those two places. It's up to you." Joan tested Stuart's resolve for a few weeks, driving an extra five miles to get the kids each time. And then she began to show up on time.

Presenting such a choice is far different from making a threat or handing down a punishment. Both threats and punishments are entirely inappropriate responses between adults—especially because it is children who suffer the consequences. In offering a choice to your ex, you are simply making a statement about what the other person's options are and about how you intend to behave in your own life. Had Stuart told Joan that the next time she was late, the kids wouldn't be there at all, that would certainly have been threatening her with punishment. Stuart would have been offering only a negative option: "You do that bad thing again and this will happen to you." In offering a choice, however, he set out the positive option first before making clear the negative consequences. Here are some more examples:

"Dave, you can treat me respectfully when you come to pick up the kids and I'll be comfortable with you coming to the door to get them, or you can decide to continue to put me down and yell at me, and I will then ask you to come no closer to my property than the end of the driveway when you come for the kids. It's up to you."

"Carol, you can call my home to speak with the children a reasonable number of times weekly, like once a day, and I will always answer the phone when you call. But if you continue to disrupt our home with four and five calls daily, I will begin to monitor my calls and not answer if you have already spoken with the children once that day. It's up to you."

When you offer a choice, you are not waiting for the other person to make a counterargument. You are simply making a statement about how things will be and about how you intend to act. That is why offering a choice can be a healthy and effective response. But it should also be a last resort. Use choice when all else has failed.

And when you do, it is critical that you follow through on what you say. If you said that the children would not be there beyond one-half hour after the appointed time, make sure you've left with them—and taken them to where you had promised. If you said that you would contact the police the next time there was an incident of harassment, make sure you contact the police. If you said that he would not be allowed any closer than the end of the driveway the next time you were mistreated, make sure that you follow through on this. Choices have consequences; make that clear by your actions.

TACTIC: TAKE AWAY THE CANDY

Does it sometimes seem that your ex-partner enjoys seeing you riled up? Certainly there are people on this earth who get a kick out of upsetting others. For some ex-partners who resent the separation, even an argument is better than no contact at all. Whatever the explanation, if you see that your ex seems to find satisfaction in upsetting you, remember that your own reactions may be reinforcing that behavior. It's logical: If making you angry is pleasurable to your ex, and insults make you angry, then the obvious thing to do is insult you as much as possible.

Take away the candy. Disengage from the conversation. Refuse to discuss the topic further until your ex acts more reasonably: "Cynthia, I'm not going to talk about the support payments anymore until you speak respectfully to me," or: "That's not an issue I'm willing to talk with you about anymore. Anything else you need to talk about?" Of course, the best form of disengagement is simply not to get trapped in the snare your ex has set for you in the first place. If you can stay calm and centered without retaliating, you take away the candy—you take the pleasure out of being hurtful by removing the reward your ex looks for in insulting you.

TACTIC: END THE HOT-TOPIC CONVERSATION—OR ESCAPE FROM IT

It is important to remember that you have the right to decide that there is certain behavior that you are unwilling to tolerate from your ex—especially if it is behavior your children might witness. You will not, for example, tolerate being called vulgar names, being sworn at, being yelled at or intimidated—behavior that may be characteristic of your ex. Once you've made that decision, then at the first sign of such behavior you must let him know that you intend to end the conversation: "Jim, I want you to know that if you continue to yell and swear at me in this way, I'll end this conversation, and we'll have to work this out in another way. I'm perfectly prepared to get up and leave if you don't treat me with respect." A woman that I know who set these limits with her ex did in fact "get up and leave"—several times—before her ex learned that his behavior wasn't working for him.

Choosing to end a conversation that is becoming abusive or overly intense models self-respect for your children.

Is it okay to hang up on someone who continues to hurl verbal abuse at you? Certainly, but believe it or not, there is a respectful way to do it, a way that shows you are not lowering yourself to the level of your ex's attacks. Give the warning we've just discussed, then simply say something like this: "Jim, you've continued to yell and swear. I'm hanging up now. We can speak again when you are more calm." *Click.* By verbally cueing your ex before the click, you maintain a bit of civility. A click with no warning is no better than yelling and swearing.

Always leave open the possibility of escape should the hot-topic conversation really go awry. You can't do anybody any good—yourself, your ex, or above all, your children—if you are overwhelmed with anxiety or anger or a feeling of being intimidated.

Prepare your escape route in advance. Sometimes it can help to state as much up front, to let your ex know that your time is limited because you have another engagement. If the time then comes when you feel you need to escape, the excuse is ready: "I'm sorry, but I've got to get to that appointment I mentioned. We'll have to continue this another time." It's indirect and not particularly assertive, but there are times when direct assertion may be too difficult—even too risky.

Remember:

When your ex becomes upset, resists your comments, or opposes what you have to say . . .

✓ Button your lips and stay calm.

✓ Use your inner Toto to understand your ex's reaction.

✓ Create a mental shield.

✓ Take a time-out.

✓ Reflect your ex's emotions.

✓ Ask a question, concede a point.

✓ Stay focused.

✓ Speak your ex-partner's language.

✓ Poke fun at yourself.

✓ Suggest an experiment.

✓ Name the game.

✓ Repeat yourself.

✓ Offer a choice.

✓ Take away the candy—disengage.

✓ End or escape.

Real Life

These ideas sound so nice and they might work if I weren't dealing with such a buffoon. There is no way in hell that my ex would ever have a reasonable or civil conversation, so why waste my time?

You have given up. Reconsider now before your children scribble in their life notebooks that when you run into challenges in adult life you should give up. It sounds as if you do feel quite helpless—and hopeless—and if you can honestly say that you have tried repeatedly to speak with your ex and have been met with nothing but disappointment, such feelings are certainly understandable. You need to detach somewhat from your struggle. Imagine that the problem with your ex was a problem with the roof in your home. You have tried three different solutions to the roof problem, and none have worked. Would you walk away from the home that you wanted repaired, leaving the roof leaking, or would you try a fourth approach? Consider the tools offered in these past several chapters as the fourth approach—a whole new set of tools that you commit to using over and over again until the repair is made. That's an important value to communicate to your children.

There are so many tools here that I'm not sure how to decide which one to use the next time things get hot with my daughter's dad. And how do I pull this all together?

Use your intuition about which tools might make sense with your ex and which ones would never fly. But keep a long-term view so that you can experiment with different tools to determine which ones work. Your ex might surprise you by responding well to approaches that you thought would never work. Also, I would try only one or two new tools at a time as you build your skills. Take one of the nagging problems between you and your ex and visualize a discussion through the template of Chapters 9 through 11. First, imagine yourself in preparation: giving the invitation, planning what you will say, becoming clear and secure about your own desired outcome, brainstorming options that may be agreeable to both of you, and so on. Next, imagine the conversation itself and hear yourself using such tools as I-statements, attentive listening, slowing down, brainstorming. Then, imagine your ex expressing some opposition to your proposals. See and hear yourself using the tools that you think make most sense in your relationship with your ex—perhaps the mental shield, or proposing a break, or disarming your ex, or conceding a point, or all of these. Finally, find a supportive friend or family member to role-play the conversation, acting the part of your ex while you experiment with the strategies and tactics you've chosen.

CHAPTER TWELVE

When Talking Doesn't Work

Suppose it fails. Suppose your hot-topic conversation with your ex has broken down, deteriorated into yelling, disintegrated into re-criminations. All your strategic planning and smart tactics have gone down the tubes, and you or your ex have actually ended up slamming down the phone or storming out of the room.

Let's put this failure in perspective:

Why did your marriage fail? If it was anything like the vast major-ity of marriages that end in divorce, it disintegrated because of serious problems in communication. Is it realistic to expect that one attempt at a mutual discussion about difficult issues will be enough to change this long-standing pattern? After all, if the problems between you and your ex were simple, you would most likely still be together.

Don't Give Up!

Remember, *one failed conversation does not mean that all is lost.* I cannot emphasize enough the importance of maintaining a hopeful, constructive attitude. It's no help at all to throw your arms up and lament that "She's ridiculous . . . It's hopeless . . . He always was a jerk and he still is." That will doom you to years of being a co-parent with a hostile partner.

Keep in mind that all important changes in life take time; you'll need to stick to this new way of talking with your ex for three to four months before you can fully evaluate its effectiveness. Remember that your new approach will be something of a surprise to your ex. Be patient while your ex adjusts to your new way of "being" in the relationship and your new techniques for resolving problems.

The new tools may feel awkward, but they will become less so with practice. Use them consistently and you will likely experience some softening on your ex-partner's part. Remember, however, that the most important criterion for success should be whether you walk away feeling you did your best to create an atmosphere of peace with your child's other parent. And if you have moments when you wonder if it is even worth trying to talk with your ex, keep in mind that everything we do as parents, including throwing up our arms in despair and giving up, is scribbled by our children in their life notebooks.

Chalk the failure up to experience and go back to the drawing board. Be constructive. Try to develop other ways of communicating with your ex that may be more effective. Consider the conversation that went down the toilet as just another class you had to attend in your "wisdom school." Ask yourself what you learned about yourself, not your ex, and use the experience to deepen your understanding about life.

Or just forget about the failure. Wipe the slate clean and determine that your next conversation with your ex is the first you are going to have. Approach it with a fresh resolve to bring out the best in him and in yourself. Old habits die hard, but they do die. Remember the principle of staying proactive, choosing to look at the dilemma with your ex as a problem to be solved rather than letting yourself wallow in painful emotions.

As was discussed earlier, you may well come to a day when you decide that this particular problem belongs in the column of dilemmas-over-which-you-have-no-control and may simply have to accept as part of your life, refocusing your attention on things that you still *can* control. Regardless of how dismal things may feel, you can always return to Chapter 3 and make the empowerment shift—a shift that for many parents represents the point at which they regain their life.

Find a Neutral Professional

It can be invaluable to seek the services of a neutral professional who can sit down with the two of you and offer you a place to try to work through some of your issues or concerns with one another— either through mediation or through what in my practice is called "co-parenting counseling."

Choose mediation if you simply want to reach agreement about certain specific issues—anything from the terms of the custodial plan, child support, and visitation concerns to how to pay for your daughter's braces. Divorce mediation involves sitting down with a person trained in conflict resolution who will help you and your ex craft your own agreement. (Contrast this with having an agreement imposed on you by a judge who is a stranger to your family.) You will leave the process with a written memorandum of agreement signed by both of you. If the issues in mediation are significant— time-sharing plans as opposed to having your daughter's raincoat returned after weekends, for instance—it's advisable to have a mediation-friendly attorney involved in the process to advise you on your memorandum before final signature. And if you are still in the early stages of divorce, your agreement document can actually be converted into a legally binding separation agreement.

Mediation can be a powerfully effective process, even with couples who are quite embattled, and it offers a wonderful, family-centered alternative to traditional litigation. You can find a mediator by searching the phone book under "mediation" or "mediators," or by contacting your local family court or dispute-resolution center. Tell the mediator about the types of issues on which you would like to reach agreement and ask about his or her level of experience with similar problems. Mediation is largely an unregulated profession, so be sure to find someone who has been practicing for a while and who has at least a minimum of forty hours of formal training.

You need "co-parenting counseling" if you are seeking to improve your relationship with your ex or to communicate better, as opposed to wanting to reach a specific agreement about specific issues. This process will require that you and your ex regularly come together in the safe environment of a professional's office to work through some of your differences. The goal is not to transform your relationship so that it works perfectly, but to soften the edges, to make the relationship more businesslike and civil for the sake of your children. Our experience with divorced couples suggests that this is usually the most effective professional intervention for separated and divorced spouses in conflict.

The most effective, best-suited professionals for this service are psychologists, clinical social workers, or licensed counselors who have substantial experience in working with divorced couples. Special expertise is needed to work with couples in high conflict, especially those who may be intersecting with the court system. If you have an attorney or your child has a law guardian, ask them for the names of skilled family therapists who they have admired for their work with divorcing families. Another strategy is to search among trained divorce mediators who are *also* psychologists or clinical social workers; such people have almost certainly had wide-ranging experience with divorced clients. Mediation centers also often have lists of professionals who they trust as family therapists. You may also have some success looking under psychologists, social workers, or licensed counselors in the phone book or by asking your physician for a referral.

In searching out the right counselor for your needs, it's perfectly okay to interview two or three candidates by phone to find out what they do and how they do it and to confirm that they have substantial experience working with divorced couples. After selecting two or three names, make your proposal to your ex—maybe along these lines:

"George, we obviously have great difficulty talking with one another about our problems, but we have to have a relationship because of our kids. I read somewhere that one thing that can be helpful to people in our spot would be to find a neutral professional both parents can agree on. We would then sit down with that person, using his office as a place to try to work through some of the problems. I've researched three local professionals, and I thought, if you had any interest in this idea, you might call them and decide on the one that seemed right for you. All three are acceptable to me. We can always change our minds once we've started and nothing is written in stone. Any interest in this?"

If the situation between you and your ex is particularly strained, you might make the same offer in a letter. If the issues are serious enough eventually to require court assistance, you might add that you want to avoid litigation and attorneys and that this would be a much more private and less expensive approach.

Unfortunately, it may be difficult to convince your ex to agree to a joint counseling approach. Occasionally, courts are willing to order such intervention, and if you are involved in litigation, you might ask your attorney or the attorney or guardian representing your children to advocate for a court order that mandates both parents to participate in this form of treatment.

If your ex is completely unwilling to consider this form of counseling, find a neutral professional for yourself. It's easy to begin feeling hopeless when nothing you are trying seems to work with your ex. Having a caring professional to lend perspective and support can help you feel less alone and can guide you to a more objective perspective on your problems. Most insurance plans have some form of coverage for counseling. You will also find that reaching out for help can be an opportunity for you to grow personally in unexpected ways.

Give yourself permission to ask for help.

Write Businesslike Letters

Another option, when talking fails, is to write letters to one another. Keep it businesslike; stick to the issue at hand—the children's school information, scheduling, the vacation schedule. Many of the high-conflict couples I have worked with find that the letter-writing habit helps them control the level of animosity between them. There are downsides, of course—for example, you can't respond to the other person spontaneously, and you can sometimes end up in an endless series of back-and-forth letters about an issue that really ought to be resolved quickly. But letters afford an opportunity to express your thoughts in a controlled and rational manner and they help you think before you respond; that makes them particularly helpful if you are worried about how you or your ex might react in a discussion.

One woman I counseled, Nancy, was persistently angry about her ex's failure to show up as scheduled for his visits with the children. Afraid of exploding in a one-on-one discussion, she turned to letter-writing, focusing on the principles we've been discussing in the last few chapters. She began her letters with compliments, always mentioned something her ex had done that she appreciated, and then went on to make I-statements explaining the frustrations and worries she had regarding her ex's behavior. In particular, the letter-writing allowed her to explain her worry about the effect she felt his not showing up was having on their children.

The letter was not a magic bullet; Nancy's ex did not become perfectly responsible, but he did begin to show up more frequently for his visits with the children—no doubt because she had had the time and space to express her worry calmly and compellingly.

Here's a sample letter that may help you compose your own.

Dear Chris,

I am writing because I want to find a way to be more involved in Joshua's activities outside of school. First, I want you to know that I appreciate your efforts to keep him involved in sports. I'm glad he has a dad who coaches his teams and is involved with him—it's easy to see how he loves having you there.

Here's my concern:

When no one lets me know about the game schedule or about where the games are being held each week, I feel left out of important parts of Joshua's life. I'm already at a disadvantage from living forty miles away, but never receiving a copy of his schedule or a call about a change of date—even though I have asked for this courtesy—makes it worse. I worry that when I'm not there, Joshua will think I don't care. I end up feeling disconnected from him. As it is, I only see him every other weekend, so seemingly little things, like sitting and clapping for him at a soccer game, are very important to me. I also worry that our inability to communicate about such simple matters puts Josh in a tough spot—that last time I missed a game, Josh blamed himself for not telling me about the date change and he felt terrible. But the problem was ours, not his.

My guess is that you have some concerns about this issue, and that it is a touchy topic for you. You may even wish that I not attend many games because of the blowup your mother and I had at T-ball last year. I understand this and can tell you that I am now committed to speaking and acting in civil ways with your family in front of Josh, even if it means that I sit quite far away from them to keep things cool. I'm also guessing that you think it should be my job, not yours, to figure out when games are—after all, that's what you have to do and you're already very busy. But since the team sends only one schedule, it goes where Josh mainly lives—with you—and it's you they notify about date and schedule changes. That's how it's happened that, more than once, I've driven forty miles only to find an empty field. I'm uncomfortable asking the already shoestring team operation to send two sheets or make two calls because you and I have difficulty talking with each other.

It means so much to Josh when we are both at games. Would you please consider sending me a copy of all sports schedules when you get them and leaving a message for me when the schedule or location

changes? I know that we both want Josh to feel he has two parents interested in his life, and I believe that he would be less tense about you
and me if he saw us regularly exchanging basic information about his
life. I think we can find a way to work this out because we both want
to do what's right for Josh.

Sincerely,
Vicky

The letter has all the ingredients that form the basis of effective
communications with a difficult ex[1]:

1. A clear statement of the letter's goal.

2. An expression of appreciation.

3. I-statements and respectful complaints.

4. Child-centered worries—not "shoulds" or demands.

5. Anticipation of the ex's objections.

6. A statement of the writer's commitment to civility.

7. An emphasis on mutual interests.

8. A specific positive request for the future.

If you're writing about urgent issues—if your letter is a last resort—imply your willingness to take serious action. Be sure to express it that way—as something you're considering, not as a threat:
"Please let me know if you are willing to consider this idea because
I am beginning to feel I have few other choices than returning to
court—and I really want to avoid this." Remember, however, that
such statements can be inflammatory and should only be made as a
last resort. Leave your ex some wiggle room so she can reach agreement with you while saving face; avoid ultimatums.

Use a Kids' Log

Some parents find it helpful to build note-writing into the regular comings and goings of their kids. The only equipment you'll need is a simple notebook; it will be passed to your ex when she takes the kids, and she'll pass it back to you when she brings them back. Each time the children leave your home, you make an entry about things you think your ex should know. Use all the good skills you have now learned about how to express these things: compliments, thank-yous, I-statements, respectful complaints, and so on.

The kids' log is a way of making letter-writing a regular part of your relationship with your ex. It can be especially helpful during the early stages of an acrimonious divorce, or when relations between you and your ex seem too brittle to risk direct conversation.

Certain guidelines are important to ensure the success of the kids' log:

1. Write something at each transition—not just occasionally.

2. Write more than a quick one-liner. For example, avoid: "Things were fine." These are your kids; surely, there's more to say.

3. Include specific comments that will make your child's transition easier—viz., "Sarah had no nap . . . she may be cranky."

4. Tell your ex things that will ensure continuity. If one of the kids is on medication, remind your ex about it: "Adam needs the ear drops every four hours."

5. Stay focused on the present in your complaints and comments, and avoid references to painful history; be businesslike.

6. Limit comments to those points necessary to make life easier for the kids and to coordinate parenting. Comments like "Your girlfriend looks like a porpoise" are off-limits.

Attorneys and the Courts:
Use with Care

Lawyers can be an invaluable resource and a source of support when the tide of anger between you and your ex is rising. They can lend clarity at a time when you are feeling lost, and they can help you avoid making things worse for yourself than they already are. For some issues—such as the final form of the separation agreement—involvement of a legal professional is a virtual necessity.

But it can be extremely expensive, both financially and emotionally, to involve attorneys in the conflicts between separating parents. For one thing, some spouses respond angrily to even the merest suggestion of a legal "remedy"; the response tends to make them even more rigidly opposed to finding a solution you can agree on.

Furthermore, some attorneys approach family problems with a sharklike attitude—useful in many types of litigation but not in family issues. In fact, such an approach is often responsible for worsening the pain in many families. That's why it's important to research local attorneys carefully. Look for specialists—matrimonial lawyers whose practices focus on families, not lawyers who defend people accused of DWI or reneging on construction contracts. There is an art to matrimonial law. Be sure you choose an attorney who has spent a lot of time honing that art in family court. Ask around. Talk to former clients. Find out if the lawyers you're considering have a reputation for fanning or dousing the flames of conflict and whether they are sensitive to the needs of children. Good resources for attorneys with a family-friendly approach are mediation centers, which often have lists of attorneys they view as oriented toward peacemaking, and friends who have been divorced.

Getting legal advice is often a critical step for a separated parent because the decisions that you make now can have implications for your child's future—and your own—and can come back to haunt you later on. So once you have found an attorney you trust, you can rely on him or her to write the needed letters to your ex—through your ex's attorney—about your worries and concerns, or about limits you want to set. Although having your attorney speak for you rather than speaking for yourself should be a last resort, there are times when it can be helpful. Certainly, when serious matters need to be resolved, saying that you must "consult with my attorney" communicates that you are taking matters very seriously.

David was powerless to control his ex-wife Sharon's tirades against him when he came to pick up the kids. What particularly distressed him was that his children were witnessing the two of them "going ballistic together," as he put it. He tried to speak with Sharon about it, but the discussions repeatedly failed. David's attorney then wrote to Sharon's attorney to say that the attorney would pursue an order of protection on behalf of his client if Sharon did not cease her out-of-control behavior. The formality and potential consequences implied in the attorney's letter caused her to be more self-controlled when she came to the door. It's a case where the presence of an attorney shifted the dynamics dramatically.

A final note about attorneys: It is important to remind yourself that, in a sense, your lawyer is like your employee. Stay in charge of what your attorney does for you and don't be afraid to ask questions about the rationale behind the decisions he or she is making. Your attorney is a legal expert—not an expert on you, your children, or your ex. And remember to be open and honest because the representation your lawyer gives you is only as good as the information he or she gets from you.

Another legal option is to pursue a court remedy to your problems with your ex-partner. Certainly, I favor people working out their problems between themselves rather than through the courts, which are not well structured to handle many family matters and are not particularly sensitive to family dynamics. Most judges agree with me; they would prefer that parents settle their differences out of court. But the court system can be an essential tool for frustrated or frightened parents whose ex-partners behave unreasonably or—worse—dangerously. In the words of a good friend of mine, the courts were meant to "supplant chaos."[2] They provide a setting in which parents can have a rationally controlled and highly structured exchange about differences. So if all the other things I have talked about here have not helped your situation, you may indeed need to go to court.

Remember to go into the court process with a realistic attitude: It is a system filled with well-intentioned yet fallible human beings. Often, these people are overwhelmed with cases; just as often, they lack the resources needed to allow full consideration of all the nuances of your particular family's particular situation. Most of the time, both parents leave litigation licking some wounds. Occasionally—but only occasionally—the courts offer the kind of solutions that people fantasize about. The best thing to expect is a controlled environment in which to try to work through your concerns with your ex.

Remember the Children . . .

Above all, remember why you're making this attempt at a hot-topic conversation in the first place. You're doing it for your children. One of the most important gifts you can give them is a healthy model of adult behavior. Certainly, one aspect of adulthood they need to be aware of is that adults are vulnerable human beings who can make mistakes. Wouldn't it be nice if they could also see adults who are able to admit to their mistakes yet continue to strive for civility?

Children need to see their parents trying to work out differences constructively and rationally. Remember, they are scribbling in their life notebooks as they watch you deal with one another. If they see you give up, they will do the same in their own relationships. If they see you come back from failure and try and try again, that is the life lesson they will learn.

Remember:
When discussions with your ex have repeatedly failed . . .

✓ Give yourself permission to seek professional assistance.

✓ Consider mediation when you need to reach agreement about specific issues.

✓ Propose co-parenting counseling when you want to improve your relationship with your ex for the sake of the children.

✓ When the level of conflict is high, use letter writing to stay civil while still being assertive.

✓ Use a kids' log to keep communication open and safe.

✓ A carefully chosen child-focused attorney can help you advocate for what you believe is best for you and your children.

✓ Consider a court remedy when the issues are important and all else has failed.

Real Life

My ex would never agree to go to counseling with me after all we've been through. Shouldn't I just go straight to the courts if she won't talk to me?

The courts are best considered a last resort for many family problems, except in situations involving domestic violence or that require court assistance by law. Although you may be right that your ex will never agree to go to counseling with you, it won't hurt to try selling the idea. Emphasize how you believe the acrimony between you may be affecting the kids. Also emphasize to your ex how much the conflicts between the two of you are messing up *her* life also and how you think it would be helpful for the two of you to have an independent person who will listen to your side of the story *and* hers. Mention how the presence of a third party might help the two of you avoid being pulled into arguments that feel hopeless. If you must turn to the courts, the law guardian for your children may be willing to advocate to the court that the parties in your family dispute be ordered or urged to participate in co-parenting counseling. You may be able to achieve an on-the-record agreement in court in which you both commit to get professional assistance together.

The last place I want to be after all of the problems we've had is in the same room with that jerk! There must be another way.

Yes, there are other ways. But it has been my professional experience that, when other attempts at communication have failed, co-parenting counseling is often the best approach to finding resolution. Skilled mental health professionals and mediators are used to sitting with angry couples and helping them feel safe and constructive. Ask yourself which is worse: several hours a month talking directly with your ex with the assistance of a counselor, or the current nagging, unresolved, possibly explosive problems between you? And finally, remember that there was a time when you and your ex ate meals together, slept together, and even loved each other. Your ex isn't from another planet, although sometimes it may seem so.

My ex and I have begun passing letters back and forth in our four-year-old's backpack. Any problems with that?

Your intentions are right on target. You are trying to contain the conflict between you and your ex by using a more civil, controlled way of communicating. Here's my advice, however: Either hand the letters to your ex yourself or mail them. The reason is simple: Children often sense the gravity of what they are carrying, and that letter in the backpack can weigh 10,000 emotional pounds to your little one, particularly if your child senses that something may be being communicated that will lead to disappointment or anger.

Sometimes my attorney acts like my parent, and I suddenly hear things coming out of her mouth in court that I never wanted said. What can I do?

Consider your attorney to be like a contractor who is wallpapering and painting your kitchen. Be very specific at all times about what you want her to do for you and what you don't want her to do. Of course, your lawyer is there to give you advice and direction, but a good attorney will also appreciate the direction you give her. When you have second thoughts about your attorney's approach, ask her for her rationale. Perhaps it will make perfect legal sense to you. If it doesn't, and if you continue to feel like you're not in control of the process, consider seeking a new lawyer.

My ex used to slap me when we were together. Now he towers over me at the door and yells and last week he even pushed me in front of the kids, so all this communication stuff seems crazy!

Any form of violence is illegal and immoral, and it terrifies children. Call the police. Get a lawyer. Consider an order of protection. Model self-protection for your kids.

PART FOUR

Your Ex and Your Children

CHAPTER THIRTEEN

When You Have Complaints about Your Ex-Partner's Parenting

What is perhaps the most emotionally challenging aspect of sharing custody with a difficult ex-spouse is the time when the children are in the custody of that other parent. The kids walk out the door to spend the weekend, and your worries begin—not just because the children are no longer within the reach of your protective embrace, but also because you're not wild about the parenting style of your ex. Maybe you never were, even when you were living together as a family under the same roof. In fact, now that you're apart, your complaints about your ex-partner's parenting may be greater than ever, causing you high anxiety whenever the kids are with your ex.

Your concerns may be well-grounded. Perhaps there are some real risks to your children. Perhaps they do need someone to intervene on their behalf. But the intensity that ratchets your concern up to anxiety—in some cases, even panic—can virtually disable your life. And let's face it, there are times when the anxiety may have more to do with your own past relationship with your ex than with any real danger to the kids. When the leftover anger or resentment or pain from a failed adult relationship is misdirected onto the children, it is quite capable of making you see major disasters where others might see minor concerns.

If Necessary, Take Protective Action!

Throughout these chapters, I'm going to recommend a number of approaches to dealing with what you perceive to be problems with your ex-partner's parenting—problems that affect the welfare or safety or disciplining of your children. Every approach I recommend, however, should go right out the window **if your children are being abused or neglected in obvious and risky ways by your ex.** As was said at the very beginning of this book and as cannot be emphasized too strongly, such extreme behavior with children is absolutely unacceptable, and should it occur, **it is your responsibility as your children's other parent to act protectively.** Do not hesitate. There's only one course of action to take, one choice. **If you have good reason to believe that your children are being mistreated by their other parent, contact the local authorities immediately**—either Child Protective Services, your local police department, or family court.

Of course, injurious behavior is difficult to determine and hard to believe. How can you be sure that the behavior that concerns you is truly abusive or neglectful? You're uncertain, and since you're uncertain, you can't be sure whether your actions will constitute assertive protection of your children or sheer overreaction. In cases of such uncertainty, I recommend that you immediately consult a mental health professional—a child psychologist or a clinical social worker, for example—to help you decide how to proceed. Your pediatrician or a lawyer with substantial experience advocating for children can also be good resources in these circumstances.

The tragedy of abusive or neglectful behavior, however, is not our primary focus in this book. Rather, I want to talk to the vast majority of the divorced population with its vastly different household routines, values, rules, and limits, all of which can create healthy, happy children—even when their parents are separated.

SPOTTING PROBLEMS THAT FALL ON YOUR SHOULDERS, NOT YOUR CHILD'S

Although I believe children should own some of the problems they have with their other parent rather than expecting you to rescue them, certain categories of problems belong to you alone. Perhaps you've discovered that your ex-wife discusses your court petitions with the children. Maybe your ex-husband is overly harsh in his discipline with the kids when they're at his home. Or perhaps your ex regularly fails to send your child's expensive asthma medication back after a visit. All these complaints concern your children, yet they belong to you alone; in each case, your ex's behavior warrants *your* concern and your complaint, and that makes these situations your burden. Indeed, there are at least two categories of situation that will always be your burden.

The first and most obvious is behavior by your ex that doesn't particularly upset your child but really upsets you. The antennae you developed in Chapter 6 should have made you pretty astute at spotting such situations. Remember the criteria?

1. Is someone other than you expressing the concern or the complaint?

2. Is someone other than you feeling most of the emotions about the problem?

3. Is it another person's life—not yours—that will most improve if the problem goes away?

4. Does the problem lie mainly between two or more other people?

For example, your ex might be feeding the kids a steady diet of junk food, and while the children are content to live on potato chips and gummy bears, you are frantic about the bad effects and bad habits these eating patterns are creating. So while this problem involves your kids and certainly concerns their welfare, it's really a complaint you have with your ex. In short, it's your burden to seek a solution.

The second category includes those situations in which your children are too young to care about the problem or to take care of themselves with their other parent. I knew a father who was furious because he knew that when his infant daughter was at her mother's, she was typically allowed to lie in the crib for long periods of time with a bottle in her mouth and with little supervision or stimulation. The father owned this problem—not his ex, who thought it was perfectly appropriate to leave the baby quiet in the crib, and certainly not the seven-month-old infant; she didn't know enough to care nor could she possibly have asserted herself. Consequently, it was up to the young father to figure out a solution.

You already have the tools to deal with either of these categories of problems'. You learned about the empowerment shift in Chapter 3 and about making your own peace in Chapter 4. You've also learned tools for nudging your ex to change. But the following special tools will help you deal with the particular problems that arise when you have complaints about your ex's parenting style.

RESPECT YOUR EX-PARTNER'S PARENTING STYLE

It's all too easy to buy into the myth that there is one appropriate way to raise children—your way, as if only you had a monopoly on the truth. In reality, children are born into an incredibly diverse array of parenting approaches, most of which produce healthy, reasonably happy children.

Maybe your children are being raised in a deeply religious household in which grace is said before each meal. Down the street is a family that pays scant attention to mealtime prayer, yet their kids are as polite, intelligent, happy, and healthy as you could wish. Some parents are strict about certain things that other parents couldn't care less about. One family serves TV dinners exclusively, while another grows and eats organic fruits and vegetables, yet the children of the two families find enough in common to be great friends—perhaps precisely because of their differences. While one parent can't imagine a night without a bath, the parent next door sees Sundays as bath day. This is a world of diversity, both within and between families.

This is not to say that "anything goes" in parenting. Certain extremes—grossly poor nutrition, harsh and hurtful discipline, extreme indulgence and laissez-faire attitudes—produce extreme results in kids. But between these extremes is where most parents reside, and their kids do just fine. The bottom line? Children can survive, grow, and thrive within a wide variety of parenting styles. That is true even when the variety occurs within one set of parents—that is, when a father is strict, a mother more easygoing. Or when one parent insists on daily baths while the other only fetches the soap twice a week. Or when one of you insists on organic vegetables while the other sprinkles the week with cupcakes.

There are many different parenting styles that create healthy, happy children.

When you are separated, however, it's easy to become overly concerned about the differences between your parenting approach and your ex's. While you two were under the same roof, you may have known that your partner was somewhat lax in discipline, or regularly forgot to give the children their vitamins, or occasionally lost her temper and was too strict, or didn't care all that much about nutrition. But life went on, and somehow you dealt with those differences. Now that you are separated, however, you find yourself suddenly uncertain about the effects of those differences on your children's welfare. What was a minor concern when you had a spouse has become a major concern now that you have an ex-spouse.

That's why the first thing to do when you're upset over the way your ex is dealing with your children is to think hard about whether the issue is important enough for a confrontation. Is it really an issue of your children's welfare—or is it simply a matter of a different style of parenting?

Evaluate honestly whether confronting your ex and airing the complaint will do more harm than good:

- Will bringing up this issue about your ex's parenting ultimately improve the quality of your child's life, or will it create more problems and tensions for your child than are already present?

- Do the benefits of bringing the issue up outweigh the costs for you and your child?

- How critical is this particular issue to your child's well-being?

If you decide that it is important to bring up the issue, remember that what you say has the potential to reinjure a person whose self-esteem has already been lowered by a failed marriage. In such cases, the manner of your complaint really can do considerable damage, as a case in point illustrates:

Jessica sat in my office in tears because her ex complained repeatedly that she seldom did anything with the children other than sit around and play indoor games with them. By contrast, when the children were with their father on weekends, as Dad asserted proudly, he would take them to all kinds of stimulating and exciting activities. For Jessica, the end of the workweek was a time of sheer exhaustion after five long days on the job, and since the job left little money for extras, stimulating and exciting activities seemed out of reach. Her ex's criticisms of her mothering, however, made her feel terrible about herself. In reality, her children loved her deeply, knew that she loved them, and found playing Chutes and Ladders in her living room as meaningful as going to a carnival. But their father's critical and rejecting way of presenting the difference between weekend activities both depressed Jessica and made her feel less cooperative altogether. So far from changing anything, his complaint succeeded mostly in hurting his ex-wife and stiffening her resistance to his suggestions. At times, she just wanted to lash back at him.

If you decide to lodge a complaint with your ex, keep in mind these tips that you learned earlier:

- Begin by mentioning a number of things that you appreciate about what your ex does before discussing the thing that's bugging you.

- Stay open to your ex's side of the story.

- Stay focused on the behavior that is concerning you; don't let the discussion turn into a broad condemnation of your ex's parenting style.

- Use I-statements to express your worries about the children rather than accusatory "you" statements.

Jessica's husband, for example, might have caused fewer hard feelings if he had presented his complaint this way: "Jessica, I wanted you to know that I'm worried, because I never hear the kids talk about getting out of the house when they're with you on weekends. I wanted to hear your side of the story."

SEPARATE SPOUSAL FROM PARENTAL CONCERNS

Very often when we believe we are advocating for our children, we are actually playing out our own resentments and personal fears:

Jane and Hal had been separated for two months when their fourteen-year-old son, Jason, was scheduled to compete in an important karate tournament, which both parents planned to attend. But on the day of the tournament, while in Jane's care, their eight-year-old daughter, Melissa, fell and broke her arm. Jane quickly notified Hal; he rushed to the emergency room so that both parents were with Melissa as the doctors reset the bone.

Jason's tournament was only three hours away, and he was certainly capable of taking a school bus to get there, but Hal felt that because the tournament was so important, and because Jason had worked hard at karate for several years, one of his parents should be there to support him. Jane was aghast when Hal left the hospital for the tournament; she thought that both parents should be at home helping their daughter settle in for the night after her painful injury. To her, as she told me in a session during which her anger was still evident, it was an example of Hal's failure as a father—a father, as Jane saw it, who was not emotionally attuned to his children and who was willing to abandon his child in her time of need.

My response was to ask Jane if she had ever considered the possibility that Hal went to the tournament because he trusted Jane to take care of their daughter. "Isn't it possible," I suggested, "that Hal decided to attend the tournament so that your son would not feel abandoned?" In fact, I proposed, wasn't it just possible that in her heart of hearts Jane knew that Hal's absence would only be a terrible trauma for Melissa if she made it so. I asked her to look at the possibility that she was really acting out her own emotional issues with her ex-husband, that abandonment was one of those issues, and that her concerns about her daughter were secondary. Eventually, after several sessions, Jane felt able to admit that she had felt abandoned by her ex-husband, that she still resented him for leaving her. It was Jane who felt abandoned, not necessarily Melissa.

Distrust your judgment the moment you can discern the shadow of a personal motive in it.
—Marie von Ebner-Eschenbach, 19th century author

Jane's story is just one example of the injuries we can imagine our ex-partners doing to our children when the real injuries are the ones done to us. If abandonment has been an issue in the marriage and its dissolution, as was the case with Jane, it's easy to find ways in which an ex-partner is abandoning our children. If we have felt neglected, it's easy to see our ex-partners neglecting our children. If we feel angry, we tend to see our children as being angry at their other parents, when this may not be the case.

Anger about past issues between you and your ex can masquerade as anger about your ex's parenting.

So take care that when you champion causes for your children, it is really their cause that is at issue, not your own adult-to-adult emotional issues with your ex.

"IF WE WERE ALL LIVING UNDER THE SAME ROOF . . ."

A good way to maintain the distinction between spousal and parental concerns is to ask yourself the following question: "If we were all living under the same roof, would I be as bothered by this situation as I am now?" Very often the answer is no. If the family had been living together, Jane may very well have at least appreciated, at most insisted, that Hal go to the karate tournament. Because the wound of the separation was still so raw, however, his decision to do so took on new meaning for her. She still felt hurt and angry about having been abandoned by Hal, and so his behavior as a father evoked the pain he had caused her as a spouse.

That is why it's useful to assess honestly how your ex's distressing behavior with your children would have affected you "if we were all living under the same roof"—that is, when you and your ex were not in the throes of a separation. If the answer is different from the response you're planning now that you're separated, think again; maybe this is not a course of action you should pursue after all. Remind yourself that even in healthy marriages, parents often have significant differences about certain aspects of parenting—and life goes on.

The Empowerment Shift: Focus on Things You Can Control

Because the empowerment shift (see page 23) is a key tool when your ex's behavior with your children is upsetting you, let's review here how to effect the shift.

Start by reminding yourself that it is highly unlikely that you will be able to influence your ex to change the way he raises your children. If you have tried and failed to get your ex to act differently as a parent, pay attention to that reality—that brick wall. Next, refocus on how *you* are raising your kids. Consider taking all the energy you're now putting into trying to change his parenting behavior and reinvesting it in your own parenting.

Such a shift may not be a perfect solution, but it is an empowering and realistic one. It means you will be reclaiming your life and your real source of power—your own good parenting.

REMEMBER THAT ONE GOOD LESSON IS BETTER THAN NONE

"So what if I'm a good parent," you might say, "the kids go over there, and everything I do is undone." But your ex-partner's bad parenting doesn't erase your good parenting. Have faith in the value and power of your own loving care for your children. Keep to what you can keep to—emphasis on both *you* and *can*. That is, keep to your own values and beliefs insofar as you're in control, and try not to make yourself crazy over what is outside your own capabilities. Remember that while your ex is at the blackboard scribbling what you view as unhealthy lessons for your children, your children are also observing the life lessons that you offer them, and these lessons can carry just as much weight—maybe even more—in shaping their souls.

Teach your children with your own example, not by pointing out what your ex is doing wrong.

ACCEPT AND RESPECT THE SEPARATE PATH YOUR CHILDREN ARE WALKING WITH YOUR EX

Bringing up children is, of course, about eventually letting them go. The way you're raising them is a prelude to that—and a preparation for it. Because you must share custody with your children's other parent, you experience some of that letting go now, as they lead a separate life whenever they are in your ex's care. It's not always easy, but that separate path they walk with your ex is something you must learn to accept and respect—if possible, even to celebrate—for your children's sake. Following is a visualization that may help you to achieve that acceptance and respect. As a metaphor, the visualization crystallizes what separated parents who share custody of their children should strive for.

The Carriage Ride

Visualize yourself both participating in this scene and hovering over it, observing everything:

You and your children are riding in a horse-drawn carriage; you are sitting on top, driving the horses, while the kids are on the seats behind you. Part of driving is, of course, the road you choose, the various twists and bumps you go around or over that toss your children back and forth, the wonderful glimpses of beautiful scenery the ride offers your children. As you hit the bumps, you apologize to your children, yet you can see that going over or around the bumps is also teaching them to learn to keep their balance in the carriage, to hold one another steady, and to brace themselves for the unexpected. You can see the smiles on their faces, can hear their laughter as you drive.

Now, from your hovering perch above this scene, you see the carriage stop. You see yourself step off and hand the reins to your ex. He or she steps into the carriage, takes over the driving; he or she chooses the road to take; he or she steers among the potholes and bumps, hitting some while avoiding others, still affording the children wonderful glimpses of beautiful scenery. You can see that the children are learning to adjust to this new way of driving; with this new driver as with you, they are still supporting each other, still bracing themselves for new, unexpected bumps, still laughing with enjoyment.

What are your options now that you've handed over the reins of the carriage to your ex? One is to worry about your ex's choice of road and deftness at steering. The other option—and I call it the *transcendent option*—is to accept that the road your children are on with their other parent is part of their own journey in life, and to affirm that even though you wish the road were straighter, or better paved, or had no bumps, it is still a valid path for your beloved children. It is the path that they have been given with their other imperfect parent, a path that will be part of the carving of their souls.

Jennifer exemplified this kind of acceptance and affirmation in the face of an ex whose lack of organization struck her as downright irresponsible parenting. "You know," she told me, "I hate the fact that Bob keeps clothes and toys and doesn't return them, and my four-year-old generally hates it too. But I started to realize that there is just about nothing I can do about it, and I began to hope that maybe she will learn something from this part of her relationship with her dad. What's interesting is that I have noticed that Tracey has begun to be a good little organizer. She has started to gather up things from her room at her dad's home before she leaves and to remember to check that she has the pants that she brought with her on Friday night. Now, I wish she didn't have to remember those things and that her dad would just be responsible about it, but I have to admit that it has helped me to remember that *this is her life with her father*, and that maybe there are some things that she will learn from it as she grows older. My parents made their fair share of dumb decisions that no one rescued me from, and I survived. Besides, Tracey comes home every weekend bubbling about the snowmobile rides that he took her on and about the fun she had with him at her grandparents' house."

Such acceptance has been an important step on the road to Jennifer's personal peace. It can do the same for you.

Remember:

- ✓ Tread lightly when preparing to complain about your ex's parenting. Carefully weigh the benefits and costs to you and your children.

- ✓ Children can survive and thrive while experiencing different approaches to parenting.

- ✓ At times, our complaints about an ex-partner's parenting really flow from hurt and resentment that we ourselves feel.

- ✓ Be respectful about the ways in which your ex differs from you as a parent; accept that your children are walking a separate path with their other parent.

- ✓ Any requests for change in your ex's parenting should be put in the form of a respectful complaint.

- ✓ Knowing when to let go of an issue requires as much wisdom or more than trying to get your ex to change.

Real Life

What difference does it make if I'm a decent parent when my kids spend three out of every seven days with a jerk who talks about me with the kids as if I'm dirt?

Please do not misunderstand the main message here: It is certainly true that a difficult ex-partner can do emotional damage to children and can drive a wedge between you and your kids. I am not minimizing how painful such situations are and how distressing and damaging, in the long run, they can be to children. You may have to try over and over again to communicate respectfully to your ex about your worries. I would recommend that in all your complaining, you emphasize your fears about the impact of your ex's behavior on *your children* rather than *your own* emotional struggle. You may eventually need to resort to more extreme kinds of intervention if talking to your ex doesn't work (see Chapter 12). And there is a small—very small—percentage of families in which the alienating behavior may be so emotionally toxic for the children that court intervention may be called for. For most parents in your situation, however, the most important message is that you must not underestimate the power of your own good parenting to positively influence your children, even while your ex is acting foolishly. One good lesson is better than none.

I'm having a hard time with this idea that I should somehow affirm or support my ex's parenthood. He lets the kids stay up an hour later on school nights so they end up exhausted, lets them watch wrestling until very late on weekends, and always forgets to give my daughter Carrie her bookbag. She ends up not having her homework sheets for her third grade class. What is there to affirm or support here?

Great question. Remember that affirming your ex-partner as a parent for your children does not mean you agree with all of his choices or that you passively accept them. Rather, it means remembering that your ex-partner is an imperfect human being who, like the rest of us, is missing certain tools in his toolbox. It means accepting the reality that this is the father that life has given to your children and that you probably cannot transform him as a person. It means looking for the gifts your ex gives your child as well as looking at all his faults and failings as a parent—maybe the way he makes your daughter giggle, or how he teaches your children about sports you may not be interested in. And, of course, it means that you invest your energy in what *you* can control—namely, the time *you* put the kids to bed.

Even if I can tolerate the wacky ways they do things over there, won't the huge differences between the two worlds we're creating for them confuse my two little kids? Isn't that kind of inconsistency harmful?

It certainly would be nice if children could experience consistency between their two homes when their parents separate. Very extreme differences between homes *can* cause distress. If your child is a temperamentally difficult youngster—overactive, frequently acting out or aggressive, reacting poorly to changes in routine, for example—consistency between the homes is even more important. However, life has given your children two different people as parents, not two clones, and even while you were under the same roof there were certainly differences in how the two of you handled the kids, just as there are in most homes. The differences between you and your ex are part of the fabric of your child's life and, in some instances, can be a source of richness. We sometimes forget that many families allow their children to spend many hours daily in child-care settings, schools, and grandparents' homes where choices made by the caregivers—about diet, when naps will occur, the consequences of misbehavior, etc.—are likely quite different from those made at home. Children in general function just fine in the face of such differences as long as basic requirements of quality pertain. If children are generally resilient enough to handle these types of transitions, why should we think they can't handle differences between their parents' homes?

CHAPTER FOURTEEN

To Protect or Not to Protect?

Nothing is more basic to parenting than the instinct to protect our children. The parental brain is wired to be vigilant for the slightest threat; it is programmed to focus on anything that might endanger our children's welfare. That protective instinct is why you must never get between a mother animal and her young in the wild or even in the farmyard. It is why we sit at the table and urge our kids to eat more, an instinct left over from a time when survival often hinged on storing up enough nutrition to weather droughts and food shortages. It is why sluggish adults can act with lightning speed when they see their children about to touch a hot stove, or cross a street without looking both ways, or explore an electrical plug with toddler fingers. It is why parents' hearts feel wrenched from their chests when they see their children cry. Protecting our little ones is as basic to being a parent as breathing is to being alive.

But as with most basic instincts, the blind impulse to protect children has its downside. Sometimes, rescue can disable our children. When the danger is not all that serious, or when the issue has more to do with the rescuing parent's fear of losing control than with an actual threat to a child's welfare, running to protect a child can actually do more harm than good.

All too frequently, one of the great difficulties parents face when they separate is an often overwhelming sense that they have lost control over aspects of their lives that they once felt they could master. This sense of loss—this feeling of powerlessness—is crystallized for many separated parents when they watch their little ones toddle out to their ex-spouse's car and see them disappear into their ex's care. It's painful to give over your beloved children to the care of their other parent when you no longer feel for that person the trust and love you once felt—especially when you know that for the next few hours, or days, or for the next week, or even for the entire summer!—the kids' safety and welfare are somebody else's business. You're out of the picture and out of the driver's seat, and you must simply trust that your ex-spouse will love and protect them. It's not easy.

This already painful process is made even more difficult if your ex is someone whose judgment you question or someone who has hurt you in the past. Such concerns add to your worry, making you even more anxious about your children's well-being while they are in the care of your ex-partner. You find yourself alert to signs of your children's discomfort or unhappiness. You may even find yourself searching for such signs, and you may respond with excessive intensity to any complaints your little ones may have about their other parent. You're always poised to strike, ready for a fight. In short, you've become hyperprotective.

It *is* your job to protect your children's basic health and safety. It *is* your job to make sure that they are not being mistreated in any way. And certainly, as has been said repeatedly, if there are any signs that they are being abused or neglected, the appropriate authorities need to be contacted immediately. But the skinned knees, the missed vitamins, and the sulking that you would have considered mundane when you and your ex lived together are not necessarily cause for alarm now that you're apart. Unfortunately, far too many separated parents treat such everyday occurrences as perilous episodes, raising them as banners as they run to do battle with the other "incompetent" parent.

**The impulse to protect our children is a natural and
critical part of being a parent. Our children just need us
to know when to apply the brakes on this impulse.**

MISSING AN IMPORTANT LESSON

Racing off to the front lines, however, can rob your children of an important opportunity—a lesson in how to solve their problems with their other parent themselves. If you're always there to fight their battles for them, they'll never learn to take care of themselves. If you take up arms on their behalf whenever they raise even a minor complaint about their other parent, they'll never learn how to manage their own relationship with that parent. If they never learn those lessons, they'll grow up without any sense of security in their own competence to cope with the difficulties life will inevitably throw their way.

Sometimes the most loving response you can give when your child is having a problem with her other parent is the message, gently delivered, that you believe in her capacity to live through, learn from, and cope with the problem. Such a response communicates an empowering, even subtly transforming message to a child, as you tell her in effect: "You can do this. You will be okay."

Two loving parents are walking on a rocky jetty by the ocean with their four-year-old child. In their concern and in their desire to protect their son, each parent holds one of the boy's hands, so that together they lift him across the gaps between boulders. As the waves sprinkle them with mist, both parents silently entertain fearsome images of their son trying to leap on his own and missing the next rock, only to fall and scrape himself.

As the little family makes its way across the jetty, the parents clinging to the small hands of their precious son, they hear conversation and laughter and turn to see children fast approaching them from behind. The sight, however, makes them stop in their tracks. Two girls, aged about ten and twelve, are making their way along the jetty with their little brother, a small and slight boy who looks to be about three years old. At first the parents are aghast that the older sisters aren't even holding the little boy's hand. And then they notice something that gives them pause. The little boy, at least a year younger than their own, is leaping from rock to rock—skillfully and easily keeping his balance. And despite a few scratches on his arms and knees, he also wears a broad, eager, confident smile as he easily passes them.

The lesson? Yes, the secure, loving presence of parents can protect a child. But taken to an extreme, it can prevent a child from learning to keep himself safe.

Try:

✓ Letting go. If you think you lean to hyperprotectiveness, look for chances to practice letting go. Examine the full breadth of the relationship that your kids have with your ex. Do they generally return to your care intact, basically content, and without injury? If so, tell yourself this: "This thing my ex does worries me, but to date, my children have been basically safe and content with her, and they have been in her care many, many times. I have made my share of mistakes with them too." Then work at keeping your mind focused on this reality and on how you, rather than your ex, can keep them safe.

EXPERIENCING AN IMPORTANT RELATIONSHIP

There's another reason it is important to find the balance between what's appropriate protectiveness and overreaction. It isn't just that hyperprotectiveness can rob your children of an opportunity to learn to take care of themselves—surely one of the greatest gifts a parent can give a child. It's also that being overly protective can rob them of their opportunity to experience the fullness of their relationship with their other parent. If you're always jumping between your child and your ex, you keep her from fully knowing her other parent—and his values, beliefs, habits, and imperfections—as well as she has a right to.

Remember The Carriage Ride visualization of the last chapter? Remind yourself that you and your ex *alternate* as the carriage driver, and that it's up to the driver of the moment to decide which turns to take, which potholes to avoid, and which rough roads to travel. In short, the carriage ride that your children take with their other parent contributes as much to shaping their character as the path that you yourself choose for them.

That is why your attempts to rescue or protect your children—as well-intentioned and as loving as those attempts may be—can sometimes curtail the children's ride with their other parent, or change its character, or derail it altogether. It's your children who may lose out when they are "protected" from the full measure of their ride with their other parent—even if the ride is a little too fast at times, or the road a bit too rough, or the carriage not in the best possible condition. After all, when you're in the driver's seat, your kids put up with *your* imperfections; they must learn to do the same with your ex.

One of our most critical jobs as parents is to protect the children we have brought into this world, and we should do the job with fervor and intensity whenever they are in serious peril. But another of our most critical responsibilities is to give our children wings with which they can explore the world, experiencing all its complexity and defects. When we do the former job to the exclusion of the latter, we cheat our children above all.

Remember:

✓ It is your job to protect your children and keep them safe when they are with you.

✓ It is your ex partner's job to protect them and keep them safe when they are with her.

✓ The lack of trust in your ex that often accompanies a marital separation can create extreme anxieties about the welfare of your children.

✓ The rush to protect your children can sometimes represent a desire to do battle with someone that you resent.

✓ There is a healthy balance between protectiveness and over-reaction.

✓ Overprotectiveness can rob your children of an opportunity to learn.

Real Life

Sometimes I can't tell if my fears about my kids being at my ex's home are sensible or not. I can't tell if I'm being overly protective or sensibly cautious. I just know that my ex hangs out with people I'd never want to have as friends. You know, people with tattoos who drink a lot and who obviously haven't seen the inside of a bathtub in a while.

Please remember to make a distinction between what you feel and what you do. Again, there is nothing wrong with a feeling, and if you are experiencing genuine fear about your children, it is fear that comes from your love for them and from your desire for them to be safe. Your fears, by themselves, can't be crazy. It is the things that we choose to *do* with our feelings that can be irrational. Ask yourself if there is objective data—real information about real events—that indicates that your children are unsafe or in peril. Examine the source or sources of the information for objectivity. If you have reliable information that your children are at real risk, you then have to explore whether the degree of risk is great enough to warrant the fallout, for you or the children, of somehow confronting your ex-partner. If it is objectively clear to you that your children are in peril, act quickly: talk to your ex, contact the appropriate authorities, see a child therapist for guidance, get legal advice. If you do not have reliable information that they are at significant risk, simply accept your fears as they are and be vigilant: Watch for any further indications of risk to your little ones, and at the same time, watch for the gifts and assets that your ex brings to your children. Refocus on the parts of your life with your children that you can control while monitoring their welfare. And remember, some of your best friends may have hidden tattoos.

My wife was generally a good mom, but she occasionally used cocaine when we were together. We had a lot of other problems, but this was one of the reasons I left her: She insisted on her freedom to use coke once a month or so. Now the kids live with me, but the court has ordered her to have visitation on Saturdays and Sundays from noon to 5 PM, and I find myself scared as hell about what might happen to the kids during that time. Do I have reason to be afraid?

The point is that you *are* afraid. Period. Now you have to decide what to do with the fear. First, you need to know what your ex-wife's patterns of drug usage are in the here and now. If you have reliable information about drug use that places your children at risk, take all reasonable measures necessary to keep them safe. Drugs, particularly drugs like cocaine, can seriously impair a person's judgment and make her act on impulse. Unfortunately, the problem for many parents in your situation is that they don't have hard evidence that clearly proves their children are at risk or they struggle with whether their kids are at *enough* risk to warrant the other problems that will arise if they intervene. You may only have your fears as evidence.

What was her drug-taking pattern when you were together? Did she ever use cocaine with the children present? Did you trust her to spend extended periods of time with the children without you, or did you view her as likely to use drugs even while caring for the children? Are you hearing stories from your children or others about *current* drug use while in the presence of your children? Without objective information of current behavior that places your children at risk, it may be hard to do much (particularly with a standing court order of visitation) except watch, wait, and remember the other things about your ex that are of value to your children. You should at least directly express your worries to your ex, emphasizing your concerns for the children, and see if she is willing to commit to avoiding any drug use while with the kids. Also, remember to refocus on the parts of your life with the children that you have control over, e.g., *your* drug-free life, the way *you* care for them, etc., remembering that your good life really is the best lecture for the kids.

CHAPTER FIFTEEN

When Your Kids Complain about Your Ex

Remember those antennae you started to grow back in Chapter 6—the ones that could spot an unnecessary burden a mile away? It's important to keep those antennae sharply upright when your kids complain about your ex.

Seven-year-old Jonathan returns home to his father's house after a weekend with his mother and is just furious. It seems his mother won't allow him to call his friends when he's at her home. Or so he says.

Sixteen-year-old Deborah returns to her mother's and immediately begins sobbing that her dad is reneging on his promise to pay for her prom dress. He had angrily told her that her mom could use the child support money for the dress; after all, it's clothing and that's what support's for.

Jonathan and Deborah had similar reactions; their parents did not. Jonathan's father was bothered by his son's discomfort, but he was not nearly as angry as Jonathan. Deborah's mother, by contrast, having been told indirectly what her parental responsibility was, flew off the handle. She began yelling that her ex had always been a pain in her butt, now was no different, and she had had enough. She picked up the phone, dialed his number, and began to bark at him.

If your antennae are sharp, you recognized that in both cases the kids' problems were unnecessary burdens for the parents. Jonathan's dad knew it too, but Deborah's mother forgot; she heard a veiled rebuff of her parenthood, instinctually felt called upon to fight for her daughter, and quickly made the problem her own, robbing Deborah of the opportunity to solve it herself. She had forgotten the four key criteria for spotting an unnecessary burden:

1. Is someone other than you expressing the concern or the complaint?

2. Is someone other than you feeling most of the emotions about the problem?

3. Is it another person's life—not yours—that will most improve if the problem goes away?

4. Does the problem lie mainly between two or more other people?

There's a wonderful sense of relief in identifying problems that are your children's and removing them from your shoulders. Just remember that once you've figured out that your child has primary responsibility for solving a problem, you *are not saying you don't care.* You may care a great deal about the problem. You are also *not saying you won't help.*

There is one condition to a child's owning a problem: He or she must be old enough to make a complaint to you about the other parent and to engage in simple forms of self-assertion, i.e., saying what he or she wants and doesn't want, and expressing such simple feelings as anger and annoyance.

Family Triangulation

When a child complains about her other parent it involves the formation of a triangle—but families are not the only place where these troublesome relationship patterns happen. Let's say I'm frustrated with my office partner because he seldom waters the indoor plants as we had agreed he would. I've got two choices for dealing with my annoyance. I can go directly to my partner, look him in the eye, and tell him I'm frustrated. "We had an agreement," I might say, "and you're not sticking to it. I wish you would water the plants more often."

Or I can create a triangle—insert someone else between my partner and me—a very common human maneuver. Maybe I'll just wander over to the secretary's desk, plunk myself down, and just in the course of conversation happen to complain out loud that my partner never seems to help around the office and that I'm really bothered by it. Maybe I'll complain to her about it tomorrow as well, and the next day, and the day after that—just because I'm uncomfortable bringing the complaint directly to him. Eventually, the secretary might drop into my partner's office at some point and just let him know that "Jeff's upset with you. You might want to water the plants."

That's a triangle. The problem lies between my partner and me, but I have triangulated my secretary into the dilemma; I'm communicating through her to my partner, rather than going to him directly and dealing with the issue. This means that I never get to fully work through the relationship issues between me and my partner, my secretary gets stuck in an uncomfortable situation that makes her anxious—conceivably anxious enough to quit, and the violets wilt anyway.

Stepping into a triangle between your ex and your child often makes things worse.

Divorced families are fertile fields for the development of triangles. With separated parents each in their own residences, it's quite common for family members at one residence to tell tales about a member of the family in the other residence. There's a difference, however, between griping about someone who is not present and complaining in order to create a triangle. The first is a common human pastime; it can occasionally help dissipate upsetting emotions, and that, in turn, may help you act more rationally the next time you see the person you're griping about. But when your child complains to you about your ex *instead of* dealing directly with her other parent herself—and especially when it is implied that you should do something about the gripe—she is bringing you into a triangle. It's a perfectly normal thing for a child of any age to do, but it's something you as a parent must guard against.

If you respond by taking your child's complaint onto your own shoulders and doing battle for her, it can be toxic for your family for a variety of reasons. First, it communicates that the child may be unable to handle the problem herself and that adults should always step in. Second, it offers you an opening to react based on historical resentments that have nothing to do with your child. And finally, doing battle for your child will only sustain rather than resolve her relationship problems with the other parent. The pattern is established: The child clearly doesn't have to work out the difficulty directly with the other parent; you'll do it for her.

Consider how your own wisdom as a parent often tells you that it is best not to fight all your child's battles with friends, teachers, and others in her life. The same wisdom tells you that rescuing your child can rob her of an opportunity to grow. Jumping in to advocate for your child with your ex teaches dependence rather than self-sufficiency and may even take away an opportunity for your child to deepen her relationship with her other parent.

That is why the healthiest and most satisfying solution is often to help your child engage directly with the other parent. It's actually a sign of respect, love, even of protection to *not* take over for your child.

LEND A SMALL EAR

When a child comes bounding in the door with complaints about his other parent, especially if the complaint is accompanied by tears or anger, it's only natural to react with strong feelings, partly out of protectiveness and partly because of old resentments that arise from your own relationship with your ex. As I've said to so many overprotective parents through the years, their ears get very, very big whenever the kids say anything negative about their other parent—as if they were particularly attuned to any condemnation of the ex-partner.

This does not escape a child's notice. He learns quickly that if he reports something bad about his other parent, you listen more intently than usual. The result? He's going to continue to say bad things about the other parent—over and over—until there's an established cycle of negative reporting about the other parent—with occasional exaggerations and expansions on reality. I have known families in which this cycle of negative reporting escalates to the point where the children are playing amateur detective when they are at the other parent's home, gathering bits of negative information they then dutifully "report," thus deepening the already profound alienation between themselves and the "bad" parent they are tattling on.

The best way to end such a cycle is to make sure it never starts. That means you must respond to your child's complaints about the other parent in an emotionally controlled, neutral, yet empathic fashion. As I tell my clients: Keep your ears small!

Reacting calmly is important too. As you become "all ears" listening to their complaint, as you respond with emotion, in effect joining with your children in their anger towards their other parent, their own feelings are amplified, and they become even more distressed than they were before they voiced the complaint. And again, an emotional response on your part signals to them that you're willing to take on this battle and that *they don't have to*, which only robs them of a valuable life lesson.

Smaller ears mean fewer tears.

Finally, it's important to remember that your child may not be giving you a full and accurate picture of the situation. A kid complaining about a parent is like a kid complaining about a sibling: details are often altered or left out, certain things that bolster the complainer's position are exaggerated, outright lying is not unknown. Remember:

- Children exaggerate.

- Children elaborate on details.

- Children leave out important details.

- And yes, although I know it's hard to believe, children sometimes lie.

Unfortunately, in our eagerness to find fault with our child's other parent, we tend to forget these important and obvious realities.

For many years Johnny's parents had waged war with each other, sometimes silently and sometimes not so silently. He lived primarily at his dad's home and visited his mother on weekends. Those visits were times of intense fighting and arguing; Johnny typically would refuse to do anything his mother asked, knowing that his father mostly approved of his obstinacy. One Sunday evening Johnny returned to his dad and angrily reported that his mother had grown so angry at him she had smashed his CD player and rendered it unusable.

Johnny's father was enraged. He immediately phoned his ex-wife, angrily accusing her of insensitivity. When he finally stopped yelling, she calmly offered her version of what had "really happened": She had an important doctor's appointment. Johnny was refusing to get into the car despite her repeated requests. All he wanted to do was listen to CDs through his headphones, which he kept plastered on his head so he could pretend not to hear anything else. Johnny's mother was now in serious danger of being late for this important appointment. She had had enough of her son's rude disobedience, so she simply pressed the STOP button on his CD player. As Johnny yanked the player from her hands, he pulled too hard, and the player flew across the room and smashed against a wall. In short, it was his own obstinacy and rudeness that caused the thing to break, not his irate mother.

Johnny's complaining to his father, of course, with its exaggerated and carefully edited interpretation, was a foregone conclusion. He had learned that his father rewarded him with significant attention and subtle approval whenever he complained about his mother, so why wouldn't he edit things a bit?

RESPOND WITH CALM CONTROL AND NEUTRALITY

Responding in an emotionally controlled and neutral way to your child's story about his other parent prevents things from getting worse than they already are. It's also a way of showing respect for your child, because it maintains what should be healthy and relatively firm boundaries between your feelings and his. Children need to know that they can have feelings without their parents necessarily feeling the same way, and parents need to know this about their own emotions. Finally, responding with neutrality also shows respect for your child's other parent, because it allows you to remember that there are always two sides to every story.

Here's a way to think about the whole issue of defining a problem as owned by your child and of helping your child develop solutions:

Imagine that your child comes running in from the playground angry, crying, looking like she has been in a scuffle. She tells you that she was having a catch with a playmate, when suddenly the other child started kicking dirt in her face and pulling her hair. What do you do? Chances are that as a rational parent, you would proceed slowly. Of course, you would express understanding about your child's feelings. But you probably wouldn't race out the door to chase down the other child in anger. Most likely, you would try to get the facts of the story straight. You might coach your child about what to do the next time something like this happened. Conceivably, you would phone the other child's parent, but you certainly wouldn't begin the conversation assuming the other child's guilt. You would want to hear both sides of the story.

There is no reason why you shouldn't take a similar approach when your child complains about her other parent. In both cases, *there is a child in the middle who is adding her interpretation to life events.*

After a weekend with her father, for example, Susanne's daughter complained to her mother that she had been made to sit in her room for four hours and could not watch any videos all weekend. When asked what she had been punished for, the little girl replied that her crime had been that she "tipped over my cranberry juice." Charging to her daughter's defense, Susanne called her ex in a rage. As soon as he could get a word in, he explained that in fact their daughter had been watching a Disney video and playing with her little stepbrother when she became angry at the boy. She began throwing cranberry juice around the living room, staining her stepbrother's clothes, a light-colored carpet, and a couch. Her father then told her she would not be able to watch the other video planned for the evening and sent her to her room for half an hour.

Susanne felt extremely foolish and then started to notice how often her child seemed to leave out important details when complaining to her about mistreatment at the hands of her dad, her friends, and her teachers. She began to respond to her child's complaints with much greater caution and became more careful to check with her ex about the other side of the story. She had taken the first step in guiding her daughter through the process of solving her own problems with her father.

The next step would be to respond to her daughter's complaint in an emotionally controlled and neutral way. To do that, Susanne—and you—would have to remember *not to do* certain things:

- *Don't* show your own emotions when your child is telling a story about his other parent.

- *Don't* let your emotions over what you are hearing become too intense.

- *Don't* rush to agree with your child that his other parent acted like an ogre.

Neutrality means listening intently to get a full understanding of what your child is saying without involving the child in your own feelings about the story. Keep your emotions in check—and wait before you respond.

WHAT ABOUT EMPATHY?

When we empathize with someone, we step into his emotional shoes so that we can understand what he is feeling. To empathize with a child who is complaining about his other parent, listen for the feelings behind what he is saying, rather than for the specific details of the story. You may hear anger, fear, disappointment, hurt, sadness, anxiety, shame, or any combination of these feelings. Whatever you hear behind the story, your goal should be to check that you are correct in your assessment of what's really bothering the child, to communicate that you understand his feelings, and to help him further clarify his own emotions.

It is very often the case that letting children know that their problems are understood virtually solves the problems. In a confusing cascade of emotions, children often lack the tools to articulate what is actually happening inside. Simply helping them put their feelings into words is often sufficient; it's just what they need to help them work through the problem. Once they know what they're feeling and know that the feeling is understood, children are often able to let go of an issue or move beyond it.

To help kids articulate what they're feeling, show them that you are listening and are interested in what's going on inside them. Ask them about their feelings: "Sometimes kids who think their mom was unfair feel sad and sometimes they feel mad. I was wondering what it felt like for you," or "When that happens to some kids they feel mad and other kids feel hurt. What feelings do you have inside?"

Showing that you understand doesn't necessarily mean agreeing with the details of the child's story or the child's interpretation of the events. Use words that show you have *heard* their anguish: "Oh, Suzy, it sounds like you feel very angry about Daddy not taking you to the movies"—not: "Suzy, what your dad did stinks!" Or "Tom, you sound disappointed that your dad didn't give you the gift you had asked for for Christmas"—not "Tom, I can't believe he didn't get that for you." Or "Tanya, it sounds like that was a difficult spot you were in with Mommy"—rather than "Tanya, your mother always did that to me too!"

HELP YOUR CHILD GENERATE POSSIBLE SOLUTIONS

The temptation, of course, is to give children firm advice about what they should do and then expect them to follow through. A different approach is called for, however, one that honors a child's capacity to learn over time how to solve their own dilemmas in their relationship with their other parent. After all, they have to find ways to solve their dilemmas with *you*. There is no reason why they shouldn't develop these skills with their other parent as well.

Learning to develop solutions is not only good life-skills training, it's also a boost for the child's self-esteem. Once a child comes up with a solution he can actually try, he will feel much more confident about his own abilities in other situations.

To begin the lesson, start by listening to your child's complaint and communicating your understanding of his feelings; then let him know that you are there to help but that you view the problem as resting on his shoulders. Ask some neutral questions: "Do you have any ideas about how you could solve this problem with your mom?" or "There must be some ways you can solve this problem.

Would you like to come up with some together?" or "What are you thinking about doing? Have you had any ideas?" You might even introduce your child to a more formal brainstorming process in which you suggest that he write his different ideas on paper. It is important to be freewheeling about this, avoiding any temptation to censor any of your child's ideas. Help him come up with as many options as possible.

Help your child view his or her dilemma with your ex as a problem to be solved rather than as a catastrophe.

There are some potential pitfalls in this process. Perhaps the biggest is your own sense of what will and what won't work. After all, you bring to the process much greater experience—in particular, experience of relationship problems with the same person your child is now complaining about. You may know, for example, that certain words on your child's part can trigger an angry reaction in the other parent. Consequently, there is a great temptation to just jump in and say, "Forget that one! She'll pop her cork!" Or, "You say that to your dad, and he won't let you watch TV for a week!" It's important to resist giving the benefit of your advice; remember that during the stage of generating ideas, you want to teach your child simply to develop a full list, not to evaluate the ideas generated, so censor yourself if you find that you're jumping in to rule out this or that possibility.

Keep the lid on even if your child comes up with some really far-out ideas—like saying she wants to let the air out of her dad's tires or screaming that he's going to pour ketchup all over his mother's white couch. Instead of nixing the idea automatically, admit that it's a possibility, and suggest writing it down on the list with all the other options. In this idea-generating phase, try hard not to be judgmental.

Of course, it is a struggle whether to declare certain solutions to be off-limits. For example, if your child were to say, "Maybe I'll just never see Daddy again" or "Maybe I'll let the air out of his tires," he is picking a very extreme response, and some parents would want to let him know it's not even an option. But I recommend including even these ideas as *potential* solutions. When it comes time to evaluate the options on the list, ask your child how he thinks the idea might make his other parent feel, what some of the consequences might be of choosing such an approach—what he would miss by not seeing his dad, how his dad might react when he finds that his tires are flat, what the implications of his action might really be.

With some solutions—especially ideas for hurting the other parent—it may also be wise to let it go onto the list while making sure you communicate that you would not tolerate such behavior when you reach the evaluation we'll outline below; this lets your child know that your disapproval would be one of the consequences of such an action and clearly communicates your moral values as a parent. But in general, a particular solution offered by your child should not be discouraged simply because you disapprove. There are always *reasons* behind our disapproval as parents, and it is these reasons that should be emphasized—for example, that ketchup on the couch would ruin property that is not your child's.

In the vast majority of cases of children coming up with extreme or unacceptable solutions, they usually choose not to act on them anyway; the proposed solution just represents their attempt to let off emotional steam. But when they do come up with such solutions, help them see why such choices will cause bad outcomes—one of which will be that they will have to deal with you.

EVALUATE THE OPTIONS WITH YOUR CHILD

Going through the different ideas that you and your child came up with and talking about what might happen if each of them were tried can be fun, because you can then talk about the more extreme ideas your child came up with, such as squirting ketchup all over the white couch, and the more rational ideas, such as sitting down with his dad or mom and talking about his feelings. This is a wonderful opportunity to let your parental wisdom shine for your child. "I wonder what would happen if you did that," you might say to start the thought process rolling, or "What do you think might go wrong if you tried that one?" or "I wonder how your mom would *feel* about it if you did that." After going through the various pluses and minuses for each of the solutions, you can see if your child is ready to choose one or simply let it be. Sometimes it can be just as helpful to say, "Well, now you've got some ideas, and I trust that you'll pick the best one." Don't feel pressured to reach closure with your child about exactly what he will or won't do about his problem. Trust the process; if he needs to resolve his dilemma, he will choose to do so in time.

It is critical to view this as a learning process that has a developmental progression to it. A child at age five, for example, may not be emotionally ready to walk up to his dad or mom and talk about his frustrations. Just going through the process repeatedly, however, can lead him to choose such a solution when he is more developmentally prepared. I know one mother who began this process when her daughter was five. She started by coaching the little girl on how she might speak with her father about trophies she had won in dance class that she wanted to put in her bedroom at her mom's home but that her father wanted to keep at *his* house. It was not until the child was seven years old that she actually chose to speak with her father. It took two years for her to learn the skills and develop the confidence, but eventually she followed through.

AS A LAST RESORT, TRY CAUTIOUS ADVOCACY

If your relationship with your ex is stable enough to tolerate mutual feedback or constructive criticism without degenerating into hostility, and if your child is too young to be comfortable asserting herself with her other parent about upsetting issues, you may be able to act as a go-between. This approach should be used very seldom and with great caution—and never in abusive or otherwise difficult relationships. But it *can* work, as it did for George and Sheila and their six-year-old daughter, Eve.

Sheila had recently taken a job in auto sales that diverted her attention from Eve on weekends, when Sheila had custody. The little girl would be dragged around from car auction to car auction, sitting on the floor while her mother worked the deals. No wonder Eve soon decided she didn't want to go to her mother's on weekends.

George was very supportive of Eve's relationship with her mother and knew she was unwilling to speak with Sheila about the problem, so he did it. "Sheila," he said over the phone, "I heard about your new job, and I'm glad for you. I thought you would want to know that Eve is struggling with it a bit, because she's missing her time with you. I'm just letting you know, so that if you wanted to talk with her about it, you could." Sheila, caught up in the new job, was surprised; she hadn't been aware of Eve's discomfort. She subsequently checked with Eve, confirmed what George had said, and made some minor but pointed adjustments in her work schedule that gave her and her daughter more time together.

Notice that George was careful not to tell Sheila that what she was doing was bad or that she should do something different—ultimately, in a wise move, he left the dilemma between mother and daughter and just nudged them to talk to each other.

Again, remember that this is not as healthy as helping your child speak for herself. It actually involves the forming of a temporary triangle, and your child loses an opportunity to step forward and make her feelings known. But it can occasionally have a positive outcome.

Another option is to suggest that the only way you can help directly is to have a meeting with the child and her other parent, reassuring the child that you will be there to help her speak with the other parent about the dilemma. When you can pull it off, this is a better approach than direct intercession because the child is empowered and supported. At the same time, the parent who first heard the complaint gets to help the child, avoids fully assuming an unnecessary burden, and has a chance to hear the ex–partner's side of the story.

RESIST TAKING THE BALL BACK

Maybe you've always been willing in the past to jump in and do battle for your child. By now, he's used to it. He trusts that you will make the call to the other parent and lodge the complaint, that you will always take his side, that you will pay lots of attention when he complains about your ex.

So if you suddenly start acting like a parent who wants to put these complaints back on his shoulders, he may try to exert all kinds of subtle and not-so-subtle pressure on you. Resist taking the ball back; don't solve his problem for him. Gently as always, keep the problem where it belongs: between your child and his other parent. If his pressure on you becomes considerable, talk it through with your child. Let him know you understand he's having a tough time, but you have confidence in his ability to get through it well—and you love him. You could try saying: "I know that what's happening between you and your mom is upsetting. I also know it's sometimes hard for you to speak with her about these things, but I believe you can do it well, and I think it's best for me not to get in the middle. Let me know if there are any other ways that I can help you."

REMEMBER THAT EMPOWERMENT ISN'T ABANDONMENT

Not shouldering the problems that rightly belong to your children is *not* passivity. On the contrary, you're empowering your children, not abandoning them. You're not failing to protect them; you're letting them learn how to cope with difficulties in human relationships—a lesson that will stand them in good stead for life.

After all, all parents are imperfect, and all children have problems with their parents—sometimes, problems that won't go away. It's all part of growing up, and that's a good way for you to view your child's troubles with his other parent. Keep it at a distance, as if your child were having difficulty with someone else in the neighborhood, and maintain an appropriate boundary between yourself and the relationship your child has with her other parent.

From that perspective, it's easier to see that your goal is not to solve the problem for your child but to help your child learn life lessons. Then if your child's attempt to speak to his other parent about the issue doesn't work out well, you will still value what *you* have done: helped your child learn how to come up with solutions to life's dilemmas, expressed your confidence in his abilities, bolstered his self-esteem, and helped him learn to adjust to disappointments.

Which outcome is more valuable for your child: having a problem solved (by you), or learning to be an effective problem-solver for life?

SEEK ACCEPTANCE, FOCUS ON WHAT YOU CAN INFLUENCE

Above all, accept the fact that you can only control so much, and focus on what you can control. This is the most basic tool of this book. Maybe you simply cannot make much of a difference to your child's problem with your ex, but you can help yourself—and your child—by focusing on things that you can control.

Katrina was brokenhearted because her child's father seldom showed up for visits, and when he did, he was often late and frequently distracted. She longed for her child to have a relationship with his father that was meaningful and consistent. It pained her that her seven-year-old had a father who acted more like an uncle who dropped into his life now and then. It took much discussion and no small spiritual struggle within herself, but Katrina eventually began to wrap her arms around the reality that her son's abandonment by his father was a problem between her son and his father—a problem she could not prevent and from which she could not protect her son. Instead of focusing on trying to convince her ex to become responsible and reliable, she instead learned to focus on remaining responsible and reliable herself and on helping her son work through his emotional struggles with his father's absence.

In doing so, Katrina embraced acceptance and helped teach it to her child. She didn't make excuses for her ex, but she did try to help her son remember that there was more to his father than the infrequent and indifferent visits. She reminded him that there were other gifts his father had brought to him, and that no human being is just his imperfections. In short, Katrina left behind the bad parenting of her ex and focused on what she could control—a lesson on life and love that she could give as her gift to her child.

Remember:

- ✓ Your child can be viewed as the primary owner of some problems in his relationship with your ex.

- ✓ You are not abandoning your child when you choose to define a problem as something your child has responsibility for solving.

- ✓ Choosing to coach rather than rescue your child is a respectful way of empowering your child to master his own life situation.

- ✓ Responding with intense emotions to your child's complaints about your ex can foster a regular cycle of complaining behavior.

- ✓ When you help your child develop possible solutions to his problem with his other parent, you have an opportunity to teach him a valuable life skill.

Real Life

The jerk that I married, and finally got the courage to leave, spends most of his time necking with his new girlfriend while my twelve-year-old tries to get a small bit of his attention. Isn't it my job to let him know that he's acting like a foolish teenager and forgetting his daughter?

Your desire to help your daughter makes perfect sense. But remember that as long as you act as her mouthpiece, she will never learn to speak for herself. If your daughter were three or four years old it would make sense for you to try some cautious advocacy on her behalf. At twelve years old, however, she most needs you to teach her how to speak, not to speak for her. If she is upset about her father's behavior and is expressing her complaints, try exploring with her different ways she might express her feelings to her dad. Remember that it may take her months or even years to find the courage to speak with him. Also, take some time to quiet your mind and explore your own feelings about his affection for his new partner. See if there are any ways in which his new relationship is causing *you* discomfort or reminding you about the things you yourself have lost with the end of your marriage. Make sure that you are not confusing your own anger or pain about his new relationship with your daughter's pain. Finally, remember that although your daughter likely has her own feelings about sharing her father with this new woman, your distress when she brings up the topic may augment her own.

My wife has almost completely evaporated from my three-year-old's life. She shows up on some of the Fridays and then blows off the next two or three scheduled times. I get Eric ready for her to arrive, he gets excited, and then I have to tell him that it looks like she's not coming. I make up excuses for her and I feel like I want to wring her neck because of what she's doing to this

little guy. Should I send him with instructions to complain to his mother? He's just a toddler! I feel like I should nip this one in the bud now so he doesn't end up with having an absent mom for the rest of his childhood. He's just starting out!

It would be nice if there were hard and fast rules about these things. First, given that he is only three years old, you might want to risk saying something to your ex, like, "I know life gets crazy and busy and I know you feel like you are stuck with a small amount of time with Eric. I just wanted you to know that he seems very sad whenever you don't come and it hurts me to see him that way. I know that you don't want him to feel hurt so I wanted to ask you if you would try and come more regularly at the times we have scheduled." Second, you may want to stop getting him excited in advance of her scheduled times so it is less of a letdown if she fails to show up. Given his emotional upset, it may make more sense to say little or nothing to him until you see that she has actually arrived. Third, remember that he is walking a separate path with your ex and that you may not be able to protect him from the pain that the relationship with his mother may cause him. Do the empowerment shift, and refocus on your own fidelity and commitment to your son as the best way of caring for him. And finally, remember that making excuses for your ex only temporarily avoids the pain for your son. Eventually, he will have to face the full reality of this relationship. If you do as I have suggested and avoid cueing him that she should be coming soon, and if he still notices that she failed to arrive and seems bothered by this, I would suggest that you simply let him know the truth rather than making up untrue excuses: It looks like his mother is not coming today and you're not sure why. Give him a chance to briefly speak about how this may be making him feel and then redirect him to other activities.

PART FIVE

Your Ex and Others in Your Life

CHAPTER SIXTEEN

Your Ex and Your New Partner

New partners can be dynamite.

Corine felt burned by the explosion. She lay in bed, staring at the ceiling, wondering whether her new husband, Chris, would be as angry when he woke up today as he had been yesterday, and the day before, and the day before. Was it just three days ago that Larry, Corine's ex-husband, had lit this fire, destroying all the happy anticipation with which Chris had looked forward to his extended family's annual reunion—and to bringing his new family together with his far-flung relatives?

Chris's family reunion had been planned for a year. Corine and Chris had asked Larry well in advance to change the visitation schedule for just one weekend to accommodate this family gathering. People were flying in from all over the country, and a highlight of the reunion would be the family's first chance to get to know Chris's new wife, Corine, and her two kids. And while Larry had never liked the idea of his kids getting close to Chris, he seemed to be in a particularly good mood on the day Corine asked to switch weekends. "No problem," Larry said.

No problem, indeed.

A few weeks later, when the kids were with Larry for the weekend, it seemed all they could talk about was the snowmobile their new stepdad was buying for the family and how much fun it was to do things and go places with him. Mostly, they were things—like snowmobiles—and places that Larry couldn't afford for them. Hurt, and worried that his children were growing close to someone else, Larry covered these feelings with a mask of anger. He called Corine to tell her that the deal was off: he wanted the kids when the court said he should have the kids, He had plans for them with his family on the weekend in question, and that was that.

As Corine lay in bed, looking at the ceiling, she wondered what Chris would do when Larry came to drop the kids off tomorrow afternoon. This reunion seemed to mean everything to him.

After a divorce, a new partner has powerful psychological meaning, not only for you but also for your children and ex-partner. Even parents who seemed secure and confident in their own parenthood can suddenly feel threatened and worried at the prospect of their children growing close to someone else, viewing someone else as a father figure or mother figure, even receiving a good-night kiss from a rival male or female. This can be particularly painful for parents whose time with their children is limited, such as those who visit their children every other weekend or for only one night a week. They often feel that their relationship with the kids is already at a disadvantage, so when someone comes along who is actually going to move in with the children and have unlimited time with them, these parents see their parenthood in danger. It can be helpful to notice that some of the emotional turbulence that your new relationship causes for your ex may actually be related to fear—specifically, fear that this new partner may replace her in the eyes of the children. The opposite can also be true: Your new partner can feel threatened by your ex, worried that the two of you still have feelings for one another, the outsider in a family situation that was formed years before he or she arrived.

Your new partner can also become a convenient dartboard for the criticisms and complaints your ex actually wants to hurl at you, and the darts can seriously confuse your children. On one hand, they may be enjoying their time with your new partner; on the other hand, they are receiving regular messages from their other parent that this new person is not to be liked. Some parents get back at their exes by insisting on their own power and authority in divisive terms: "I'm your dad, and you only have to do what I say; don't worry about listening to him. . . ." "She's not your mom. . . . I am. Don't let her decide how your hair is styled. *I* decide that."

Pay attention to the emotional meaning that your new partner has for your ex.

Exacerbating these difficult psychological responses are all the complexities of stepfamily life. It was complicated enough before you ever met your new partner just to worry about how your ex would react to your decisions and actions vis-à-vis your children. Now that you are involved in a new relationship, a third party is on the scene, someone with his or her own thoughts and desires. So when it comes time to decide on where and when to take a summer vacation, you have to coordinate your schedule not only with your ex's schedule but also with your new partner's.

In some families, these new complexities increase the possibility of conflict. A new relationship, that between your ex and your new partner, has entered the mix. Even if the relationship is distant and silent, either or both of these two parties can make decisions that affect the other, potentially creating cycles of reaction and counterreaction between your households.

Remember Who the Parents Are

The basic tool for maintaining your emotional balance and clarity in the face of all these complications is to remember that the primary responsibilities of parenting belong equally to you and your ex. Yes, a new and loving partner is on the scene, but *you* share the primary responsibilities of parenting with *your ex*. So when it comes to making significant decisions regarding your child, or solving children-related problems, the line of communication should be between you and your ex; the decisions should be made jointly by you and your children's other parent.

When Your New Partner Has Complaints About Your Ex

Suddenly, there are three grown-ups in the equation—although sometimes, you can't tell it from their behavior. But it's a new situation, with new dynamics. The first step, as always, is to decide who owns the problem and whether or not you share it.

SHARED OWNERSHIP?

In Corine and Chris's case, it's clear that Chris is not the sole owner of this problem. True, it was Chris who first complained about the interference with his reunion, who was likely the one most upset about it, whose life would most significantly improve if the problem went away; overwhelmingly, this was a problem between Chris, the new husband, and Larry, his wife's ex-partner.

But it was Corine who lay in bed staring at the ceiling and feeling a mix of anxiety and anger over Larry's behavior. Corine, too, thought Larry had acted badly; she, too, felt angry and hurt. In a very real sense, she shared the problem her husband was having with her ex. The question is: Should she participate in trying to find a solution? Should she reach out to Larry? Should she try to find a way for her children to attend their new stepfather's family reunion?

Corine did not own the problem between Chris and Larry, but she was not simply a neutral outside observer. She too had a stake in the problem's resolution—and in the manner of its resolution. For those reasons, she had both justification and reason to take some assertive action. Should you determine that you have reason to take assertive action, rely on the skills taught throughout this book—working on your own mind-set, using I-statements in lodging complaints, and so on.

At other times, however, the problem will lie primarily between your current partner and your ex. In that case, it may make most sense for you to stay out of it.

Eric's new wife, Samantha, as well as ex-wife Jennifer both worked in the same insurance company. It made it easy for Jennifer to send E-mail after E-mail to Samantha, warning her to remember that *she* was the children's mom and it was not Samantha's place to discipline them. For a while, Samantha did nothing; she understood the threat that Eric's recent marriage posed for Jennifer, and perhaps she hoped that Jennifer would simply "get it out of her system." For his part, Eric made it clear that he wanted to stay out of the conflict. Finally, as the messages kept coming, Samantha decided to confront Jennifer directly. It didn't work, and Samantha eventually felt forced to file a complaint with the personnel office.

Avoid being pulled into a triangle between your ex and your current partner.

The messages in Samantha's E-mail box did *not* affect Eric directly. The problem was between his wife and his ex. The option he had chosen was to stay out of it. He wasn't going to rush into battle with his ex-wife because, he reasoned, both she and his new partner were adults. Surely, he could leave it to them to somehow work it out for themselves. He was sympathetic about the difficulties Samantha faced. He commiserated with her, agreed that Jennifer's behavior was ridiculous, even helped brainstorm options for solving the problem—all the while resisting the impulse to enter the fray.

In doing so, Eric spelled out a clear message to his ex-wife that he would not act as a buffer or messenger between her and Samantha. Her actions, he effectively told her, would engender consequences—i.e., Samantha's anger—that she would have to deal with herself. In short, by keeping his distance, Eric kept himself out of the triangle and left the problem where it belonged.

Try:

✓ Noticing any slight—or not so slight—pressure to simultaneously please your partner, your ex, and your children. Be aware of the ways in which you feel tugged in different directions and accept the feelings that follow. Check to see if some of the demands being placed on you by those around you are unreasonable, then work toward letting go of these concerns. Let those around you know—in an assertive way—what you will and won't keep on your shoulders.

The Overly Involved New Partner

Betty had been a single mom for ten years. Her ex had left when their daughters were three and four years old. Now young teenagers, the girls had grown up in chaos, their mother barely able to make ends meet—partially because her ex seldom paid support—and often leaving them alone while she worked at night. Eventually, the girls learned to run their own lives. While they loved their mother, they had little respect for her. As to their father, although they saw him every other weekend, they did not feel particularly close to him.

Then Betty met Sam, a longtime bachelor who had always longed to have a family of his own. Sam was also financially stable, and when he fell in love with Betty, he invested his whole person in the task of helping her family. He thought her life was thoroughly disorganized and that her daughters, for whom he cared deeply, were out of control. And so he came on like gangbusters, trying to fix everything that he saw wrong with Betty's family. At first, this felt wonderful; for Betty, someone was at last bringing order to the disorder of her life. Sam began to discipline the girls, developed a list of household rules that he posted on the refrigerator, regularly sent them to their rooms when they were fighting or disobeying, and demanded that they respect their mom.

Sam also noticed that Betty's ex paid support only about half the time and that he was regularly late picking up the girls—often, as much as an hour late. He confronted the ex-husband, both on the phone and in the driveway when he came to get the kids, and relations between the two deteriorated into one ongoing battle.

The pattern is seen frequently in stepfamilies. For a variety of psychological reasons and out of genuine concern, a new partner becomes overly involved in his new family's preexisting problems, causing ripples of hostility and sparks of tension between his home and the home of the children's other parent.

You may have to tame your new partner.

If your new partner is like Sam, by all means welcome his support of you; thank him for his well-intentioned attempts to help you and your children. At the same time, however, it is critically important to encourage him to establish appropriate boundaries between himself, your children, and your ex. Remember, new partners can be emotional dynamite for ex-spouses, arousing all kinds of confusing emotions. Helping your new partner learn to let go of certain issues and to leave them in your lap can go a long way toward reducing the conflict in the family.

For Betty, this meant realizing that she was allowing her new partner to rescue her from situations that she was quite competent to handle. Her children's behavior had gotten out of control because of her persistent fatigue and frequent absences from home. Sam taking on the task of being their disciplinarian was not the solution to the problem—in fact, it spurred the kids to resistance. Similarly, Sam could not rescue her from her ex's failure to pay the child support the law required him to pay. Rather, with support from Sam, Betty was quite capable of handling both problems—and it was up to her, not Sam, to do so.

ENCOURAGE A RELATIONSHIP BETWEEN YOUR EX AND YOUR NEW PARTNER

Although it may sound like a far-out idea that should only be tried on a distant planet, it might actually be possible in your family—provided the level of hostility between ex-partners and new partners is not too high.

And it isn't always high. Dennis's new wife, Andrea, tended to be overly concerned about his children and about his ex. She had never had children herself, and this new family was an opportunity for her to have what she had always longed for. However, she came on a little strong in her new role as stepmother, and this was threatening to Dennis' ex-wife, Pam. Pam was also very threatening to Andrea, because Andrea knew, at least unconsciously, that she could never have as special or as close a relationship with the children as did their real mom. As for Dennis, he had specifically told Andrea that, for his children's sake, he wanted her to find a way to get along with his ex—despite all the things about her that drove them both crazy.

The way this family resolved some of these tensions was wonderful. At one point in a session, a lightbulb seemed to go off in Dennis's head. "I just had a crazy idea," he announced. "Why don't you two get together and have coffee some night?" Pam and Andrea looked at each other, and their jaws dropped for a moment. Then Andrea said, "I never thought of that. I think I'd like it." The two agreed to meet and did so on several occasions, sharing both coffee and thoughts about the kids and their relationships with them. Both women walked away from these times together feeling less frightened by the other person and more able to support each other's place in the children's lives. The tensions and jealousy didn't disappear, but they certainly softened.

If it is at all possible, encourage your new partner to establish a basic working relationship with your ex-spouse. They don't have to become fast friends or share intimacies and confidences. But a handshake sealing an avowal from both that they will support one another's relationship with the children can go a long way toward laying a foundation of respect in their relationship.

AFFIRMING YOUR CHILDREN'S RELATIONSHIP WITH THEIR OTHER PARENT

Maybe your new partner is angry with your ex-partner—and maybe she has good reasons for her anger. The problem comes when she yields to the temptation to put your ex down around the home, in front of the kids.

It's up to you to make sure that your children's relationship with their other parent is supported and affirmed in your home, despite that other parent's upsetting behavior. It can be emotionally toxic for children to be in a place where they don't feel comfortable openly expressing affection for the parent who is not present.

Insist on a home environment that honors and affirms your child's relationship with her other parent.

If your new partner behaves in ways that are critical or disparaging of your ex, remember that it is your role to make it clear to her that this is inappropriate and disturbing for the children. Any frustrated or angry feelings that you and your new partner have about your ex should be expressed well away from your children, so that their relationship with their other parent can be as relaxed and comfortable as possible.

When Your Ex Has a Complaint about Your New Partner

Cindy was frightened because the tensions between her ex and her new husband were mounting. Dan, her ex, had been complaining to her recently about how her husband acted when Dan brought the children back to the home on Sundays. Because Cindy worked a Sunday night shift, it was her new husband, Brad, who was there at home when Dan returned the children. Dan complained that Brad would reach out the door, grab the children by the shoulder, and lead them into the house—as if rescuing them from their father's clutches.

"Who does he think he is anyway?" Dan yelled. "I'm their dad, and he's just a guy you slept around with." Cindy agreed that her new husband went overboard and that his behavior wasn't good for the kids.

Who owns this problem? It's Dan who has the complaint and who is most upset. While Cindy is understandably distressed, the problem is primarily between her new spouse and her ex; in that sense, it's an unnecessary burden for her. But unfortunately, where a new partner is involved, treating such a problem as an unnecessary burden may be unrealistic. After all, Cindy is the common element for all the parties involved, so she may not be able to avoid part-ownership of the problem.

One option is for Cindy to deal only with the piece of the dilemma that really disturbs *her*—in this case, the way Brad shuttles the children away from their dad as if they needed to be protected from him. She decided to speak with Brad to try to convince him that such behavior was not helping the children but in fact was likely distressing them.

INVITE DIALOGUE

If you are sure the dilemma lies between your new partner and your ex, invite a dialogue between the two.

Doing so raises several challenges. First, because your ex is probably more comfortable speaking with you than with your new partner, he may aim all of his complaints about your new partner at you. This is somewhat understandable, but unless you fear there could be violence between your ex and your new partner, defuse it: "This sounds like something that's really between you and my husband. I'd like to avoid being in the middle. Here's his number at work if you want to talk to him about it."

Maybe you're pretty certain that your ex wouldn't call your current spouse in a million years. Still, by making it clear that you're not going to take his problem onto your shoulders, and by offering the phone number for direct dialogue, you not only encourage the two to work it out between them, you also erect a boundary between yourself and your ex's complaints.

OFFER REASSURANCE

If your ex's complaints stem from his feeling threatened by your new partner's place in the children's lives, or from genuine concern that your new partner is behaving inappropriately with the kids, offer reassurance. Show him that you will continue to do your job as a parent. Let him know in the strongest possible way that he need not worry. Remind him that in your house he will always be respected and you will make sure that his children are always well cared for. Tell him you're committed to keeping him fully informed about the children, answering his messages, having the children return his calls, getting them ready on time to go to his home, and the like. One mother I counseled anticipated her ex's anxieties about her new relationship and reassured him about these matters in advance. It relaxed the father and made him feel less bothered by her new boyfriend.

SOMETIMES NO CONTACT IS BEST

There is sometimes open hostility between ex-partners and new partners; it can occasionally be so intense that it is simply best for them to have little or no contact. If you are aware of any potential for violence between them, or if you fear they will not be able to control themselves in the presence of the children, structure the family arrangements so that the two parties do not intersect. I know one family in which the mother, having seen one violent exchange between her new husband and her ex, determined that she would always be present for the transfer of the children between her ex's home and hers. She stopped letting her new partner go to her ex's house to drop off the children or pick them up—because she feared it placed the children at too much risk—and she always went to her own door when her ex arrived, asking her partner to stay out of view.

Remember:

✓ New partners have powerful psychological meaning for your children and your ex.

✓ Despite the presence of a new and loving partner, you share the primary responsibilities of parenting with your ex.

✓ You can choose whether or not to become involved in a problem that lies between your new partner and your ex.

✓ New partners who become overly involved in trying to change family life or insert themselves as problem-solvers between you and your ex can add fuel to the family fire.

✓ Encouraging a relationship between your ex and your current partner can be a healthy way of staying out of an unhealthy triangle.

✓ Your new partner should support your child's relationship with the other parent.

✓ When your ex has a complaint about your new partner and voices it to you, you are being invited into a difficult triangle.

✓ Your ex may need reassurance that he or she will be honored and respected in your home.

Real Life

My ex approaches all conversations with me the way a flyswatter approaches a bug, and I always feel squashed when the ex-

change is over. **My boyfriend now accompanies me so that my ex can't get the best of me in the conversation. Is this wrong?**

Your desire for the protection and security of your partner makes perfect sense. But you will do better in the long run—for both yourself and your children—if you work at developing ways assertively to protect yourself from being verbally squashed in your conversations with your ex. The presence of your partner sends a message that you are unable to take care of yourself in conversation and may actually reinforce your ex's tendency to overrun you verbally when your partner isn't around. Consider taking an assertiveness class, and reread the chapter on hot topics to build your strength and confidence. Try visualizing yourself as an agile butterfly that easily fools the "swatter"—rather than as a slow-moving bug that is an easy target.

My partner means well, but she keeps slipping and bad-mouthing my ex in front of the children. My ex can be a jerk, but I know in my heart that my girlfriend's comments are not helping my kids. What can I do?

Let your girlfriend know that you appreciate how she backs you up and supports you in your struggles with your ex, but that you do have a concern about making the lives of your children as peaceful and conflict-free as possible. Help your partner view her comments about your ex through the eyes of your children, emphasizing how, despite your ex's imperfections, your little ones want to be able to love their other parent *and* their father's new girlfriend. Ask her to refrain from put-downs about your ex as a way of taking care of the kids.

CHAPTER SEVENTEEN

Your Ex and Your Family

The ending of a marriage is painful for all involved. It represents the death of a dream. Once, you hoped to build a life with this particular person, share children, and grow old together. That dream has been fractured, and the love and trust you and your spouse once shared have given way to anger, hurt, fear, even depression. Under the circumstances, it's natural to seek the comfort and solace of your family of origin. Even people who have been distant from family during their marriage find themselves drifting back, seeking the security, advice, and support of familiar people and places. On a more practical level, separated spouses, their financial wherewithal diminished by the separation, may need the actual shelter families can provide, along with the emotional shelter.

And just as it's natural for you to reach out to mother, father, brothers, and sisters, it's natural for them to rise to your defense. Sensing that you've been hurt, family members are poised to strike back on your behalf. And since the blood-is-thicker-than-water syndrome is probably taking place in your ex-spouse's family as well, a kind of tribal warfare may ensue, in which the two families of origin beat their war drums and actively seek out opportunities to criticize or attack the other ex-spouse.

Sometimes they may do so in front of your children. And on occasion, the conflict can be very open and very loud, as your family "gets back" at your ex as he picks up the kids or drops them off. While it feels good to know that your family is backing you up, there may also be moments when you feel that your loved ones are only making things worse, either for you or for your children.

Loving family members can fan the flames of conflict.

When your family's defense of you takes this turn, it can easily rile your ex-spouse and strain relations between the two of you even further. When your ex complains about members of your family, or is certain they're saying terrible things about him, or objects to the way your children are treated when in the care of your relatives, when he believes that your family is interfering in his relationship with the children, then your family has become, in his mind, his enemies.

In short, families can play a dual role in your life as an ex-spouse sharing custody. They can be an island of security and love in the middle of family conflict, but in their well-intentioned zeal to take your part, they can also fan the flames of conflict and raise the level of distress—in your life, their own lives, and worst of all, in the lives of your children.

When Family Members Have Complaints about Your Ex

Randy told me how painful it was to see his son Colin begin to reject Randy's father, the child's grandfather, Patrick. The rejection was particularly noticeable after Colin's week with his mother, Carol. Randy typically spent a lot of time with his father, so during his week of custody, Colin would be with his grandfather fairly continually. He would refuse to do what his grandfather asked, would even speak to him disrespectfully, and once actually said: "My mommy told me I don't have to do what you say." At first, Patrick was angry over his grandson's behavior, but mostly, it broke his heart to see this child to whom he had once felt so close draw further and further away from him.

Eventually, Patrick approached Randy about the problem. "When are you going to do something about this?" he demanded. "Carol is wrecking your son; my grandson is starting to hate me." Randy sensed that his father was increasingly preoccupied with losing his grandson's affection and was depressed by it. Randy was upset too, angry with his ex for damaging his son's relationship with granddad.

One option we explored was encouraging Patrick himself to take action. Randy would suggest to his father that "since he and Carol used to be able to talk well together," in Randy's words, Patrick might consider calling her or writing her a letter to discuss his concerns and express his unhappiness. As Randy and I mulled this option, we were aware that it was a good step for Randy because he would be taking himself out of the triangle between his own father and his ex; he'd be letting the two adults work out an adult-to-adult problem.

On further reflection, however, Randy decided that his father was so unable to be assertive about this issue that it was unlikely he would ever follow through on the suggestion. Randy also decided that it was in his son's best interests for him to say something to his ex, to let her know that what she was doing was causing her own child great distress. He did that, and while Carol didn't completely give up complaining about Patrick, she lowered the intensity of her rancor. Eventually, Colin was once again able to relax with his grandfather.

In this kind of situation—as in just about every situation in this book—it is important to begin by determining if the problem is an unnecessary burden for you. Even if it is, that doesn't mean you have to exit the situation. In Randy's situation, since he shared his father's concern, he partially owned the problem. Still, the primary issue was between his father and his ex. Once he understood this, Randy had great freedom of choice. He knew he did not *have* to act.

After all, the problem was not primarily on his shoulders, and one option—usually the healthiest—was to encourage the adults to work things out among themselves. But because Randy shared his father's concern, and because the concern was for his son as well as for his father, his decision to place himself *temporarily* in the middle as an advocate for his child made sense.

Remember that it is usually best to try to get the adults who have the problem to work it out together while you stay out of the middle. But certainly, your children being negatively affected is an acceptable reason to allow yourself to step in and try to improve the situation. When you do, and you approach your ex with complaints or concerns on behalf of your parents or your siblings, remember to use I-statements and to focus your comments on your children's welfare.

KEEPING YOUR FAMILY FROM FANNING THE FLAMES

John became completely exasperated every time he spoke about his inability to keep his own mother from getting in a dig at his ex whenever the ex came to pick up the kids. Barbara told me that her father never mentioned her ex's name without appending the formula, "that bum." There are a thousand different ways that loving family members, overflowing with good intentions, can inadvertently or purposely fan the flames of conflict between your children and your ex-partners. It's important to set boundaries for these family members—to let them know first, that upsetting behavior by your ex is a problem between you and your ex, and second, that they can help most by staying out of it. Talking about these boundaries can be challenging, but it is very important. You must make it clear to family members that crossing certain lines makes things worse for your children and makes your life more difficult in the long run. After all, it instills anger in your ex that *you* have to live with. So thank them very much for their love and concern, and ask them politely to button their lips. For your part, it will help if you also quit complaining about your ex in front of them.

You may have to tame your family.

BE CLEAR WITH YOUR FAMILY ABOUT THE HELP YOU WANT—AND THE "HELP" YOU DON'T WANT

Nina was a passive, shy, dependent woman who had recently separated from a controlling and verbally harsh husband. Ever since she was a little girl, her parents had done battle for her with her friends and teachers; they simply assumed she would never do so for herself. It taught Nina a lesson she had learned well, to the point where it was almost unconscious: shed a few tears, complain to her parents about how someone was being unfair to her, and they would rally to her cause, confront the offending person, and handle their daughter's defense. Her parents had become her sword, and after she separated and returned to the bosom of her family, things were pretty much the same. Nina would sit in her parents' living room, bring forth some tears over her ex-husband's latest bit of foolish or insensitive behavior, and her dad and mom would seize the next opportunity to confront their son-in-law, often while the kids were within earshot.

If you have a tendency to use those around you to fight your battles, is it because you are unprepared to do so yourself? Convincing family members that we are incapable of handling our own relationship problems can fire them up so intensely that they will behave in ways that fan the flames of conflict. Burdening them with our emotional complaints makes it almost impossible for them to remain detached from our family drama. Unconsciously, we are asking them to step in where they really don't belong; the consequence may be a worsening of the situation for all involved.

Tell your parents or brothers and sisters exactly what is helpful and exactly what is not. There is a big difference between a grandmother who listens to you in a nonjudgmental way, lets you lean on her, offers you gentle advice, but stays out of the middle, and the grandmother who actively puts your ex down when he comes to the door. Let your loved ones know that you need them to listen, provide support, possibly help you financially—but tell them there are certain kinds of help that actually makes things worse for you.

COACH THE FAMILY ON SUPPORTING THE KIDS' RELATIONSHIPS WITH THEIR OTHER PARENT

Relatives filled with good intentions—loving grandparents, aunts, uncles, others—can unconsciously do a lot to damage your children's relationship with their other parent. It is your role, as your children's parent, to coach your family on supporting the kids' relationships with their other parent. Be straightforward and precise with your family about the kinds of behavior that place your children in difficult emotional situations, such as putting their father or mother down, or engaging in openly hostile exchanges.

Sometimes it is the subtler behavior on the part of your family that speaks the loudest. Family members often tell me: "Oh, we don't put her down at all. We just don't talk about her around here." Imagine the message it sends to the children to know that the other parent that they love and cherish is not even mentioned in one of the worlds in which they live. Such silence communicates that the other parent is looked on with disdain. For children, who naturally have unconflicted feelings of love for the other parent, it can be perplexing indeed that that parent is never spoken of. Your children need you and your family enthusiastically to support their relationship with their other parent—despite that parent's imperfections— even if it means "faking" small talk about the other parent that is positive. "That's a cool car your daddy bought" can go a long way toward relaxing the tension inside your child.

Insist that your family support your child's relationship with your ex.

It can be particularly difficult to confront your family and ask them to behave differently if you feel dependent on them or if you are uncomfortable being assertive with them. Some people feel such a deep sense of gratitude for the ways in which their family has supported them through their divorce process that they find it difficult to express complaints to their parents or siblings. It may be hard to do, but it is essential for your children.

When Your Ex Has a Complaint about Your Family

Jerry's ex was always complaining to him that when the children were at Jerry's parents' home, they had to listen to their grandparents put her down. She felt that the grandparents were helping to poison the children's minds against her, and it caused her great pain because she knew the children loved their grandparents but also loved her.

In my office, Jerry expressed frustration above all. He had some sense that his parents *were* making things worse for the children, yet he didn't know how to respond to his ex-wife's complaints. Hearing his parents mutter complaints about "the bitch" he had finally left made him feel relieved that he was not alone anymore in his frustrations with his ex, but it also saddened him to see the pained look on his kids' faces as they heard another "bad word" used to describe the mom they loved.

What a spot Jerry's in! His parents, on whom he relies and whose resentments stem from the many things he has told them about his ex, are acting out of a desire to protect and are rallying behind him as their son. But Jerry knows that he has many years of co-parenting ahead of him and that if the children keep reporting his parents' behavior to his ex-wife, his relationship with her is likely to be an endless war. The result? Further pain for his little ones.

Jerry and I spent some time focusing on how his parents' behavior could be toxic for his children. Then Jerry took two important steps. First, to protect his children, he let his parents know that he wanted them to stop their behavior. Second, he invited his ex to speak directly to his parents about how she felt rather than complaining through him.

The tools for dealing with situations in which your ex is at loggerheads with your family are the same techniques we have been stressing throughout this book. Start by determining whether or not the situation is a necessary burden for you. Chances are, if your ex is upset about something that your parents have done, it is most likely a problem that lies primarily between your ex and your family; it does not reside on your shoulders. It may be a problem that you have concerns about, but that doesn't necessarily make it your problem.

When confronted by conflicts between your ex and your family, don't be defensive. Instead, invite dialogue. The temptation is always to bark back—the vestige of a primitive response to seeing one's own "tribe" attacked, even if only verbally. But it's a response that usually does not help matters, and it *can* make things worse. Remind yourself that this problem lies on your ex's shoulders, and suggest that she have a dialogue with the family member she feels has offended her (assuming, of course, that there is no risk of violence). It's probable that your ex used to have regular contact with the very family members about whom she now has a complaint. Before you and she were separated, she shared holidays with them, prepared and ate meals with them, watched the big game on television with them. We tend to forget that, just as we tend to forget that the adults who have these complaints about one another are just that: adults. They will not implode if they have to have a conversation with one another. Gently reminding your ex that she can speak with your family directly to register a complaint—not through you—can communicate boundaries and your own well justified unwillingness to get into a problem you simply can't resolve.

At the same time, it's important to reassure your ex that you will follow through on your responsibilities—and when your family's behavior places your children at emotional risk, you certainly have a responsibility. For example, if your ex complains that your family is talking about him in front of the children or behaving disdainfully at transition times, you probably should take some responsibility. After all, these things affect your children. You can still let your ex know that you would encourage him to have direct dialogue with your family. Giving reassurance, after all, is not giving in.

Try saying it like this: "I know that you're ticked off about things my parents may be saying about you to the kids. I haven't heard them say those things, but I want you to know that I see it as my job to make sure your relationship with the kids is supported by my family. I think you should contact my parents and talk with them directly about the things you want them to stop doing, but I want to reassure you that, when I am present, I will not allow you to be put down in front of our kids. Despite the mess that you and I have had with each other, in my home I am committed to honoring your relationship with our children."

Then go back and speak with your family about the issue, letting them know that you think they are damaging the children's relationship with your ex and causing them unnecessary distress. Or, ask your ex if there is a particular way he would like you to help with the problem.

This type of response can help your ex relax about the security of his relationship with your children and can go a long way toward creating harmony between the two of you in the best interests of your children. The important thing is the emotionally powerful effect that your reassurance can provide—reassurance that you are committed to ensuring that your ex is always spoken of respectfully and in positive terms in your home, reassurance that you see it as your responsibility to encourage and protect your children's relationship with him.

Reassure your ex about how you will support him or her in your home.

Of course, there *are* times when it will make most sense simply to eliminate contact between your family members and your ex because of the effect it can have on your children. If the history of the relationship between your family and your ex–partner is particularly volatile—or worse, violent—asking them to stay clear of one another when the children are anywhere near is prudent. You can let your family members know that you understand they are acting out of concern for you, but that it is the emotional health of your children that is your priority; it is their welfare you are committed to.

Remember:

✓ Loving family members can be sources of both support and increased conflict.

✓ One way of caring for your children is to ensure that your family does not intensify the conflict with your ex.

✓ Your children need your family to support their relationship with their other parent.

✓ You can choose whether or not to become involved in a problem that lies between your family and your ex.

✓ Your ex may need reassurance that he will be honored and respected by your family when the children are present.

Real Life

My parents can't stand the sight of my ex because of what she did to me. She drove away from my home with most of our belongings and both children and relocated to another town without giving me any warning. It's hard to get them to shut their mouths about her around the kids, but what they say is certainly understandable. You expect me to suggest they speak directly with my ex when things are this hot? And isn't it important for the kids to know the truth about her?

There's no reason for your family to have any conversation with your ex unless there are ongoing problems between them. If you're hearing a lot of complaints from your ex or from your family and you don't want to get in the middle, please remember the following: There was a time when your ex and your family talked with one another, sent each other birthday cards, and passed the remote control back and forth. Just because there's been a divorce doesn't mean they're not still responsible for working out their own problems. Also, please remember that while your parents are putting down your ex—even if her behavior was despicable—it is still your responsibility to protect your children from this kind of insensitive behavior. As to whether the kids should "know the truth about" your ex, ask yourself the following question: Which would you rather for your children: that they transition between your homes with a sense of peace and well-being, or that they have knots in their stomachs because they have learned from your parents that their natural feelings of love for their mom are somehow forbidden? The truth that you want them to "know" is *your* interpretation of their mother; there's no reason it has to become *their* truth.

It's hard for me to make my sister be more positive about my ex when he isn't returning the favor. My child adores her aunt and her father keeps telling her that our divorce happened because my sister didn't keep her nose out of out of our business. Why should she treat this guy with respect?

Again, back to the blackboard! One healthy lesson for your child to scribble in her life notebook is better than none. Which is preferable, having your daughter experience *both* her aunt's hatred for her father and her father's hatred for her aunt, or for her at least to see her aunt behave in a civil way that honors her relationship with her dad?

CHAPTER EIGHTEEN

Final Thoughts: The Path to Freedom and Contentment

You've learned a lot in this book about how to carve personal peace out of custody chaos. No matter how complicated, infuriating, or hopeless your relationship with your ex may be, you've learned essential lessons about defining what's really at issue, assigning responsibility for the issue, finding peace between your ears or nudging your ex-partner to change, and dealing with very specific problems that afflict the relationship between you and your child's other parent.

There's a lot here. As you work through it, remember that Rome was not built in a day, and that finding peace in your relationship with your ex will take time and effort. But remember this as well: Your children will surely reap the fruits of your work.

My real aim has been to help you reclaim part of your life in the midst of a troubled relationship with your ex. Please remember that it is *your* way of being with your children, whether your ex is present or not, that is your greatest hope, your source of real power, and your best opportunity to make a difference for your them. In practicing the lessons offered here with your child's other parent, you can achieve a great reward for yourself—peace within—not just for this difficulty but for any other difficulty life may send you. And being at peace as a parent means that you will be able to be an island of strength and compassion for your children in the midst of the sometimes turbulent waters of divorce.

Notes

Chapter 3

[1]An elaboration on the "divorce eclipse" concept first presented in *Kids First after Divorce: Simple Tips for Helping Your Children Cope with Divorce* (Wittmann & Cale, 1995). Dr. Randy Cale, who co-conceived the "eclipse" concept, was a central and significant contributor to the ideas in this chapter and was co-author of the work from which it is drawn. Parts of the model are elaboration on concepts presented by Stephen Covey in *The 7 Habits of Highly Effective People*, Fireside, 1990.

Chapter 4

[1]The first two irrationalities (catastrophizing, and absolutist thinking) were presented by Albert Ellis and Arthur Lange in their work, *How to Keep People from Pushing Your Buttons*, Birch Lane Press, 1994.

[2]For a more detailed summary of the power of "preference" thinking, please see *Handbook to Higher Consciousness* by Ken Keyes, Jr., Love Line Books, 1990.

Chapter 5

[1]Rechtschaffen, Stephan, M.D. *Time Shifting*. Doubleday, New York, 1997.

[2]Gold, Lois. *Between Love and Hate: A Guide to Civilized Divorce*. Plume, 1996. Pages 7–8.

[3]See *Forgiveness: A Bold Choice for a Peaceful Heart* by Robin Casarjian

(Bantam Doubleday Dell, New York, 1992), a wonderful book offering a more extended discussion of this topic. Strongly recommended reading for those struggling with whether or not they can forgive an ex-partner.

[4]Jampolsky, Gerald G. *Goodbye to Guilt: Releasing Fear through Forgiveness*. New York: Bantam Books, 1985.

[5]Dass, Ram. *Spiritual Awakening*. Audiotape series: Nightingale Conant, 1993.

Chapter 6

[1]In *Joint Custody with a Jerk: Raising a Child with an Uncooperative Ex* (St. Martin's Press, 1996), authors Julia A. Ross and Judy Corcoran also recognize the importance of discerning problem ownership. The alternate decision model they offer, entitled "The Problem Pyramid," may prove useful to readers.

[2]I again want to thank Julia A. Ross and Judy Corcoran, authors of *Joint Custody with a Jerk: Raising a Child with an Uncooperative Ex* (St. Martin's Press, 1996), for their mention of this response as an option.

Chapter 8

[1]*Matthew*, 7:12.

[2]Covey, Stephen (1999). *Living the 7 Habits: The Courage to Change.* New York: Fireside.

[3]The differences between proactive and reactive people are discussed at greater length by Stephen R. Covey in his widely acclaimed book *The 7 Habits of Highly Effective People : Powerful Lessons in Personal Change*. Fireside, 1990.

Chapter 10

[1]The tools offered in this chapter and the one that follows combine techniques that I have found helpful with clients, along with the fine ideas offered by Lois Gold, Ross and Corcoran, and John Gottman. Their works are listed in the additional resources section.

[2]Lois Gold makes this suggestion in her helpful book *Between Love and Hate: A Guide to Civilized Divorce,* published by Plenum in 1992.

Chapter 11

[1]Driscoll, Richard. *Mental Shielding to Brush Off Hostility*. Frontiers, 1995.

[2]I want to thank Henry Grayson for his suggestion of this use of the Toto event in his tape series *The New Physics of Love: The Power of Mind and Spirit in Relationships,* Sounds True, 2000.

[3]A good way to learn these techniques is with the assistance of audio-tapes. *Mental Shielding to Brush Off Hostility,* Dr. Robert Driscoll's book referred to earlier, is accompanied by audio cassettes that provide this kind of training.

[4]Gottman, John, et al. *Why Marriages Succeed or Fail: And How You Can Make Yours Last.* New York: Fireside, 1995.

[5]This phrase was originally attributed to the late Carl Sagan.

[6]Lois Gold proposes similar "argument busters" in her book *Between Love and Hate: A Guide to Civilized Divorce.*

[7]Ross and Corcoran, in *Joint Custody with a Jerk: Raising a Child with an Uncooperative Ex,* also give examples of the creative use of metaphors with difficult ex-partners.

[8]Sam Horn, in her wonderful book entitled *Tongue Fu!* from St. Martin's Press, developed this strategy within the area of general communication principles. I have borrowed her concept here and applied it to the specific area of conversations with a difficult ex.

Chapter 12

[1]See Lois Gold's work *Beyond Love and Hate* for another presentation regarding letters to ex partners.

[2]I want to thank my good friend Jeffrey Cohen, Esq. for sharing his understanding of the legal system.

Additional Resources

Casarjian, Robin. *Forgiveness: A Bold Choice for a Peaceful Heart.* New York: Bantam Doubleday Dell, 1992.

Covey, Stephen R. *The 7 Habits of Highly Effective People: Powerful Lessons to Personal Change.* New York: Fireside, 1990.

Covey, Stephen R. *Living the 7 Habits: The Courage to Change.* New York: Simon & Schuster, 2000.

Dass, Ram. *Spiritual Awakening.* Audiotapes. Illinois: Nightengale Conant, 1993.

Driscoll, Richard. *Mental Shielding to Brush Off Hostility.* Knoxville: Frontiers Press, 1995.

Ellis, Albert & Lange, Arthur. *How To Keep People From Pushing Your Buttons.* New York: Citadel Press, 1994.

Fisher, Robert & Ury, William. *Getting to Yes.* Boston: Houghton Mifflin, 1981.

Gold, Lois. *Between Love & Hate: A Guide to Civilized Divorce.* New York: Plume, 1996.

Gottman, John. *Why Marriages Succeed or Fail: And How You Can Make Yours Last.* New York: Fireside, 1995.

Horn, Sam. *Tongue Fu!: How to Deflect, Disarm, and Defuse any Verbal Conflict.* New York: St. Martin's Press, 1996.

Jampolsky, Gerald. *Goodbye to Guilt: Releasing Fear through Forgiveness.* New York: Bantam Books, 1985.

Keyes, Kenneth. *Handbook to Higher Consciousness.* Oregon: Love Line Books, 1975.

Rechtschaffen, Stephan. *Time Shifting.* New York: Doubleday, 1996.

Ross, Julia A. & Corcoran, Judy. *Joint Custody with a Jerk: Raising a Child with an Uncooperative Ex.* New York: St. Martin's Press, 1996.

Wittmann, Jeffrey & Cale, Randy. *Kids First: Simple Tips for Helping your Children Cope With Divorce.* New York: Child & Family Insights, 1995.

Index

Page numbers in *italics* indicate illustrations.

About the Author

Dr. Jeffrey Wittmann is a psychologist in private practice in Albany, New York, and is co-director of Child & Family Psychological Services and of The Center for Forensic Psychology. He has worked almost exclusively with divorcing families for over seventeen years, is a trained divorce mediator, and has provided invited testimony to the New York State Senate on matrimonial statutes. Dr. Wittmann lectures widely to public and professional groups and is the author of scholarly works in the areas of psychotherapy, religious motivation, and both forensic and family psychology. Together with Dr. Randy Cale, he has authored and taught the acclaimed "Kids First after Divorce" program to hundreds of separated parents. Most important, he is the proud dad of two wonderful kids.

Dr. Wittmann can be reached for public presentations, private consultation, or for a list of his self-help materials for separated parents at 1-800-846-0080 (number to be provided) or at his Web site at www.exproblems.com.